SWIFT SWORD

THE TRUE STORY OF THE MARINES OF MIKE 3/5 IN VIETNAM, 4 SEPTEMBER 1967

DOYLE GLASS

Coleche Press, Dallas TX

Swift Sword: The True Story of the Marines of MIKE 3/5
in Vietnam 4 September 1967
By Doyle D. Glass

Published by

Coleche Press
Dallas, Texas 75205

Note: Passages in italics reflect the recollections of Marine and
Navy Corpsmen veterans during interviews with the
author or in after-action reports.

Editing by Cynde Christie, WritingCoachCynde.com
Cover Design by Jun Ares
Interior Layout by Nick Zelinger, NZGraphics.com

ISBN: 979-8-9860316-0-6 (print)
LCCN: data on file

Second Edition

Printed in the United States of America

TABLE OF CONTENTS

TABLE OF FIGURES

DEDICATION

To the 127 Marines and Navy Corpsmen
killed on Operation Swift,
September 4-15, 1967,
and to the survivors haunted forever
by the memories of that battle.

INTRODUCTION

A friend asked me, "Why do you feel the need to write a new edition of *Swift Sword*? Since you published it in 2014, your book has been an unqualified success. Why take the time and effort to fix what clearly isn't broken?"

The question was a good one.

Why wasn't I satisfied? What was missing? Was I simply falling prey to my perfectionist self? "Don't let perfect be the enemy of good!" a wise person once said. That had to be it, but still, I delayed.

As I struggled, I began to delve into the past, back to the genesis of *Swift Sword*. I found old emails from veterans, as well as the transcripts of their interviews, and simply began to read. A flood of memories came back, both good and difficult, from a time seemingly so long ago, when I came across an email from 2008.

"I was hardened to death, torn bodies, and friends being killed. I realized on Operation Hastings (July 18–30, 1966), when a handful of my 2nd Platoon M Co 3/5 were killed in the DMZ and a young man by the name of Denny LaNore was killed on July 22, 1966, that I had to disassociate myself as much as possible with death and the horrors of fighting in order to best do my job as a commander. Callus, but stoic, I had to ignore the tragedies for the sake of my unit."

Retired Marine Lieutenant Colonel JD Murray wrote that email. As a young lieutenant, he was the commander of Mike Company 3/5 on Operation Swift in September of 1967. The email was his response to me when I told him of my desire to tell the true story of combat during the Vietnam War. His response was a glimpse of what that meant for him, an insight often hidden by veterans of the terror of war.

"The tone of your book," he continued, "*must* contain what the troops on the ground felt, endured, and carried with them all these years."

Murray went on to recommend, in fact insist, that if I truly wanted to capture the realities of combat that I read EB Sledge's seminal memoir of combat in the Pacific during WWII, *With the Old Breed: At Peleliu and Okinawa.*

"It is unvarnished, brutal, without a shred of sentimentality or false patriotism," Murray said, "a profound primer on what it actually was like to be in that war. Read it closely—it reflects an eerie resemblance to what happened with M Co on Swift."

I read *With the Old Breed* and came away with the realization that, for me, Sledge's memoir was the single best and most profound epic of what it was truly like to experience combat during WWII, and I wasn't alone in that assessment. Famed documentarian Ken Burns relied heavily on *With the Old Breed* for his PBS documentary *The War* (2007). The writers of the HBO war drama miniseries *The Pacific* (2010) also partially based their story on Sledge's memoir.

Sledge, a front-line combat Marine with K Company 3/5, based his work on notes he kept secured in a small Bible he carried with him during combat. In his preface, it struck me as to why he chose to relive the harsh memories and write the memoir.

"In writing, I am fulfilling an obligation I have long felt to my comrades in the 1st Marine Division, all of whom suffered so much for our country," Sledge wrote. "None came out unscathed. Many gave their lives, many their health, and some their sanity. All who survived will long remember the horror they would rather forget. But they suffered and they did their duty so a sheltered homeland can enjoy the peace that was purchased at such high cost. We owe those Marines a profound debt of gratitude."

I didn't serve. I am not a veteran. I am the personal beneficiary, like millions of other Americans and freedom loving peoples, of the sacrifice of those who fought and suffered for me. As such, I also have an obligation, a debt far greater than Sledge felt he had. For me, personally, as a child of the 1960s, I owe my deep gratitude to the men who fought in Vietnam.

My goal was now clear. What Sledge did for the combat service-man during WWII, I would attempt to do for the combat veterans of Vietnam.

However, there was no way, no possibility, that I could match Sledge's memoir. He had experienced the horror that I had never seen. But I could, at least I thought, come close. What I could do was record the experiences of those who fought on Swift and present their memories in the clearest way possible.

From 2008 to 2011, I conducted forty-nine personal interviews of Marine veterans of Swift, spoke with friends and families of veterans, reviewed twelve after-action reports of the battle of September 4, 1967, and read numerous accounts on the battles in Vietnam's Quế Sơn Valley. This included a visit to Vietnam in 2009 as well as an interview with a veteran of the NVA command.

I would compare my task to that of a thousand-piece jigsaw puzzle with each piece unknown and hidden, not unlike an archae-ologist beginning a new dig. Not only did I have to fit each piece together in the proper order, I had to find them first.

As I began to discover and unearth those pieces with each interview I conducted, I began to sift through what was relevant to the story and discard what was not, find which pieces fit, as veteran accounts differ. There was even the case of one veteran who gave false testimony that I had to evaluate and ultimately remove from the story line.

As the pieces were unearthed, it also became clear that this was not a linear puzzle, one that I could lay out two-dimensionally on a table as the piecing together of a coherent timeline proved to be a difficult challenge throughout. This jigsaw had three dimensions with moving parts, with pieces being placed simultaneously on different parts of the battlefield. This would create an entirely new set of issues, as accounts had to be presented in sequence for the reader even though those events written about often occurred at the same time on different parts of the battlefield. That sequencing alone distorts reality, coupled with the inevitable mistakes in fact and disagreement over certain facts as the memories of each veteran differ.

"It is very difficult to adequately portray actual combat in a 3D environment," Murray said. "It's like floating on air in an out-of-body experience. You will do things you have never done before, experience the unthinkable, and witness the unbelievable, followed by total exhaustion but with the will to continue again, knowing you will see it all again."

In 2011, after the interviews were complete and a rough outline created, I began to work with the veterans and my editors to create *Swift Sword*, specifically the events experienced by the Marines of Mike 3/5 on September 4, 1967. Right at the time that the book was finally coming together, however, I was thrust into my own personal tragedy when my wife was diagnosed with aggressive, and ultimately terminal, breast cancer. Together, we were plunged into a four-year battle that we fought as we tried to raise a young son and daughter.

I was committed to finishing *Swift Sword,* but saving my wife's life and caring for the children was the top priority. With the help of many, I carried on with the book, completing and publishing it the fall of 2014. That December, my wife lost her battle with cancer.

I grieved, moved on with my life, and tried to put behind me the pain of my recent past. I buried my old life deep, locking those memories in a box with a padlock, and in many ways, I locked my memories of *Swift Sword* away as well.

I moved, met a beautiful and amazing woman, remarried, unofficially adopted her daughter—as she adopted mine—and began a new life. With my son in college, my life stable and happy, I began to write again, and in anticipation of the release of my new book, *Benoist's War*, my editor and I decided to re-release *Lions of Medina* (my first book about Marines in Vietnam) and *Swift Sword* to a new audience of readers.

And on reading that first paragraph, after locking *Swift Sword* away for eight long years, I knew that my job wasn't finished. Somehow, someway, I knew that I had more to do.

Then, as it is at times with the nature of epiphanies, it came, a realization now so obvious that if it had been a snake, it would have bit me. With the benefit of time and distance, of grieving and a return to the blessings of a happy and fulfilled life, the reason became crystal clear when few things were clear for me at the end of 2014.

While the first edition and my subsequent initial re-write both do an admirable job in the telling of the events of the battle, it did little to convey what the troops on the ground felt, endured, and carried with them all these years. The book did not convey the brutal essence of combat as Sledge did so admirably in *With the Old Breed*. In short, I had done a commendable job in presenting the facts, but the story was far from complete. The most important element, the true experience of the veterans, was often missing. I had failed fully to illustrate what Sledge had done so well.

Instead of falling into the writer's despair in not having fulfilled my years long mission, I was galvanized. Buried deep in the recesses of my email, stored in the eternal and wonderful cloud, were the transcripts of each and every veteran whom I had interviewed, every after-action report, and every email written to me since this journey began. A treasure trove of memories and emotions, many from men now gone, was there.

I had not given voice to the men themselves. I had not allowed the veterans to tell the story *themselves*. That was the missing *something* that had gnawed at me for so long.

It was then, with a renewed heart and a sense of profound gratitude, that I re-read every interview and allowed the veterans, not me, to tell the story of Operation Swift, September 4, 1967. *Their* words convey the horror; *their* emotions convey the profound love of their brothers in arms; *their* war told because it was they who fought it, both at home and in Vietnam, and it is to them that we owe a profound debt of gratitude.

To that end, the actual quotes of the veterans from the interviews I conducted over forty years after the battle are in italics, while the action or dialogue that took place on the battlefield of Operation Swift in September 1967 is in the regular font. I want to make it easy for the reader to follow the stories of then and now, what the Marines lived and what they carried on in their memories.

"War is brutish, inglorious, and a terrible waste—" Sledge wrote. "The only redeeming factors were my comrades' incredible bravery and their devotion to each other. Marine Corps training taught us to kill efficiently and to try to survive. But it also taught us loyalty to each other—and love. That esprit de corps sustained us."

Swift Sword is that story. As charged by JD Murray fourteen years ago, it is now my profound hope that what *With the Old Breed* was for the combat Marine of WWII, *Swift Sword* will be for the combat Marine of the Vietnam War.

Doyle Glass
November 2022

PROLOGUE

They shall grow not old, as we that are left grow old;
Age shall not weary them, nor the years condemn.
At the going down of the sun and in the morning
We will remember them.

—Laurence Binyon from "For the Fallen"

By 1967, the war between the communist Democratic Republic of Vietnam, (in the north), and the Republic of Vietnam and its principal ally, the United States, (in the south), had been long and costly. Determined to reunite the country under communist rule, the North Vietnamese embarked on a plan of action aimed at inflicting large numbers of casualties on the Americans in an effort to turn public opinion in the United States against the conflict. To execute this strategy, the leaders in Hanoi authorized a series of division-level, centralized attacks on specific American targets in preparation for the Tet Offensive, which they had planned for January of 1968.

Located along the border of the Quảng Nam and Quảng Tin provinces, the Quế Sơn Valley was produce-rich and long considered as the key to gaining control of South Vietnam's five Northern provinces. Hanoi viewed the area known as Doi Cam, near the village of Đông Sơn along the Ly Ly River, as a springboard from which the United States could gain control of the valley. To counter this perceived threat, the North Vietnamese deployed two regiments of the vaunted 2nd Division of the People's Army of Vietnam and the 1st Regiment of the National Liberation Army (Viet Cong) to Doi

Cam to seize the vital rice harvest, disrupt the presidential election planned for that September, and engage the Americans in decisive and deadly combat.

At 04:30, on September 4, 1967, the North Vietnamese Army (NVA) struck.

Delta 1/5, Near the Village of Đông Sơn

Dug in near the village of Đông Sơn, the night had been a relatively quiet one for Captain (CPT) Robert Morgan's two platoons of Marines. Numbering between seventy and ninety men, the leathernecks belonging to Delta Company, 1st Battalion, 5th Marines (1/5) had detailed to South Vietnam's Quế Sơn Valley to provide security for local voters in the previous day's presidential election.

Having crossed the Ly Ly River at dusk, CPT Morgan established a perimeter in an open field facing a large boulder and a long trench line on a piece of high ground to the left. With their backs to the river, Morgan chose not to take that high ground or encamp in a copse of trees on the opposite bank, and instead, as darkness fell, ordered his tired Marines to dig in where they were, two men per position about thirty yards apart with a three-man listening post (LP) out front.

After dark, the leathernecks were put on edge when three Vietnamese children, each carrying torches, were brought into the perimeter. The Marines considered their story, that they were checking fishing traps, dubious since the North Vietnamese routinely used children as scouts to provide intelligence about American positions and strength. Once they stowed the children into the safety of a trench, the Marines waited for first light.

It was still dark when the sound of barking dogs, whistles and bells, and the now familiar crack of enemy small arms fire shattered the silence. The attack, about one hundred meters from the Marine perimeter, was light and inaccurate, creating the impression that the enemy was most likely a small band of Viet Cong (local guerrilla fighters) sent to harass the Americans.

In command of Delta Company for only a month and not well-known to his Marines, the twenty-eight-year old Morgan was a tough, stocky officer who had the look of authority that one might expect of a Marine company commander. After ordering the LP positioned beyond the perimeter to return, he ordered his Marines to respond. The leathernecks answered with a fierce defense, quickly overwhelming the enemy with their own outgoing rifle and grenade fire.

Almost as if the NVA had planned the initial sortie to bait the Americans into revealing their positions, assault troops of the 1st Viet Cong Regiment charged forward. Red and green tracers crisscrossed the night sky as the valley erupted with blinding flashes and deafening blasts as heavy machine guns and mortars joined the offensive.

"We've got control of the situation," Morgan radioed 1/5 Battalion Headquarters at Hill 51 about a kilometer away. "We need help, but we've got control—"

"*It was like being in a wagon wheel,*" said Lance Corporal (LCpl) Steve Wilson, Morgan's radio operator, "*with spokes running toward the center, bullets coming from every direction. It was like you were in the middle of a box of fireworks that somebody had set off.*"

Colt .45 pistol in hand, the captain crouched behind several tall rocks for cover. "*I'd never heard that amount of firing going on the whole time I was in Vietnam,*" said squad leader Corporal (Cpl) Bill Dubose. "*It was just—it sounded like a hundred machine guns going off.*"

"Reposition that rocket squad," Morgan yelled, "and direct your fire there!"

Squad leaders shouted orders over the roar of gunfire, the whistles of the NVA, and the cries of wounded men as mortar blasts exploded inside the perimeter, spraying deadly shrapnel into the Americans.

"Update Battalion," the captain ordered his radio operator, "we have engaged the enemy from at least two sides in heavy combat."

Five to seven hundred enemy combatants quickly mushroomed to twelve to fifteen hundred as elements of the 2nd NVA Division converged on Morgan's two platoons.

"*There was a little hedgerow that run along the river,*" Dubose said, "*and they was coming up that hedgerow and slipping in right there at the corner of the perimeter. And they was just strung over, you could see them running all over, and you could see them inside the perimeter running, so you didn't know, it being dark, you didn't know whether to shoot, whether you're going to hit one of your own men.*"

"Get down, Captain!" A Marine shouted. "Get down!"

As he rose from the cover of the boulders to get a better view of the battle, CPT Morgan came face to face with an NVA rifleman who now appeared inside the Marine perimeter. "There he is!" Morgan shouted. "Get him!"

The enemy soldier fired, and the captain fell to his knees.

"Delta 6 is down!" Wilson shouted into the radio. "Delta 6 is down!"

The leathernecks hunkered down in fighting holes and behind rocks, fighting to maintain their position, and as more VC assault troops breached the perimeter, the fighting soon was hand-to-hand.

Cpl Dubose led a five-man squad that held that portion of the perimeter facing the huge boulder and the high ground to the left.

From that rock, an NVA soldier had now set up a machine gun and, firing down on Dubose's men, proceeded to decimate his squad.

"It was a clear shot from the rock to the side that we were set in on, and we had no cover. I know it killed everyone in my squad except myself and a guy we called Frenchie."

What the Marines needed, before the NVA completely overran them, was artillery support. With the captain and the forward observer (FO) now dead, 2nd Lieutenant (2LT) Carlton Fulford took charge of the company, ordered another operator to access the correct radio frequency, and called the artillery battery on Hill 51.

"We need artillery support!"

"We can send someone for you—"

"If you don't fire at these coordinates, there won't be enough of us left to come after!"

Minutes later, American artillery began to rain on the Viet Cong just outside the Marine perimeter. Huey gunships also arrived, firing 50 caliber machine gun rounds into the attacking enemy, followed by helicopters with CS gas, all causing the enemy attack to subside—but only slightly.

Back on Hill 51, about a "klick" (kilometer) away, the Marines at the battalion firebase watched the night attack intensify as heavy rounds boomed across the valley and radios blasted out the chatter of desperate men. It was obvious that artillery and gunship support would not be enough, as the two platoons of Delta Company needed more reinforcements before the NVA annihilated them. The battalion commander for 1/5, Colonel (Col) Peter Hilgartner, immediately ordered Bravo Company and the remaining Delta Platoon, about 140 men, to reinforce Fulford's beleaguered troops.

As the sun began to rise over what was left of Delta Company, another Huey gunship arrived to provide covering fire for a UH-34 helicopter sent in to evacuate Fulford's critically wounded Marines.

Despite the gunship's protection, enemy fire quickly overwhelmed the medical evacuation transportation (medevac) chopper, causing it to spiral down, like a seedling falling from a pine tree, into the center of the Marine perimeter. Landing beyond a hedgerow and on top of the hole dug for the protection of the Vietnamese children brought in the night before, without harming the children, the pilot was able to run from the wreckage for the nearest shelter and join the fight.

Moments later, a new enemy mortar barrage rocked the area with explosions and shrapnel, striking the Huey gunship, and it too careened down to a hard landing, its crew also escaping into the fray.

Bravo 1/5, Ly Ly River

At about the same time, the men of Bravo 1/5 were in the mess hall at Hill 51 when word came that Delta was in trouble.

"*I was down getting breakfast, powdered eggs on a piece of bread with ketchup,*" Sergeant (Sgt) Jim Dougherty said, "*when these guys come running up hollering 'Bravo Company, we're mounting up; everybody go! Delta Company's in trouble again.'*"

Since Operations Union I and II, earlier in the year, Delta 1/5 had acquired a reputation for bad luck in the Quế Sơn Valley.

"*Delta Company's name,*" Dougherty said, "*was Dying Delta 1/5. They couldn't walk around the block without running into an enemy regiment. We figured, 'Okay, here we go; grab our shit, run out, get Delta out of trouble, and we're back this afternoon.' That was what everybody thought. You know, the old story: run out, and help Delta Company out, and then come back.*"

At about 08:20, as they crossed the deep, swiftly flowing Ly Ly River, Bravo Company, with the remaining platoon of Delta on point, radioed their approach to Lt Fulford's besieged men. After climbing up the bank onto dry land, the point squad of Delta's 2nd Platoon surged forward through a tree line and emerged onto an open dry rice paddy, the ground cracked and rock hard.

"*The river was flowing pretty fast, from our left to right,*" Navy Corpsman Larry Casselman said, "*and it was close to chest deep. We were holding our gas masks and our gear over our heads, the point was already across the river, and we were just about to the first tree line when they opened fire on us, small arms on full automatic. It was a curtain of automatic fire for five minutes.*"

Knowing that any reinforcements coming to Delta's aid would take a direct line from the firebase at Hill 51, the enemy had secured riflemen in the tree line and machine gun squads behind rocks in the path of the oncoming Americans. Now, with a distinct home field advantage, the NVA opened up with every weapon they had.

"*As was their practice, they had the position that they wanted back in a tree line,*" said Cpl Brian Spradling, a squad leader with Delta's 2nd Platoon. "*As we approached, the NVA opened up with real heavy small arms and automatic weapons. We probably got to within maybe half a kilometer of our other two platoons from Delta, and we really ran into a buzz saw.*"

Suddenly under attack from several directions, the thirty-five men of 2nd Platoon scrambled for cover and tried to return fire as they formed a hasty perimeter away from the open rice paddy at the end of the tree line. Caught by a flood of bullets while still crossing the river, the remaining Marines scrambled onto land and took shelter behind a paddy dike on the riverside, with the tree line to their left and the dry rice paddy beyond. Pinned down by a machine gun at their front, a sniper at their rear, and a growing number of NVA soldiers who were converging on their position, the Americans threw grenades, tried to set up machine gun positions of their own, and began to fire mortars almost vertically, causing the shells to fall within a hair's breadth of their own positions.

"*We spread out, we returned fire, and we tried to drag those hit back to some cover,*" Spradling said, "*and we did some maneuvering, but it seemed like with every little move that we made we just received more intense fire—every time we exposed ourselves at all. We finally just tried to hold our position to avoid being overrun.*"

The hunter had become the hunted, the rescuers now in need of their own rescue as four thousand veterans of the NVA's 2nd Division executed a battle plan that had one objective in mind: to annihilate every single United States Marine in the Quế Sơn Valley.

1

BALD EAGLE

Mike Company, 3/5 Battalion Headquarters, Hill 63

It was still dark when 1st Lieutenant (LT1) J.D. Murray, commander of Mike Company, 3rd Battalion, 5th Marines (3/5), called his officers to his command post on Hill 63, a fire support base located northwest of Chu Lai and about twenty kilometers from Hill 51. Due to the vastness of the region, when Marine units ran into trouble in the Quế Sơn Valley, few forces were available to provide backup. One of those was Mike 3/5, a Bald Eagle company designated as a quick reaction force on standby for immediate help as needed.

In command of Mike Company for less than two months, when Murray first arrived in Vietnam, the twenty-eight-year old had 160 pounds on his short, stocky frame and looked like the former college football player that he was. After months of field combat, an arduous climate, and lack of sleep, he now weighed a paltry 135.

A captain normally commanded a rifle company in the Marine Corps, but most available officers lacked combat experience. Having already completed one tour of duty in Vietnam, Lieutenant (Lt) Murray had plenty of experience, so his commander wisely placed him in charge of Mike Company. Of the officers under his command, only Murray and Lt Mike Hayden, leader of the weapons platoon, had actually seen combat. Lts Ed Combs, Ed Blecksmith, and Randy Cernick, the respective heads of 1st, 2nd, and 3rd Platoons, were fresh out of infantry leadership training at The Basic School and had each been in Vietnam for less than three months.

Murray hardly knew his platoon commanders, and to further complicate matters, his platoons were not in one location, with one on bridge security duty several miles away and two rotating between sweeps of roads near the base.

"The Quế Sơn Valley is very large," Murray remembered, *"and the Marine battalions that tried to control the valley were meager for the size of the terrain. Those units tied to defensive positions (Hill 51 for 1/5, Hill 63 for 3/5) that required troops for protection resulted in the deployment of understrength units when trouble arose. Command had split my three platoons up, I didn't have a good feel for my platoon commanders, and we didn't have the opportunity to train. Our training was on-the-job training in combat. In the long run, that really hurt because I may have been able to use them a little bit better than the way that I did."*

In addition, under normal circumstances, Murray would rely on an executive officer (or second in command) and a gunnery sergeant (a non-commissioned officer who provided logistical support to the company), but on that morning, Lt Murray had neither.

At full strength, a rifle platoon consisted of about forty-five men organized into three squads, each composed of a squad leader, grenadier, three four-man fire teams, and a platoon sergeant. Platoons in Vietnam, however, were rarely at full strength. The leathernecks' arsenal of weapons included the new M16 rifles, Colt .45 pistols, grenades, and M79 grenade launchers. The weapons platoon, divided between the rifle platoons, provided crew-served weapons and gunners (M60 machine guns, 60mm mortars, and M72 LAW or M20 3.5 inch rocket launchers) to each rifle platoon, with two machine guns and a rocket team assigned to each, while the 60mm mortar team remained together as a unit. Two Navy corpsmen, men who had basic training in combat medicine, also accompanied each platoon in the field.

"It was early in the morning and still dark when I was awakened and told to go to the battalion pen," 2LT Ed Combs said. *"JD, Mike Hayden, and Blecksmith—all the officers—were there, and they had the radio going. It was obvious that one of the other companies was in a heavy battle."*

"Early in the morning of the fourth, we were told that B and D Co 1/5 were in trouble and we were to stand down our day operation," Murray said. *"Around 09:30, I was summoned to the 3/5 command bunker and briefed that the Regiment (5th Marines) had ordered 3/5 to provide two companies (K and M) to go operational control under 1/5 to help relieve the pressure on B and D Companies. I prepared a five-paragraph order and immediately returned to the company area, where the lieutenants, platoon sergeants, and attached personnel were assembled, and briefed them on our mission."*

"Delta and Bravo 1/5 are in trouble," Murray told his officers. "Ready your men and await further orders."

Under normal circumstances, companies from the same battalion would provide support operations for their sister units, but in this case, no units from 1/5 were available. Mike and Kilo 3/5 were "chopped" (reassigned) to the command of Col Hilgartner, commander of 1/5, and ordered to meet up with his command group. As September 4 dawned clear, bright, humid, and hot, Mike and Kilo 3/5 received their orders to come to the aid of Bravo and Delta 1/5. The plan was to helicopter the two relief companies to within a few kilometers of Bravo and Delta and land in the same landing zone (LZ), at which time the combined units would come under the command of Col Hilgartner.

Due to the urgency of the mission and the distance between units, there was no time for Lt Murray and the commander of Kilo to receive a briefing in person from Col Hilgartner at Hill 51. This was a rescue mission, pure and simple. Time was of the essence, and details were—at best—sketchy.

1st Platoon

"We're in trouble."

That was the first thought that crossed the mind of Platoon Sgt Craig "Sully" Sullivan when he saw the face of Lt Combs. The commander of 1st Platoon, hastily summoned to Murray's command bunker, had returned to his men with unusual urgency.

"Delta and Bravo 1/5 have really stepped in it," Lt Combs said. "We're going to have to go out and rescue them. We have about twenty minutes to get ready to go."

Sully called up his platoon's three squad leaders, which included the man he relied on most in tight situations, 1st Squad leader, Cpl Bill Vandergriff. Vandergriff, a member of the Odawa Indian tribe who had joined the Corps on a five-dollar bet, described his platoon sergeant as a "swashbuckler."

"*Sully had that swagger about him,*" he said, "*that confidence.*"

"Saddle up," Sullivan said. "We got to go help out 1/5."

"What's going on?"

"They're in it bad. Take extra water—and extra ammo."

. . .

LCpl Ryan Hooley, a grunt in Sergeant (Sgt) Sims's 2nd Squad, threw out his C-Rations and stuffed his backpack with cans of fruit when he received word that 1st Platoon was headed out.

"Over there, one of the things you could never get enough of was fruit," he said. *"We had the C-rats, and as terrible as they were, there were certain things that were really prized, and one of those was canned peaches in syrup. Those things were gold, along with the chocolate and the cake, so I had my parents send me a bunch of canned fruit in syrup."*

As he stuffed his backpack, another Marine, a new guy, stepped up.

"Hooley—I'm not making it back from this. Take my stuff, and mail it home to my mom."

The Marine was holding a handful of personal items.

"Pruett, get the hell away from me. You know this is like bad mojo, you know. You're going to make it home; now, what the hell are you talking about—"

"No. I'm not making it out of this, so would you send it home?"

Hooley shook his head.

"I'm not touching that stuff. It might rub off."

2nd Platoon

On another part of the hill, Private 1st Class (Pfc) Tony Martinez, a grunt in Sgt Larry Peters' 1st Squad in 2nd Platoon, nervously checked his gear. He had packed three days' worth of C-rations, a poncho, two bandoleers of machine gun ammunition, magazines for his M16, a gas mask, and helmet. Like the other men, he carried about forty pounds of gear in his pack.

The five-foot-five Martinez had been in Vietnam only for a few weeks. He wore military-issue black-framed glasses that collected moisture in the humid climate, and instead of the lighter-weight jungle utilities worn by the "salts" (experienced Marines), he was still wearing the uniform issued to him stateside, which was made of heavy cotton that didn't shed moisture easily. His sweat would no doubt ruin the picture he carried of his high school sweetheart, and to make matters worse, instead of lighter canvas jungle boots with treads to help handle the terrain, he still wore heavy leather boots with smooth soles and no vents to get rid of water.

As a "fucking new guy" (FNG), Martinez stood out, and he knew it. He tried to keep his mouth shut and learn from the others, but when the salts mixed with green additions fresh from the states, unit solidarity was severely undermined. Inexperienced and prone to make mistakes that would get him or the man next to him killed, the FNG often took the place of a recently wounded or killed salt.

Martinez's squad leader, by contrast, was a veteran who had already served a full tour of duty in Vietnam in a combined action platoon, acting as an advisor to South Vietnamese militia, and was now on his second tour. A down-to-earth sergeant called "Larry" by his men, the twenty-year-old Peters, who had lost quite a bit of weight during his time "in-country," always wore the sleeves of his jungle utilities rolled up his arms.

"*He used to draw martini glasses on all his gear,*" Combat Engineer Lief Ericson remembered. "*He had drawn 'em on his boots, his pack, his helmet liner, everything. Everybody had their own talisman to ward off the evil over there, and that happened to be his.*"

"*He looked like Custer,*" LCpl Eliot Rubenfeld said. "*Good-looking, dirty blonde hair, and a nice, big, fat mustache. He was gung-ho, and he looked to me like he was destined to be some sort of hero.*"

"*He became a Catholic,*" his sister Shirley said, "*and he spent a lot of time on his first tour helping the nuns at an orphanage in D'Nang. He wanted to go back to his unit and to the kids that he had sort of adopted and to work with the sisters at the orphanage. That is why he wanted to be back there.*"

When Shirley learned that her younger brother had volunteered for a second tour, Peters sought to assure her that his orders would be for Da Nang and that he wouldn't see combat. But when he wrote that summer that the Marines were short on sergeants and needed help on the front line, she felt a sense of dread.

"*My heart went right down to my toes, and I thought, 'Oh god, you're never coming back.' I could have banged his head against the wall if I'd been near him for doing such a dumb thing when he had said he would not.*"

"*Being new in-country,*" Martinez remembered, "*I looked up to him, and every word he said I followed to the letter because, of course, I wanted to survive.*"

As he prepared his squad, Peters gave Martinez's gear a quick check, taking special care to inspect his M16.

"Make sure to clean your rifle three times a day to reduce jamming."

"Yes, sir."

He then gestured to the photo of the pretty, young girl.

"The rain might get to that—"

Peters took the picture and zipped it into a plastic bag he carried with his own personal items.

"I'll watch it for you."

"Thank you, sir."

"You're good to go."

Attached to Sgt Pete's squad was a machine gun team led by Cpl Carlton Clark ("CC from DC"), a nineteen-year-old combat veteran with one Purple Heart accustomed to receiving assignments to different squads in various platoons as needed. Clark had worked with a number of non-coms but had a different feeling when he looked at Peters.

"This guy looks real gung-ho," he thought. "Hey, Sarge, you ain't going to go up here and try to get medals, are you?"

• • •

Rocket Squad leader Sgt Howard "Red" Manfra (also in Lt Blecksmith's 2nd Platoon) had been in-country since April and had converted his savings, close to six hundred dollars, into cash for a well-earned seven-day leave to Hawaii.

"Saddle up, Red!"

"Shit—can't I stay back? I'm going on R&R."

"No. We need everybody out there. We'll chopper you back in on the fifth, and you can go on R&R on the sixth. Let's go!"

As Red started to tuck his cash into his sea bag for safekeeping, he had a strange premonition that he wouldn't make it back to Hill 63 for his long-awaited leave. He tried to shake off the feeling that he might die in combat. Maybe he just didn't trust that the company would get him back on time in the middle of a mission.

"We'll go out," he pondered, "set up a perimeter for 1/5, get their wounded and dead, and get the choppers in—and get them out. That will be it."

He thought for a moment, ran his hand through his hair, and then hurried over to the company clerk.

"If anything happens to me, make sure that this money gets home to my mother in New Jersey."

"Uh, sure."

Manfra darted away to prepare his men and equipment, leaving the bewildered clerk holding five hundred and seventy-five dollars.

3rd Platoon

Cpl Chuck Cummings, one of three squad leaders in Cernick's 3rd Platoon, was resting on his rack when another leatherneck rushed into his tent.

"D Company 1/5's been hit! The gooks zapped their six. We're moving out!"

Cummings came to his feet as the men scrambled to check their gear and assemble into squads. The stress was palpable and immediate. With Delta's company commander killed in action (KIA), the Marines knew that they were likely in for a fierce fight.

As a squad leader, Cummings was in charge of three four-man fire teams and a machine gun team. He carried a Colt .45 pistol and an M79 grenade launcher. After receiving his orders, Cummings had ammunition, grenades, and C-Ration meals distributed to his men and had each of them fill both of their canteens with water. In addition to their normal equipment, Cummings men also packed extra mortar, machine gun ammunition, and rocket rounds for the weapons squads.

Cummings, a salt who had been in-country for almost eleven months, knew that many of the thirteen men in his squad had never seen combat.

"Listen to your fire team leaders," he said. "You'll be all right. If we get hit, don't shoot your own people. Watch what other people do. If you run, run low. Don't stand up. Make sure you've got water and all your gear."

Cummings also knew that his men's principal firearm, the M16 semiautomatic rifle, was unreliable and would often malfunction in combat.

"Make sure that each of you has your cleaning rod to eject jammed cartridges. A knife won't do the job. Remember—no more than fifteen or sixteen rounds in the magazine. I know that it holds twenty, but it's more likely to jam if you load it up. And for God's sake, keep those magazines clean."

Cummings was walking a fine line. He knew that the new rifles, issued to the Marines in April and May, had often jammed in combat on Operations Union I and II, and he believed that the enemy's AK-47 was a superior weapon, but he didn't want to demoralize his men. Trust in a weapon empowered them, and he didn't want his leathernecks to waste energy being concerned about their rifles.

As the men prepared to move out, Cummings introduced them to a new member of the squad, nineteen-year-old Pfc Tony Gabaldon.

"*I looked at the kid,*" said Cpl Dennis Tylinski, a short-timer with two months left on his tour, "*and I think I was like twenty-one, then somebody younger than you, you think of them as kids back then, and I says, 'Gabaldon, do you pronounce that as Ga-bal-don?'*"

"Yeah."

"Where are you from?"

"California."

"*When I was a kid,*" Tylinski said, "*I remember watching the movie* Hell to Eternity *starring Tab Hunter, and Hunter played Guy Gabaldon, a kid that grew up with a Japanese family just prior to World War II, so he knew the Japanese language. He went through the Marine Corps and got on Saipan, and a lot of the Japanese civilians were committing suicide by jumping off mountains and cliffs. And he used his language of Japanese to talk a lot of them out of it.*"

"You any relation to Guy Gabaldon?" Tylinski asked the new arrival.

"Yeah," the kid said. "I think that he's a distant cousin."

"The kid looked real young," Tylinski said. *"Tony was a real young kid."*

Company Command

Back with the company command group, Cpl Chuck Goebel checked and rechecked the two radios that he would take into combat. As forward air controller (FAC), it was Goebel's job to communicate with critical fixed-wing aircraft and helicopter support should the company need it. Through Goebel, Lt Murray had a variety of airborne resources at his disposal: helicopters delivering rockets, machine gun fire or smoke and gas canisters, jet aircraft with high explosive bombs and napalm, and "Spooky" (also known as Puff the Magic Dragon), the deadly C-130 gunship armed with Gatling guns.

With all of that firepower just a radio call away, Goebel didn't think to check his pistol.

Departure Landing Zone, Hill 63

"I was sitting on the ground, and I just had this sinking feeling," LCpl Ryan Hooley of 1st Platoon said. *"I knew something bad was going to happen. I didn't know exactly what, but I had this feeling in the pit of my gut. It's just like electric. You can feel it there, and you know, you can almost smell it."*

As Hooley looked at the ground, he saw a pair of legs walk by and stop. He looked up to see a man in his late thirties with the bars of an officer on his collar. Hooley started to come to his feet.

"No, sit down, son. You don't get up."

The officer sat down beside Hooley, asked if he could bum a smoke, and said— "You don't look so good. What's wrong?"

"I just have this feeling. I don't know what's gonna happen, but it's not good, and I got—I know something's gonna happen to me today—"

"You know, you shouldn't feel that way—"

"*And I'm thinking to myself 'Yeah, yeah, yeah—I'm not gonna kill myself or run away. I just got this feeling, and it's not good.' Up to that point, I always thought I was going to come home fine, but that was the first time in my life that I ever felt that I might not be coming home.*"

"Can I say a word of prayer with you?"

"Sure."

"*The officer said a prayer, blessed me, said 'You'll be alright, son,' and got up and walked off.*"

Despite the assurance and blessing of the battalion chaplain, LCpl Hooley was still ill at ease.

"*Did it calm my fears? No. Did it do anything for me? No, but he was trying to reassure me, and as one man to another, I appreciated that.*"

Soft-spoken, yet gruff enough to keep the leathernecks' attention, Navy Chaplain Father Vincent Capodanno continued to walk among the Marines as they prepared their equipment and began to make their way to the departure/landing LZ to await transport helicopters. Like he had with LCpl Hooley, the chain-smoking Catholic priest sensed tension and fear among the men, and he sought to provide what comfort he could. At thirty-eight, the tall and leathery Staten Island native had already served one tour of duty in Vietnam and had requested, and been granted, an extension. His assignment was to the battalion's headquarters and supply company (H&S), known as "the group," and he had been told that H&S was to remain behind when Mike and Kilo were sent out.

"*I was given an order to give to Father Capodanno that the main group wasn't moving out the following morning,*" Pete Morales said, "*because the line companies were going to meet heavy enemy resistance, and that the group was going to move out later when it was safer.*"

"Fine," the padre told Morales, "but my Marines need me in time of pain, sorrow, and dying. I'm getting short, but I'm planning to extend for six more months. I love them, and they need me."

"*He was our priest, and he was there for you when you needed him,*" said LCpl Nick Duca, a machine gunner with 2nd Platoon. "*He would talk to you, console you, give you whatever kind of spiritual guidance you needed because we were young, we were scared, and we never knew what bullet had our name on it.*"

"*He had a reputation,*" 1st Platoon Sgt Sullivan said, "*of going out in the bush. He wasn't supposed to, but he did.*"

As he walked among the leathernecks, Capodanno found Sullivan and his men.

"*I had my 1st Platoon over in a group checking all their equipment, and Father Capodanno comes walking up. And he asked me would I mind if we got the troops together and he had a little prayer for them. And he told me that he felt that we would need it. So I said, 'Well, certainly.'*"

"There's a lot going on and a lot you can't control," Capodanno would say in a simple message to his Marines. "It's really in God's hands, so the best you can do to prepare is to try to stay in the state of grace because you can't control what might happen once something starts. Keep in mind that you'll be judged someday. You can't control what's going to happen, but the best you can do is prepare, and that's by living the best life you can. We are all doing noble duty."

After saying a prayer, the battalion chaplain took the platoon sergeant's hand.

"We might be stepping into it," Capodanno said, "and I want to make sure that all of you know that God is on our side."

After praying with Sullivan's men, the leathernecks began to line up as the priest began to hand out Saint Christopher medals rumored to have been cast from silver candleholders from his church in New York. Many Marines already carried medals of the protective saint of travelers, but not all of them.

Cpl Larry Nunez of 2nd Platoon joined the line, but the chaplain had distributed all of his medals by the time Nunez had reached the front. As the other Marines dispersed, Nunez approached the priest.

"Do you need my services?"

"No, Father. I'm Protestant, but I really wanted one of your medals."

Capodanno removed his own Saint Christopher medal from his dog tags and handed it to Nunez.

"If you want one, you're going to have it."

• • •

At 11:10, less than two hours after the Marines of Mike and Kilo 3/5 received orders to rescue their comrades in Delta and Bravo 1/5, the last transport helicopter carrying the men of Kilo Company from the departure LZ on Hill 63 disappeared across the countryside. For the leathernecks of Mike Company, it was now "hurry up and wait," as there were not enough choppers available for all of the Marines. Loaded with gear, the men sat on the grass in the hot, sun-drenched LZ for another nerve racking thirty minutes, anxiously guessing about the mission ahead.

"I hear they got it bad."

"Yeah, outnumbered."

"What do you think's gonna happen?"

"Maybe it'll be over by the time we get there."

"Yeah—we'll just set up a perimeter, help clean up."

"*It sounded like it was really bad,*" said Cpl George Phillips, leader of a rocket squad attached to 1st Platoon and a salt with nine months in-country. "*I saw Father Capodanno. You know, the chaplains; when the chaplains show up, you know it's not good.*"

A veteran who had mentored Phillips when he was an FNG put it more succinctly:

"*When the chaplains show up, you're going to get fucked.*"

While waiting for the transport helicopters, LCpl Fred Permenter, with 3rd Squad of 3rd Platoon, noticed Pfc Steve Wright from 2nd Platoon, whom he had met a few days before, standing by himself with a worried look on his face.

"What's going on, Steve? Are you alright, buddy?"

"I didn't get any letters at mail call this morning."

"*I could see that he was visibly worried about something. We talked for a few minutes about home, and as we did, a Marine came out with more mail and called Steve's name. I could see relief come across his face, and as he read the letter, I could see the weight of concern leave his shoulders.*"

At about the same time, Lt Col Charles B. Webster, commander of the 3rd Battalion, 5th Marines, arrived at the LZ to address the waiting men. Machine Gunner Clark usually didn't pay too much attention when officers gave pep talks, but this time, some of what Webster said stuck.

"Your fellow Marines are relying on you today. You are up against the 2nd NVA Division: about two thousand regulars."

Clark didn't need to hear any more. He wasn't an FNG. Even though he was only nineteen, he had seen fierce fighting and taken wounds on Union I, so he knew that they weren't going on a picnic. Clark rechecked his gear and tried to push what Webster said from his mind, but LCpl Fred Tancke, who was laying on his pack with a towel covering the bolt of his rifle, couldn't. The 2nd Platoon rifleman could do the math, and to him, the odds didn't look good. With a little over three hundred men combined, the NVA outnumbered Mike and Kilo Companies at least five to one.

"Colonel, don't you think that's a lot for us to take on? One company doesn't seem like it is enough Marines to go against that big of a force."

"Kilo will be going out with you," Webster said and added, as he saw the concerned look on the nineteen-year-old's face, "You will make us proud today."

As the colonel spoke, the whirling blades of the second set of transport helicopters whipped a cloud of sand around the waiting men. Lt Murray watched with concern, having given orders for the Marines to keep their rifle breaches covered to protect them from dust. Some men, like Tancke, used towels wrapped around the rifle's receiver so that debris could not get in through the ejection port, as well as the plastic that wrapped their C-Ration spoon over the end of the rifle barrel. When the M16 would inevitably jam, those Marines with experience would also attach the cleaning rod to the upper and lower sling swivels for easy access.

"*When we got into fire fights,*" George Phillips said, "*the towels came off, the little plastic you could shoot right through, and you used the cleaning rods to punch out the rounds.*"

Despite these precautions, as well as orders for each grunt to clean his M16 at least twice a day, Murray knew that the rifles his men were equipped with were not reliable. When first issued in limited numbers in 1965, the M16 was dependable, but as the weapon moved into wide-scale use in the fall of 1966, reports came in that the rifle tended to jam during combat. Some soldiers wrote their congressmen pleading for help, fearing for their lives if the weapons continued to fail. Journalists caught wind of the controversy and ran stories on the evening news.

In October of 1966, the government investigated the problem, and it was determined that the weapons jammed due to poor maintenance by the fighting men in the field. An edict went out: Army and Marine Corps commanders received orders to insure that their men had proper training in rifle maintenance with a more even and consistent distribution of rifle cleaning rods.

Lt Murray received those orders, and as he watched his men guard their rifles from the flying sand, he gritted his teeth. Those higher in command blamed the problem with the M16 on poor leadership at the fire team, squad, and platoon levels, but Murray knew better. He had led the forward fighting units, and he knew damn well that his devil dogs knew how to clean their weapons, but despite their efforts, the rifles continued to malfunction.

The issue was not maintenance but a tendency for the rifle's extractor to rip off the lip of a cartridge, leaving it in the barrel and then double feeding a second live round behind it, causing the M16 to jam. The only way to clear the rounds was to pull back the bolt, knock out each cartridge with a cleaning rod, and then manually reload: a dangerous, time-consuming process in a place where Marine lives depended on the reliability of their rifles.

Of additional concern was the safety of the CH-46 transport helicopters tasked to take the men into the Quế Sơn Valley. The large, tandem-rotor Sea Knights could quickly carry twenty-five grunts into battle, but the arriving fleet had been grounded after several of the choppers had crashed due to tail rotor problems. The leathernecks didn't bother to ask if the arriving helicopters had passed inspection—or even if they had had one. There simply were not enough transports available to carry Mike Company to the battlefield in time to save Delta and Bravo. Potentially crashing in a Sea Knight was just another risk that the Marines had to take.

1st Platoon boarded first, with half of the men in one chopper with Lt Combs and the other half in a second Sea Knight under Sully's supervision. Combs moved to the front of his transport, handed the pilot a map with the destination LZ marked on it, and put on a headset. The pilot looked at the map and nodded.

• • •

"Padre," Dave Magnenat asked, "did you forget about the Bible you were going to give me?"

Father Capodanno acknowledged that he had, dropped his gear to the dirt, ran back to his hooch, and was back in a flash with a small Bible for the Navy corpsman who was remaining behind.

"Padre—good luck," John Costello of India Company called out, "and be careful!"

Costello watched with concern as the chaplain boarded one of the helicopters, knowing that Capodanno likely did not have permission to join Mike Company in the field. "*They would have never let him go out there unless he was with the battalion command.*"

"*He went out on the same airship that I was on,*" FAC Chuck Goebel said. "*He was sitting forward, port (left) side, and looking very somber as we flew.*"

At 11:50 hours, when the last of the Marines of Mike 3/5 climbed aboard the Sea Knights, and as his chopper was flying to an LZ somewhere in the Quế Sơn Valley, Lt Murray had a bad feeling about the rescue mission. The fact that he and his men were now officially under the operational control of Col Hilgartner and his 1/5 Command didn't sit well with him.

"You just don't take units, split them up, give them to somebody else, and expect them to run fluidly."

The plan was for Mike and Kilo 3/5 and the 1/5 Command Group under Col Hilgartner to link up in the same LZ where Hilgartner would give the two companies a thorough briefing of their combined mission.

Events in Vietnam, however, rarely went according to plan.

2

THE KNOLL

En Route to the Quế Sơn Valley

"Sit on your helmet."

Pfc Martinez, in a chopper with 2nd Platoon, gave his sergeant a confused look. Peters gestured to the other salts, who were all sitting on their helmets.

"In case you get rounds coming up from the bottom."

Martinez did as ordered.

"We were told that we were going into a hot LZ," said Cpl Don Goulet, a fire team leader with 3rd Squad of 3rd Platoon, *"and that made everybody pucker and prepare themselves."*

On another airship with 1st Platoon, LCpl Jack Swan sat in silence. As point man in Vandergriff's 1st Squad, the well-muscled twenty-year-old led the platoon, and at times the entire company, in the field, and he had no interest in making friends. He especially had no interest in striking up a conversation with the five-foot-seven, one hundred-pound nineteen-year- old FNG in his squad, Pfc Howard Haney, who sat quietly nearby, weighed down with a fifty pound pack, flak jacket, an M16, and as much ammo as he could carry.

"The new guy doesn't understand," Murray explained. *"He doesn't have the proper training, and that makes him a danger to everybody. It takes a while to assimilate him. He is a foreigner, so after he is there for a period of time and he has demonstrated his merit that he is a team player, then he becomes part of the unit, but it takes a while."*

Swan greeted the FNG with silence, but he showed a different side to his squad leader.

"Jack was very outgoing," Vandergriff said. *"He was very lean, wiry, and a lot of fun to be around back in the 'rear with the gear.' In the field, he was extremely intense, a damn good Marine, and I put my life in his hands many times. I didn't have to worry about anybody having my back as long as Jack was around."*

As he pondered the new guy, Haney, Swan eyed LCpl Thomas Fisher, leader of one of the three four-man fire teams that made up the squad. Fisher was a stocky, powerfully built salt with the eagle, globe, and anchor emblem of the Marine Corps tattooed on his left arm. Fisher had taught Swan the ropes of survival in Vietnam when Swan himself was an FNG.

"He didn't fuck with you like a lot of the other guys did," Swan said. *"He just said, 'Now, listen up. Pay attention to this. This is how you want to do it; this is what you want to look for—' He was a great teacher, cared about his men, and a hell of a good guy."*

On the transport carrying the command group, the pilot turned to Lt Murray. "We're going to the alternate LZ."

Kilo Company and the 1/5 Command Group had come under fire at the original landing zone. That LZ was "hot," so the pilot of the Sea Knight had to quickly find a different place to offload Murray's leathernecks.

"Alternate LZ? I was never briefed on an alternate LZ!"

There was no time to argue, much less process the new information, as moments later, the Sea Knight landed. At about noon, Murray jumped from the chopper, looked around, and tried to figure out where the hell he was. Despite the urgent orders and the threat of imminent danger, the alternate LZ was quiet except for the beating of chopper blades as more Marines leaped out onto the ground. Most commanders would have been grateful to land in a deserted

LZ, but Murray knew instantly that something was wrong. His orders were to land Mike Company in the same location as Kilo and the 1/5 Command Group, but those Marines were nowhere to be found.

Murray ordered his men to set up security while he waited for the rest of the company. As choppers continued to bring in men to the LZ, he studied his map and tried to make it make sense.

"We were probably fifteen hundred to two thousand meters away from Kilo," Murray said. *"Col Hilgartner and the 1/5 Command Group did not land in the same LZ as Kilo, and neither one of them landed in the same LZ as us. The thing that bothered me was that I was never briefed on an alternate LZ. When I know the LZ I am going in, I know certain ways to get out of there, I know how to set up my security, and I've got a plan of action. When you put me in an alternate LZ and I don't really know where it is, it takes time to be able to figure out where you are at."*

To further complicate matters, the 1/5 Command Group and Kilo Company had already landed and moved out of their respective LZs.

Murray's radio crackled.

"Where are you?"

It was the operations officer for 1/5. Murray read the coordinates of where he thought he was.

"No, no, no. That is not your location. You landed in the same LZ that we did."

"No, I'm at the alternate LZ."

"No, no, no! What is your location?"

Murray repeated his location and got the distinct feeling that the operations officer for 1/5 had no confidence in his ability to read a map. Quickly realizing that the 1/5 Command Group had no idea where Mike Company had landed, Murray improvised. He knew that the 12th Marine Artillery Unit was in the valley and requested that a "Willie Peter" (white phosphorous) round be fired on Mike 3/5's objective.

As Murray and his platoon commanders watched, a trail of white smoke rose from a hill four kilometers away to the southwest. Consulting his map, Murray realized that Kilo Company was fifteen hundred meters closer than Mike Company and he were to the men of Delta and Bravo 1/5 at Đông Sơn. The bad news did not sit well with 1/5 Battalion Commander (Cmdr) Hilgartner.

"Get your butt up here ASAP!"

The new plan of action was for Kilo to link up with the 1/5 command and take a position to the west (the left side) of Route 534, a single lane dirt road, while Mike Company took the east (right side). The units would sweep west five to six kilometers (three to four miles) to the village of Đông Sơn and the beleaguered men of Bravo and Delta 1/5. Landing about forty minutes after Kilo and the command group, Mike Company had now separated from Kilo and Command by fifteen hundred to two thousand meters (about a mile). Rather than move as one unit, the two companies moved separately into enemy territory and were now vulnerable to a piecemeal attack by the numerically superior NVA.

Murray ordered Lt Combs and 1st Platoon to take point, with Blecksmith's 2nd and Cernick's 3rd following behind in a staggered column. Since the weapons platoon had split up into rocket and machine gun squads assigned individually to the three rifle platoons, Lt Mike Hayden and the 60mm mortars would follow behind the command group along with some engineers and a helicopter support team.

Despite the near one-hundred-percent humidity, one-hundred-degree weather, and carrying forty pounds of gear per man, the leathernecks moved quickly through low bushes, over slightly rolling hills, and past scattered huts and trees that dotted the landscape.

1st Squad of 1st Platoon, commanded by Cpl Vandergriff, took point as expected with LCpl Jack Swan, carrying an M79 grenade launcher, as point man for the entire company. In his four months in Vietnam, Swan had developed a reputation as a reliable point man, the eyes and ears of the company who could save lives. As point, Swan faced the most danger, as he would be the one to trip any booby traps, set off any land mines, or come face-to-face with any enemy troops waiting in ambush.

"We picked him because he was the skinniest and littlest," Lt Combs said, *"and he just liked it; he volunteered to do it. He'd get upset unless he was the point man."*

As a salt attached to 2nd Platoon, Cpl Carlton Clark knew the rules when moving in enemy territory. Each grunt was to maintain an interval of ten to fifteen meters while staying within eye contact of each other so that a sweep of enemy machine gun fire or a single mortar round wouldn't wipe out several Marines with one salvo. Even though he had his doubts about the dangerous mission, he felt confident, even a bit cocky, about being with such a powerful platoon of devil dogs.

"I knew how hard we hit, and I felt like they had to fear us. That takes a lot of fear away, knowing that you're a strong fighting force, so it gives you confidence to hit—and hit hard."

At one point, the fast-moving staggered column stopped, and Clark scanned the area for signs of trouble while keeping an eye on the grunt to his front. He turned to see the man behind him, Pfc Dennis Fisher, who was carrying two belts of machine gun ammo, still walking forward and looking up at the sky. Clark opened his mouth to say something but then decided to see how long it would take the FNG to realize that the column had stopped. That happened when the private bumped into Clark.

"Fisher—keep your eyes open, and maintain your interval!"

The stunned nineteen-year-old did as ordered.

After about two hours of tactical movement under the hot sun, Murray's men had made good progress, covering three-and-a-half to four kilometers (about two miles), so he issued orders to stop in a small village for a quick break. The Marines had travelled just over half the distance to their objective and were now within a few klicks of Kilo's position. Something, however, wasn't right.

The village, nothing more than a few houses surrounded by banana and breadfruit trees, was eerily quiet and appeared deserted. For the veterans, the absence of people and animals was a sure indication that enemy troops were nearby. Murray sensed it and sent out a combat patrol to scout the surrounding territory.

As he did, his radio lit up.

"I think we're gonna have action here soon," Col Hilgartner said. "How soon can you get here?"

"We should be there shortly," Murray replied, giving Mike Company's coordinates. Kilo was still ahead of them, guiding on the opposite side of Route 534, which was only a few klicks to the left of Mike Company's march. Then, the radio crackled again.

"We just found an AK on a boulder. We need you here now!"

Murray recalled the patrol and ordered his company to move out, now in a combat wedge formation with 1st Platoon on point, Blecksmith's 2nd Platoon on the left side of the wedge (the side closest to Route 534), and Cernick's 3rd Platoon on the right side of the wedge, both slightly behind 1st Platoon. The company's formation resembled a triangle. Murray and his command group would take position just behind 1st Platoon in the center of the wedge.

Cpl Don Goulet, who had been a Catholic altar boy for seven years and didn't swear much before joining the Corps, was near the rear of the company with 3rd Platoon and had just dropped down to rest when the order came to move out.

"Jesus Christ—fuck this shit!"

"And he (Capodanno) was standing right behind me. I looked up at him, he looked down at me, and I felt extremely embarrassed."

He sat down and said, "How are you boys doing?"

"Fine, Father."

The chaplain smiled and gave Goulet a look that said, "It's OK. I understand the Marine Corps language."

Cappadonna came to his feet and continued up the line with 3rd Platoon. Goulet, feeling reassured, also came to his feet to continue the march.

"If I get killed," he thought, "at least a priest will be there for me."

The leathernecks left the village and the cover of trees for a flat, open area that dipped into a slight valley of rocky terrain. As the valley sloped to the north, the land consisted of small brush and hedgerows that lead to a thick line of trees near the bank of the Ly Ly River, which was about a kilometer to the north (or right) of Mike Company's march.

An eerie stillness engulfed the Marines as they walked quickly through the valley and low brush. The Quế Sơn Basin was a populated area, yet there were no villagers, animals, or birds present. There was no noise; not even the air moved.

"Hold up!"

Cpl Vandergriff walked up to his point man, who he often keyed off simply by exchanging looks.

"Jack, this is not good."

"I got you."

"Keep your eyes peeled."

Back with the command group, Murray's radio blared again.

"Kilo has contact! Get here as soon as you can!"

Murray sent the order forward for 1st Platoon to pick up the pace. That was one command that point man Swan did not want to hear.

"We were being pushed pretty fast," Swan said, *"which myself and my squad leader, Bill Vandegriff—we didn't like that push thing because it didn't give us a chance to look at things that were moving."*

About three hundred meters from the village and separated from it by a draw, a knoll, about two hundred meters long and 150 meters wide, gradually rose from the dry, flat terrain. Long, narrow, and shaped like a football, it ascended about fifteen meters and blocked the view of the land on the other side. Starting at the narrow end and walking lengthwise, it was dry and rocky, pockmarked with bomb craters with only scattered bushes for cover. Vandergriff's point squad, followed by 1st Platoon and the rest of the company, reached its top at about 14:30 hours.

"My radioman and I were in the middle of the squad," Lt Combs said. *"Cpl Fisher was on my right side fire team, and we were spread out pretty well, about fifty feet away from each other. On my left, we had a point man (Swan) out with a couple of Marines behind him, and then the 1st Squad leader was out there on up to the left of me, Bill Vandergriff. Sully was back with the 2nd Squad over to the left of us, and the 3rd Squad (Cpl Sims) was to the right. It was a diamond formation, with me being in the middle of that diamond."*

With most likely Pfc Gene Mortensen behind him to his right, Swan sensed the FNG to his left, Pfc Haney, creeping ahead.

"*We were doing a V (inverted) shape,*" Swan said, "*and I kept yelling at the kid on the left, 'Don't get ahead of me!'*"

At the crest of the knoll, Swan could now see that the barren hillside dropped down sharply into a giant rice paddy.

"*When we came down the knoll to this huge rice paddy in front of us, and I mean huge, buddy, my brain was going one hundred miles an hour,*" Swan said, "*but I didn't pick up on the fact that there weren't any people in that rice paddy and there were no water buffalo. I noticed out to my 11:00 a young couple, a male and female Vietnamese. She was carrying the buckets over her shoulder type thing, and he was walking behind her. And I said to myself, 'That looks really serene.'*"

"*I was walking to his left,*" Haney said. "*It was real quiet. Things didn't seem right to me.*"

Just behind Vandergriff's point squad, Lt Combs spotted a group of men moving through the brush to the left of the rice paddy about five hundred meters to the south. Although he couldn't see them clearly, he thought he had spotted Kilo Company.

"6," he radioed Murray, "Do we have other Marines in our area? I think I see Kilo."

As the point squad reached the bottom of the front side of the knoll, Swan saw a bush move off to this left—with what looked like a foot at its base.

"*I saw a civilian jump up and run about three or four feet,*" Haney said, "*and then drop back down. At that time, I heard Jack off to my right front say—*"

"Oh shit!"

"Bill," Swan called back to his squad leader, "there's brush moving on the hill at about our 10:30."

Cpl Vandergriff saw the same movement and relayed the message to his platoon sergeant, who had just reached the crest.

"If that son of a bitch moves again," Sgt Sullivan said, "you shoot it!"

The bush moved, and Vandergriff and Swan didn't hesitate. Vandergriff hit the "bush" with two rounds from his M16, and Swan let loose with his M79 grenade launcher.

"I turned around and fired," Swan said. *"I watched the round as it took off from the tube, and watched it arc, and it was headed that way, and that is when all hell broke loose."*

"I thought I had stepped on a bees nest," Lt Combs said, *"because I heard this buzzing, just this constant buzzing, and then you hear the crack: the report of the round. I glanced to my right, and it was like this whole field was alive. They were NVA, and they had bushes on their back and the whole bit, the camouflaged face, and they were coming right for us."*

A swarm of bullets, both rifle and machine gun fire, came from nowhere and yet everywhere, tearing into the exposed men.

"The whole friggin' world came down on top of us," Sullivan said. *"They were firing rockets, and they were firing RPG, and they were firing machine guns. Mortars started coming in. I mean, the whole shebang came in on us at one time."*

The leathernecks scrambled for cover, but the few scant bushes on the knoll offered few places to hide. Vandergriff dived into an old bomb crater about five meters off the front of the knoll. Sgt Sullivan and his radio operator, Cpl Mercereuio, found another as bullets zipped across the top. As an enemy round shot one of his grenades off his hip, Swan dropped behind a paddy dike sixty to eighty feet from Haney, with two dikes between them.

"When the shit hit the fan, I went straight down," Swan said, *"and probably about twenty feet in front of me was probably the last rice paddy dike before you entered that huge rice paddy."*

A man to the left of Vandergriff took three rounds of machine gun fire in his back as he dove for cover.

"When they opened up, it looked like a wall of smoke hit me in the face," Haney said. *"I dove, and I got hit in mid-air in my left shoulder, and it kind of bounced me into the ground, back up to my feet, and I was falling forward face-first."*

The round tore through Haney's chest and out his back an inch from his spine. He fell forward, unable to move his arm or shoulder or even turn his head.

"I tried to scream for a corpsman, and I just blew blood out of my lungs," Haney said. *"The guy to my right and back: he was hit, and he went down, and he was hit quite a few more times after that and died."*

That Marine was likely Pfc Gene Mortensen. Others hit the deck and tried to lay down suppressing fire in the enemy's direction.

"I would say they weren't over thirty yards from us," Haney said. *"I think they opened up because we were walking right into them. If we would have went past there and made it out into the large rice paddy, I think they would have annihilated us."*

The young couple that Swan had spotted broke into a run and took shelter in a large hootch. Once inside, the barrel of a VC machine gun appeared out the front door and opened up.

"What they were was a ploy to make it look serene out there," Swan said, *"and they almost had me."*

Swan put a round from his M79 grenade launcher through the door of the hootch. He saw a lot of movement, so he concentrated rounds into the brush to the left and right at the rear of the hut.

"I figured I'd get down, and fire some rounds off, and bail back up the hill, but I turned around, and everybody was running back up the hill."

"I was on the radio with JD," Combs said, "and our first reaction was to get our machine guns up and then the sixty mortars."

Due to the adrenaline that flooded his body, Lt Combs didn't realize that he had taken a round through the elbow.

"The only cover that we had were two-and-a-half foot bushes. We were down low, almost into the paddy area, and we were trying to move back. I was trying to move back up the side of the knoll, just so I could see."

1st Platoon Sgt Sullivan, just behind the point squad, peered over the edge of the hole he was in with his radio operator.

"They were moving in a V-type formation, four or five man fire teams with a lot of camouflage, carrying their weapons at port arms. Some crawled through the rice paddy, others would stand up and shoot, firing from the hip, while most of them were running in a shuffle, firing as they ran."

The NVA wore green uniforms, and many had small, round bamboo mats attached to their chests and backs with twigs, branches, and banana leaves inserted into slots. The camouflage was so effective that, when not moving, the only way that Sully could detect their presence was when he saw a puff of smoke from an enemy rifle.

"What can you see?" Murray radioed Lt Combs. "Where are your people?"

With a fire team at his front, Combs watched as LCpl Thomas Fisher bought his men up on the right.

"I remember seeing him get hit," Combs said. "He seemed okay. He was yelling at someone to pull back."

Cpl Bob Matteson with 1st Platoon took an AK-47 round to his left leg, through and through, as he attempted to hump machine gun ammo to one of the guns. Cpl Ken Fields, an M60 machine gunner whose squad was attached to 1st Platoon, had skirted the knoll, slapped a large volcanic rock, and was about to step into the rice paddy when rounds started coming in from the front. As he took cover behind the boulder, bullets hit the ground near his feet and then began to come in from several directions. He spotted his team leader and ammo carrier twenty-five meters to his right behind a hedgerow.

"They've got me pinned down. I'm going to come down there with you!"

As machine gun rounds churned the dirt around him, Fields ran, lost his balance, and slid into his team leader. As he landed, slicing his hand on a thorn, the entire knoll exploded with a deafening roar as the NVA opened up with sweeping and intense fire from mortars, rocket propelled grenades, machine guns, and AK-47s.

2nd Platoon

Blecksmith's 2nd Platoon, at the left side of the wedge formation and behind 1st Platoon, had spread out when Swan triggered the ambush. Cpl Nunez, still wearing the Saint Christopher medal given to him by Father Capodanno, was taking a short break with 2nd Squad leader Cpl Bill Young as the forward Marines, who were ascending the knoll, slowed their pace. The two had just sat at the base of an old masonry well at the edge of the draw between the knoll and the village when they heard shots in the distance. At first, the two were unconcerned, as sniper fire was common, but then a bullet smacked into the well between their heads. As they exchanged wide-eyed looks, more rounds came in, and word came over the radio that the point squad had engaged the enemy.

3rd Platoon

Cernick's 3rd Platoon, at the right side of the wedge behind 1st Platoon, had spread out between the village and the draw. Father Capodanno, who was with the lead elements of 3rd Platoon just behind the command group, hit the deck. When he heard cries for help ring out from farther up the right side of the knoll, he began to creep in that direction.

Cpl Cummings had just set out from the village with his squad when he heard the gunfire coming from the direction of the knoll. As the roar to their front increased, he led his men forward until 3rd Platoon itself came under intense machine gun fire as camouflaged squads of NVA tried to sweep through the open draw. He and his men fell to the ground and returned fire.

3

FACING ANNIHILATION

Command Crater

As he rushed forward with the sound of the ambush, Lt Murray caught a glimpse of a dead enemy soldier, the body so well camouflaged that only his hand and weapon were visible. The command group, which consisted of Murray, his radio operator, a sniper team, a FAC, and a FO for artillery, jumped into a giant bomb crater at the top of the knoll. The crater, about 150 meters behind where the NVA had Swan and Haney pinned down, was deep enough to stand in.

Goebel, the FAC, put his radios in front of him and peered over the edge. As he did, the beehive became a hornet's nest as AK-47 and machine gun rounds, rocket-propelled grenades, mortars, and rockets exploded from the well-hidden enemy.

Murray's radio lit up.

"We're being hit! Dead and wounded all around!"

"We're being overrun!"

"Taking heavy fire!"

The messages from his platoon commanders came on top of each other amidst the din of battle. In fifteen months of combat, Murray had never witnessed such a barrage of fire, and by experience, he knew that fear was his greatest enemy.

"Knock it off!"

"Report in order, 1st Platoon—"

As the reports came in, Murray was able assess the approximate location of incoming fire and the number of casualties. The heaviest attacks were coming from the north, the area near the Ly Ly River (to the right of the knoll) and the west (where the NVA had the 1st Platoon pinned down at the front).

To Murray, it seemed as if the leathernecks had tripped the ambush early, as hundreds of NVA were still maneuvering across the rice paddies and out of the hedgerows toward the knoll. If the Marines had continued forward without detecting the enemy presence, the North Vietnamese could have trapped the entire company and possibly wiped it out. Now, Lt Murray had to consolidate his company's position before they were overrun on the knoll.

"Anybody in the military knows that if you get into a fight, the first thing you want to do is suppress the enemy's fire," Murray said, *"and you want to move against them. The people that are moving against them have to have some type of protection, and that protection is you firing your weapons so that the enemy keeps their heads down as your assault force moves forward.*

"My head was down," he remembered, *"and I am looking up, and I see bushes moving all over the place. The 'bushes' get up, and then they settle. I don't see them running, but a little bit later they get up and move again, and the NVA are moving all across our front in clumps of four, five, or maybe ten with bushes on their backs. When they are down on the ground, and you are looking from above or from the side, they are bushes. Then those bushes would move ten to fifteen yards and would then sit down. They shoot, move, get down, fire, shoot, and move, and I could see it in multiple areas out in front of us. It reminded me of a training film, but this was the real thing."*

The objective of the NVA "fire and maneuver" was to get close to the devil dogs and overwhelm them with firepower. The assaulting NVA infantrymen had support from an additional battalion of their comrades who laid down a withering fire to keep the Marines heads down, thereby allowing their infantry to advance relatively protected. If the enemy kept the Marines pinned down, they would be able to advance across the open draw between the village and knoll and surround Mike Company with relative ease. If that happened without a defensive perimeter, the NVA, once in the American's front and rear, could trap the Marines in a vice and wipe them out piecemeal.

Murray couldn't let that happen. He had to tighten his men into a reasonable perimeter in order to repel the attack coming from the west and any onslaught coming across the rice paddies and hedgerows to the north.

"If firing is coming from one side, what you try to do is overwhelm that fire," Murray said, *"but in this case, it was coming from multiple directions, so if you can't overwhelm them, then you want to get into defensive positions and go from there. It's called 'rally around the wagons,' and basically, that is what we did. We stayed right where we were and tried to establish a perimeter so that everybody is in contact with everybody else."*

"Machine guns, up!"

The gun squads began to fight their way forward to support the platoons.

"Have Lt Hayden support the company with mortars."

Along with the 60mm mortars, two hundred meters behind Murray, aircraft support was also available and waiting on station in both Chu Lai (sixteen kilometers to the south) and Da Nang (thirty-two kilometers to the north) and could be over the battlefield in ten minutes. Air and artillery support, however, could only do so much, as the enemy was on top of Mike Company and Kilo was nearby.

Weapons Platoon Cmdr Lt Hayden, the 60mm mortars, and one squad from 3rd Platoon were still in the village, cut off from the remainder of the company and unable to fight their way through the NVA in the draw between their location and the knoll. With an effective range of 3.5 klicks (a little over two miles), however, Hayden's mortars could still provide adequate support where needed. With a team of devil dogs providing covering fire, Hayden moved his mortars into an open area about twenty-five meters behind the main perimeter and awaited orders.

The 60mm M2 mortar is a smoothbore, muzzle-loaded weapon that consists of a heavy metal tube and baseplate. Firing a high explosive fragmentation round at a high angle, Hayden's team could fire over the leathernecks and into the enemy positions but never did so without receiving specific orders. Otherwise, the rounds might strike Marines.

"Combat is mass confusion," Murray said. *"As a Marine officer, I am trained to try and deal with it, but basically, I know things that I have that are available to me to support my company. When you are in a situation like that where it is coming from all different directions, if I don't know where the extremities of Bravo and Delta Companies are and I don't know where the extremities of Kilo and 1/5 Command are located, it really gets dicey. I can deal with the northern part, the Ly Ly River, the one I can't deal with is south, which is toward the road where somewhere in there Kilo is located, as well as the headquarters for 1/5."*

"1," Murray radioed Lt Combs, "where do you need sixty support (mortars)?"

"6, they're all across the front on our right and left side. We are surrounded."

"Give me some locations."

Combs, his elbow wound now bandaged by a corpsman, pulled out his map.

"6, I need it most at 092339."

The rounds were Willie Peter, which confirmed the coordinates with trails of white smoke.

"1, do we need to adjust?"

"I had to protect the whole company, and it was very difficult," Murray said. *"There was a lot of low scrub and small trees, so you could only see so far. I could see out into the rice paddies in some locations, but others, I couldn't. I would assume from where I was located to where the initial platoons were up north was about fifty meters. So there was a lot of coordination over the phone under a very difficult situation."*

Lt Combs also had to be careful. The coordinates he had given Murray to relay back to Lt Hayden with the mortars put the rounds close to his point squad, especially Swan and Haney, still pinned down in the paddy. He shouted down to Cpl Vandergriff, point squad leader, still trapped in a crater at the front of the knoll, who reported that the motors were landing only fifty meters away. Combs backed the coordinates out another fifty meters and shouted into the radio:

"Fire for effect!"

A barrage of high explosive mortar rounds, complimented by their longer range 81mm cousins located back at Hill 51, arced through the air over the knoll and exploded among the enemy, taking out three positions of NVA automatic weapons.

The enemy fire slowed but not for long.

"FAC, get Airborne on the net. We need fixed-wing and artillery at COORS to follow."

Looking at his map, Murray read off the coordinates, and Goebel relayed the message.

While Murray was doing his best to keep the enemy from breaching the Marine perimeter from the outside, what he didn't know was that the NVA were about to attack the leathernecks from within it. The terrain on which the Americans advanced was not only potted with craters and fighting holes dug by the NVA to provide cover as they advanced, but it was also honeycombed with tunnels from which they could emerge, attack the Americans, and just as quickly disappear.

LCpl Hooley was with Cpl Sim's squad of 1st Platoon, to the right and behind Vandergriff's squad and in the open, when the ambush hit. When his squad leader took a round to the leg and the wounded started to pile up, Hooley dashed back to the command crater in search of a corpsman, while what remained of his squad laid down suppressing fire.

"What the hell are you doing here?" a staff sergeant asked him.

"I come to get a corpsman. We got guys out in the front that are hit and hurt."

"Hell, the fire's too intense. We're not sending a corpsman down there."

Hooley began to crawl back out of the crater.

"Where the hell are you going?" the sergeant asked.

"I'm going back to my squad."

"I'll go with you—" said an unknown corpsman.

As Hooley and the corpsman leapt from the command crater, a round from a grenade launcher landed nearby, knocking both men to the ground.

"I looked around to see if the corpsman was dead, and he was okay, and then I looked back, and there was gooks running around by the command post—"

Hooley started to fire with his M16.

"We've got gooks in the perimeter! They're in the perimeter!"

"And I kept shooting these guys and kept hollering, and it scared the shit out of me, you know. I thought, 'Oh my god, they're inside of the perimeter,' and that's the worst thing that can happen to a company. If you get overrun, that's how they kill everybody in the company is they attack from the back, and you can't defend both the front and the back."

As he fired, Hooley watched as NVA in groups of four or five rushed between the command post and a large boulder nearby.

"They were running to this big rock, and they were crouching down like they were getting down into something."

At the base of that boulder was the entrance to a tunnel. As Hooley burned through magazines of ammunition that the corpsman loaded for him, his M16 jammed. As he slammed the cleaning rod down the barrel to knock out the jammed cartridges, the NVA opened up with a machine gun smuggled from the tunnel, slicing bullets through his jungle utilities, canteen, first-aid kit, helmet, and the bone of his lower left arm.

"I felt as if I had been hit by a sledgehammer, and this stuff started running down my back, and I thought, 'That's blood.' So I reached around with my left hand, and I brought it back around, and it was clear. There was no doubt in my mind that I was going to die. I never thought I'd see the next day."

Cpl Fred Riddle, FO for the large 81mm mortars located back at Hill 51, was advancing with his radioman and Father Capodanno when orders came for him to join Lt Murray in the command crater. Riddle did as ordered, but the Navy chaplain remained behind with 2nd Platoon and a corpsman.

"The last I saw of them, they were attending a wounded Marine. The corpsman was working on him, and the padre was giving last rites."

Back at the command crater, Murray again radioed 1st Platoon Cmdr Combs.

"1, where are the NVA?"

"They are all across the front, and they are on our right side, they're on our left side. JD, 6, we are surrounded!"

A Huey gunship appeared over the NVA to the right of the knoll, unloaded all of its ammunition, and swept away. It was the first of the air support called in by Murray from his command post in the crater. He now had to assess whether the gunship, mortars, and outgoing Marine fire were keeping the enemy at bay.

"1, can you see? How effective is the artillery?"

From his exposed position at the front of the knoll, Lt Combs and his radioman, LCpl Larry Lukens, who carried the PRC-77 radio with a conspicuous antenna, crawled up a little higher to get a better view. Most of the devil dogs were on their stomachs, in craters, or behind any rock, bush, or mound of earth they could find. The only way that Combs could see over the bushes where artillery and mortar rounds were landing was to rise up on his knees.

That made him and his radioman a target.

"What the enemy wants to do is to take out our leadership," Murray said. *"They look for the 'antenna farm,' and they know that where the antenna farm is, that is where the leader is. And the best thing to do is take out that antenna farm."*

"I was marking the artillery to see how effective we were doing," Combs said, *"and I got on my left side, and I had the radio in my right hand on the side of the small hill. As I leaned down to stand up,*

hunched over, I saw the impact of a bullet in the dirt in front of me, and I thought it was a ricochet."

Combs was wrong. A large caliber bullet had entered his back, blasted through his left shoulder, blew out the front of his chest, and hit the dirt in front of him.

"It went right through, and you could see the dirt explode. It was like somebody took a baseball bat and hit me as hard as they could and on my crazy bone; my whole body was my crazy bone. All my nerves were reacting, and that took me down. It was like all the wind had been knocked out of my body, and I started sucking air, trying to get my breath. I looked down at the hole in my chest, and I thought I was dead. I asked Him (God) to forgive me for all my sins I had done. And that was kind of it."

LCpl Lukens tried to pull his lieutenant to cover.

"Mike 1 is down!" he shouted into the radio, "Mike 1 is down!"

"He grabbed a hold of me and pulled me over into his lap, and that is about the time he got hit—"

"The platoon commander has been hit," Murray heard over the radio, "and I don't know where the platoon sergeant is."

With the commander of 1st Platoon now out of the fight, Murray was suddenly blind as to what was happening at his front. The Marines had formed an irregular oval perimeter on the knoll about one hundred meters across, but the company was strung out some 350 meters from Swan and Haney and 1st Squad to 3rd Platoon in the village. In addition to their heavy attack at the west (front) and north (right) of the small hill, the enemy was pushing machine gun teams and infantry into the draw in an attempt to isolate the Americans in the village and surround those on the knoll.

If the company did not pull back and tighten its perimeter, the enemy would break through and wipe out the Marines one at a time. 1st Platoon couldn't maneuver without a commander, so Murray had to remedy that situation fast as well as assess what obstacles the platoon was facing.

"I'm going to find Sgt Sullivan and tell him to take over—"

Several men offered to go in his place, but Murray shook his head. In the heat of battle, he didn't want to send a runner through the automatic weapons and incoming mortars to find the 1st Platoon sergeant, but he failed to see the ramifications of his decision. With Lt Hayden back with the mortars and Lts Blecksmith and Cernick pinned down on the left and backside of the knoll, the artillery FO was the only remaining officer in the command crater. As company commander, if Murray were to die or receive life-threatening wounds, Mike Company would be without a leader at the most critical time.

Murray scrambled out of the crater and headed forward toward 1st Platoon, located along the left front side of the knoll. Bushes and small trees lay splintered and leveled to the ground as rounds flew in every direction. As he ran over the crest, Murray saw countless squads of well-camouflaged NVA soldiers teeming in the open rice paddies and fields, all converging on his outnumbered Marines.

"Rounds were just cracking all over the place," Murray said. *"I ran as low as I could and as fast as I could. I think it was like one hundred to 125 yards, and I can remember seeing all these bushes and trees that were cut down by the fire. It was really scary because here I am trying to find a platoon sergeant, and I didn't know if I was going to be able to find him."*

After a full one-hundred-meter dash, Murray dropped into a shallow crater filled with Marines, and one of them was Platoon Sergeant Sullivan.

"Then out of nowhere, and to this day, I still haven't figured out how in the hell he did it, JD, the company commander came down

and kneeled down beside me in that hole, and them bullets was just flying all across the top of it."

"I don't know where you came from, and I don't know how you got here," Sully began.

"Sully, Ed is hit. He needs you, and you now got it. You got to get these people together!"

"It sounded like a beehive just kept going over us, just like bees, flying and swarming and he was just as calm as a damn cucumber, I just looked at him, said, 'Aye-aye, sir,' and flew out of that friggin' hole."

After giving the order, Murray realized that he would now have to return to the command crater through the same withering fire that he had just braved. Murray had been a halfback in high school, but he had never covered one hundred meters faster than he did on the return trip. As he slid safely back into the crater, it dawned on him that his personal mission to find Sully was not the wisest decision of his military career.

Leaving his radioman behind in order to safeguard contact with Murray, 1st Platoon Sgt Sullivan flew out of his crater toward the front of the knoll to assess the positions of the men now under his charge and organize them into a defensive position.

"I was trying to pull out troops into some type of perimeter defense," Sullivan said. *"I was running to every place where I could grab people, and I would start putting them into different positions to defend ourselves."*

Sullivan tried to run from one position to another, but due to the intense fire, he had to crawl instead. His goal was to place his men, two to a group, in an inverted U-shape around the outside portion of the knoll, but some of the men didn't want to move.

"We got to get up here and form a defense!" he shouted. "You got to get out here and fight this. We're not going to make it if you don't move. We got to help each other and work together as a team!"

As Sullivan moved off to the right, an enemy machine gun opened up, and he hit the deck. Under covering fire from Cpl Little, he was able to get up and move again, and as he did, he saw LCpl Thomas Fisher, a fire team leader in Vandergriff's 1st Squad, in front of him.

"I saw Fisher running, and he was firing his M16, and then he went down, and then I went down again. While I was laying there, I looked up and saw him run off to the left, and he was firing again, but at that time, I didn't know that he had been hit."

In the face of withering enemy fire, Fisher single-handedly decimated an NVA machine gun team with his M16, only to face an immediate assault from a second NVA automatic weapon nearby. Fisher, still alone, ran toward that weapon and took out the second gunner as well.

"He was standing up in all of that fire. I could see the bushes get whittled away because they had his fire team pinned down," Sullivan said. *"He was firing like crazy as he moved toward the enemy positions."*

A round cut through Fisher's left arm and cracked his rifle, and he went down. Despite his wound and now lack of a weapon, he came to his feet and continued to run forward through the barrage.

"He wasn't backing up or getting down. He was going after them."

Off to his right to the north, Sullivan was shocked to see Father Capodanno, who had orders not to accompany Marines into the field and a corpsman working on a downed Marine. The sergeant scrambled toward several large black rocks, hoping his Marines could give the chaplain and corpsman some cover, but an NVA machine gun quickly pinned him down before he could reach the boulders.

"I figured if I got over there I could get in between them rocks, and it would give me a little cover, and maybe I could see where everybody was at so I could get them organized."

"I'll cover you to the rocks!"

As the Marine opened a volley of gunfire, Sully made another dash toward the boulders when an NVA mortar blasted him to the ground.

"I get over by the rocks, and the next thing you know, a mortar went off in front of me, and it blew my damn eye out. Yeah, it blew my eye out, and I couldn't hardly hear."

Only moments after assuming command, 1st Platoon was almost, once again, without a leader. The explosion had jarred an eye out of its socket, and Sullivan's face burned where the shrapnel seared his skin. A corpsman was quickly at his side, did what he could for Sully's eye with a salve and dressing, then bandaged a deep gash on his forehead.

"I was just kind of numb. I was tingling all over, and I burned where the shrapnel had hit me. My adrenaline was just pumping at eight hundred miles an hour. It (the mortar blast) almost knocked me out because it got real, real dark, and it got real black, and I was seeing these stars. I really thought I was going down."

Sully ignored his injury as best he could, and while Cpl Fields and his machine gun provided covering fire, he began to crawl the ground in front of the knoll to assess the condition of 1st Platoon. Due to the enemy onslaught, there was no way to maneuver his troops into a more effective perimeter, and there was no removing the many wounded men to the rear. Instead, he directed the corpsman to take the wounded to a giant crater he had discovered on the lower part of the knoll. Sullivan remained in that forward crater, soon occupied by ten wounded men, and helped target machine gun and M79 grenade launcher fire against enemy positions.

2nd Platoon

"From what I could picture," Murray said, *"1st Platoon was being hit pretty bad. I wasn't sure about 2nd Platoon, but it became obvious that there was help needed on the north side, which was the Ly Ly River side. I told Ed Blecksmith to send people around to support that north side because they were being hit fairly bad."*

Having called in air and artillery support and having placed Sgt Sullivan in command of 1st Platoon, Murray now radioed 2nd Platoon Cmdr Lt Blecksmith.

"Move around the knoll toward the north and cover the right flank. Support 1st Platoon; they're in deep trouble. A lot of wounded. Fill in the gap."

As a fresh "boot lieutenant" who had never seen combat, Lt Blecksmith was fortunate to have in 2nd Platoon a strong cadre of leaders in Sgt Marbury and in squad leaders Sgt Peters, Sgt Manfra, as well as Cpls Young and Nunez. Blecksmith turned to his most experienced squad leader, Sgt Pete, to lead 1st and 2nd Squad forward: eighteen to twenty Marines reinforced by a rocket and two machine gun teams.

Murray ordered a squad from Cernick's 3rd Platoon, strung out in the draw on the right side of the wedge near the village, to reinforce 1st Platoon while the remaining squads created a loose defensive perimeter at the south side (the back) of the knoll.

"Rockets up!"

Accompanied by Platoon Sergeant Marbury, Sgt Peters led the two squads forward using squad and fire team tactics, mainly two man and team rushes, across the lower side of the knoll, where they had some protection from the sheets of fire coming across the top until they reached the side facing the Ly Ly River (to the north).

With Peters was Sgt Red Manfra, the Marine who was due to go on R&R in Hawaii the next day, and his rocket squad. LCpl John Lobur paused to assemble a M20 3.5 inch rocket launcher and then turned to Red.

"How's this for R&R?"

Manfra said nothing as they moved forward.

3rd Platoon

Lt Cernick's 3rd Platoon and Lt Hayden's mortar team remained strung out at the right side of the wedge between the village and the draw. Cpl Don Baima, leader of a machine gun team attached to 3rd Platoon, was still in the village when the ambush hit. A machine gun team consisted of the team leader, gunner, assistant gunner, and ammo humper. Baima's duty as team leader was to find the most advantageous place to put the M60, point out targets for the gunner, and provide security in order to ensure that the enemy didn't sneak up on the flank of the gun.

"Naturally, the enemy would try to knock out the machine gun just as we would try and knock out their machine gun."

What Baima didn't expect was friendly fire. As his squad began to move out, a Marine accidentally popped a red smoke grenade, the signal to American gunships that enemy, instead of friendly, troops were on the ground. To his horror, Baima watched as the hulking form of a Huey gunship appeared over his head and began to blast the ground around him with its heavy guns, then surge forward to rain bullets onto the Marines in the open draw.

"Who's got a panel?" Baima shouted.

An air panel, about two-by-four feet, consisted of rectangular pieces of brightly colored cloth that, when laid out, would mark Marine positions in order to avoid friendly fire.

"Who's got an air panel?" No one answered.

Baima hit the deck as the giant helicopter returned to sew another line of bullets within a few feet of the men. As the chopper circled for another strike he remembered that just before lifting off at Hill 63, he had packed a panel himself. As the Huey's blades beat louder for another approach, Baima pulled it from his pack, placed it onto the ground, and began to waive his arms back and forth.

"Holy shit! I hope he sees it!" he thought.

"It was like rain falling," Goulet said, *"coming from above you, going through the leaves. It was pretty scary, as we were getting it from the rear and from the air, our own people. The platoon commander (Lt Cernick) popped a yellow smoke to identify us as friendly troops, and that marked our position. The helicopter moved forward and began to fire on the North Vietnamese who was shooting at us, and they suppressed them enough so we could get up and move out of there."*

4

HANGIN' ON

1st Platoon

By the time the mortar rounds had landed, Point Man Jack Swan, pinned down by a machine gun at his 11:00 position, an NVA sniper at his 1:00, and small arms fire in the rice paddy beyond the front of the knoll, was running low on ammunition for his M79 grenade launcher.

Swan was now isolated and cut off from his comrades. Each time he moved, the enemy sniper fired, knocking dirt into his face. Within half an hour, he was completely out of ammunition—no rifle or pistol and armed only with one white phosphorous grenade.

"And it was just a play-fuck-fuck-with-me after that. We had mortars coming in, 82s and the smaller ones, and I guess they had 60 or 61s: 'mike-mike.' So I spent the day just lying there in the corner and just looking up the hill. I couldn't see anybody up over the knoll."

A dead Marine lay to his right, but the fire was too intense for Swan to reach the man's rifle, and he couldn't reach Haney, the first man hit, who was still lying to his left about eighteen meters away, unable to move.

"I thought I was hit in the lungs," Haney said. *"I was choking and coughing up blood, and that went on about fifteen minutes, and then it stopped."*

Separated by two rice paddy dikes from his point man, Haney lay immobilized by his shoulder wound and the weight of his fifty-pound pack.

"When I fell forward, that pack slid up over the top of me and acted as a compression. Believe me, I hated that pack all day long, and I wanted it off me, but I couldn't get it off. It was lucky I couldn't because if I would have got the pack off, I know I would have bled to death."

Haney couldn't stand, he couldn't crawl, and he couldn't move his head. It felt as if someone was holding it in place. He was angry with his body for not doing what he wanted it to do.

"I would try and get up and try to move. I tried to find my M16, but I never saw it after I was hit. It went out in front of me, and I couldn't move enough to get to it, I couldn't turn my head to get up, and I couldn't crawl. It was frustrating because of that."

When he did try to move to find his M16, the sniper, not over thirty yards away, fired and the round struck his pack.

"My pack got hit one more time while I was lying there. The only thing I can come up with is that they thought I was dead so they didn't mess with me. I had no cover. I mean, there's no reason for me to be alive other than the grace of God."

His body filled with dull pain, Haney wasn't able to see what was going on around him, and each time he thought that the roar of battle couldn't get any worse, the air exploded with more noise.

"It just escalated to the point that it was just beyond belief. It was a deafening roar, and you know about the time you think it can't get any louder, then it just triples. It's hard to lay there and listen to the bullets going over your head. It's phenomenal, and it still amazes me to this day. It was a deafening, deafening roar."

When Swan turned to look back up the hill, an enemy mortar round detonated near LCpl Fields's machine gun team, who'd been out in the open.

"And I remember turning around, and an 82mm mortar burst behind them: him and his A gunner," Swan said, *"and all I saw was a cloud of dust, and here he and his A gunner went with a 'Hi-dee-hi-ho, Silver!' back up the fucking hill, neither one of them hit!"*

Fields and his team were able leap unharmed into a large crater, about four meters across and not quite two meters deep. He set up his M60 "Pig" and started firing toward the right, where most of the incoming rounds now originated and over the heads of those men trapped in the rice paddy and front of the knoll.

• • •

In a nearby hole, about two meters deep with soft sand at the bottom, Cpl Vandergriff, like Swan, felt cut off from the world. The crater he had found was six- to seven-feet deep and eight-feet wide with soft sand at the bottom. He was about fifteen yards behind Haney and Swan, and about fifty yards in front of the command crater.

Prior to the 60mm mortar barrage, Vandergriff had been able to communicate with Lt Combs further up the knoll, but now he heard nothing from his platoon commander, and he couldn't stick his head above the crater without getting shot at.

"Mortar rounds were just landing all over," he said, *"and I kept hearing, 'Corpsman, up! Corpsman, up!' and I knew people were getting hurt pretty bad back there."*

As point squad leader, his Marine training had prepared him to use weapons, follow orders, and work as a team, but it hadn't prepared him for this kind of terror and helplessness.

"I remember being so terrified, so afraid, that I could actually taste bile in my throat: that bitter, terrible taste of fear. I'm the first to tell you that I was scared shitless."

Vandergriff's terror skyrocketed when he heard someone shout, "They're coming in!"

"I thought 'Awe shit. Here I am in this hole, and I don't know where they're coming from. I don't know what direction I am going to be able to get off a shot. Are they coming from my front side or back?' I thought of my wife, my mom and dad, brothers and sisters, just wondering if this is it."

Spotting movement out of the corner of his eye, Vandergriff swung his M16 around toward the rim of the crater. LCpl Thomas Fisher, the fire team leader who, when the ambush first hit faced down the barrage of enemy fire to single-handedly take out not one but two enemy machine guns, dropped into Vandergriff's hole. Without a rifle, shirt, or helmet, Vandergriff noticed a battle dressing on the upper part of his left arm.

"What's going on?"

Fisher said nothing.

"He just sat there with his right leg bent underneath him, and he just kind of looked at me. After about two—maybe three—minutes, he got up, and I said, 'Where in the hell you going?' and he was gone. He didn't say a word to me. He just seemed like he was dazed or in shock, to be walking around out there and all that shit is going on. I was amazed."

Exposed once again to enemy fire, Fisher spotted Swan trapped in the rice paddy. He also saw the enemy sniper and machine gunners who had him pinned down.

"Fire there!" he ordered a nearby fire team, pointing out the enemy positions, and then headed toward Swan. As the point man watched Fisher approach to about thirty feet behind him and to his right, the enemy machine gun ceased fire.

"Get down! There are snipers out here, man!"

As Swan yelled, an NVA bullet slammed dead center into Fisher's chest, knocking him to the ground. Swan crawled down the side of the rice paddy dike toward Fisher, raised his head above the dike, and the sniper put a round in front of his face, kicking dirt into his eyes. Swan jumped back to wipe out the dust, popped his head over again, and as he did, the sniper put a second round into Fisher's chest.

"*I heard the gurgle,*" Swan said, "*and he was gone.*"

Just meters away, up the hill in a crater, Sgt Sullivan received word that Lt Murray was sending a squad from 2nd Platoon to link up with him and provide reinforcement for 1st Platoon's position.

"*I never saw a one of them,*" Sullivan said. "*They never made it.*"

5

SERGEANT PETE AND THE CHAPLAIN

Company Command

Back at the command crater, Lt Murray was dealing with the mass confusion of battle. With enemy mortars and grenades now landing within the company perimeter and machine gun and small-arms fire cutting across the knoll, the NVA were beginning to pierce his defense. With the company still strung out and pinned down, he was quickly losing men, and with hundreds of NVA advancing from the north, they could easily overrun his position.

Not only did the North Vietnamese have supremacy in numbers, they held a tactical advantage as well. With the ability to maneuver, small and large units of NVA could advance and attack the Marines while their comrades provided fire suppression. The Americans, outnumbered, outgunned, and outmaneuvered by an expertly camouflaged enemy, were doing their best to hold on.

As an experienced combat leader, Murray's mind ticked through a checklist of problems and possible solutions.

How do I counter the NVA organic mortars and weapons within the company?

What are the dimensions of my forces?

Where is the first immediate need to suppress the NVA?

Where am I most vulnerable?

How many wounded and KIA do I have?

How many effective troops do I still have?

How much ammunition remains?

When will the flow of assaulting infantry stop?

In addition to a company of courageous devil dogs on the ground, Murray had one asset that the enemy did not possess: air support. Fixed-wing aircraft that could drop bombs and napalm, helicopter gunships that could spray death from the air with their machine guns, and long-range artillery were all strong options, but Murray had to be careful with close air support. With the enemy now on top of his position and without knowing the exact location of other Marine units in the area, he risked calling in devastating air strikes on his own men.

Over 160 Marines of Kilo 3/5 and the 1/5 Command Group, all under the command of Col Hilgatner, had taken defensive positions in a trench line about five hundred meters or less to the southwest of Murray's men. With the brunt of the NVA attack coming directly at Mike Company on the knoll and not at the men under Hilgartner's command, it was now Murray, the would-be rescuer of Delta and Bravo 1/5, who called for help.

"I called the battalion commander for 1/5 and told him, 'We are being overrun. I need help immediately.'"

"Well, so are we," was Hilgartner's terse reply. "I can't send anybody over."

"I was really bent out of shape because they said they couldn't help us. We would have been a hell of a lot better off if all of us could have gotten together, but they said they couldn't do it, that they were under fire."

Murray had no time to waste ruminating over the disappointing news.

"My thought was to bring in tear gas, knowing clear well that we had people wounded out there. They might not be able to get their gas masks on, and they might die, but I am not looking at the individual; I am looking at the company as a whole. Do you want to get wiped out, or do you want to try something that may change the conduct of the fight?"

"Okay, we are going to bring in gas," he thought as he turned to FAC Goebel with the radio. "We are going to bring it right into our position and see what happens."

1st Platoon

Lt Combs still lay exposed on the front of the knoll, his chest laid wide open by a heavy enemy round, when he heard the call.

"Tell everybody to put on their gas masks!"

"Well shit!" Combs thought. *"I had dropped my pack, and I had no gas mask. All I could think about was CS coming down, and with an open chest wound and everything else, it was going to be a mess."*

Still motionless down in the rice paddy off to the front of the knoll, Haney also heard the call to put on gas masks. His mask was on his left side, and he struggled to remove the heavy pack to retrieve it but to no avail.

Minutes later, a Marine A-4 Skyhawk jet flew high over the knoll and dropped three 500- gallon napalm tanks filled with micro-pulverized CS gas powder at locations around Mike Company's perimeter but not directly onto the knoll itself. Murray's hope was that the gas would debilitate the enemy by burning their eyes, throat, lungs, and skin, and with any luck, force the NVA to pull back or at least pause their relentless attack.

From his fighting hole on the backside of the knoll, to the right of 2nd Platoon's line, Combat Engineer Ericson was laying down a base of fire at the oncoming NVA when the tear gas rolled over him.

"I didn't have a gas mask, and half of the grunts didn't have their gas masks either so we're sitting there, and I'm choking and coughing and right on the edge of panic, when somebody taps me on the shoulder, and I turned around, and there was a guy on the other side of me who I really hadn't taken much notice of before. He's holding out his gas mask, so I goes to grab it, and when I looks first thing I realize is this guy's old."

When Ericson noticed the cross on the man's collar, he thought, "What the hell is the chaplain doing out here in all of this?"

"He hands his gas mask to me, so I grab it, and I take maybe three or four breaths, put some fresh air in my lungs, hand it back to him, and we handed it back and forth until the gas dissipated."

Once the CS lifted, Father Capodanno made his way forward to 2nd Platoon and Sgt Pete's position at the front side of the knoll.

"CS drop ineffective at our position," Murray radioed. "Enemy continues to advance on our position—we are about to be overrun!"

• • •

As Sgt Sullivan's 1st Platoon fought to hold back the NVA at the west (or front) of the knoll, two squads from 2nd, reinforced by one rocket and two machine gun teams, would take the fight to the enemy at the north (or right). If Sgt Pete's eighteen to twenty leathernecks could put some fire on the enemy's flank, 1st Platoon might be able to pull back.

"Get on line!" Peters shouted. "Everybody, move up! Move up!"

Peters's two squads began to form a line facing the enemy positions to the north. The terrain at the base of the knoll consisted of a small grouping of trees, open fields beyond, and another larger cluster of woods farther out. The NVA were using the farther woods to provide supporting fire for their troops attacking 1st Platoon at the front. With Sgt Sullivan's leathernecks in danger of being overrun, there was no time to assess the strength of the enemy in the far woods. There was only time to act.

"We were ordered," 2nd Platoon Cmdr Lt Blecksmith said, *"to go around the knoll and envelope the tree line."*

"Gun ammo, up!"

As the order came down the line, Pfc Martinez, carrying two bandoliers of M60 ammunition, ran forward to one of the two machine gun teams.

"I delivered the ammo, and then I turned to my two o'clock and noticed that Sgt Peters had started to string the squad to the right of the knoll."

Once the two squads had linked up, Peters led them forward into the open field between the base of the knoll and the far cluster of woods, with Clark and Duca's machine guns providing covering fire.

"We shouldn't do this," someone said. "We're going to be sitting ducks!"

"I remember there was tree lines on our left, tree lines on our right, and such a wide open area," Duca said. *"We were pretty much in a straight line, advancing forward."*

As the Marines entered the open field, enemy guns, most likely 7.62mm RPD machine guns of Soviet design and AK-47s, opened up on Sgt Pete's men from the far tree line.

"Keep moving!" Peters shouted. "Keep moving!"

And then came the mortars.

"As they were stringing us out on a line in the open to assault," Martinez said, *"I heard the first explosion, which was a mortar round at the very end of the line of Marines. I noticed another one go off and another—they were walking mortars down the line—"*

As bullets poured in, enemy mortars began to rain in on the two reinforced squads, the range zeroed in, and the fire deadly accurate, one round taking out an entire Marine fire team.

"I remember seeing McKenzie," Martinez said, *"an FNG I had gotten to the unit with at the same time, go down with one of the first mortar rounds that went off."*

"In about thirty seconds," Lobur said, *"Manfra, Gundlach, myself, and Steve Blackwood were at the very top of the knoll firing as fast as we could at the enemy mortar positions to the east. This is when I saw the chaplain run behind us going to the northeast. In less than a minute, we had fired all our rockets and Sgt Peters was screaming for us and the rest of the 2nd Platoon to take up positions on the right flank."*

As Cpls. Nunez and Young crested the small hill, a hidden machine gun about twenty-five yards away raked them. Nunez heard three sharp pops from an RPD, a light automatic weapon of Russian design, and saw Young drop to the ground. With blood at his utilities just under the waist, Nunez unbuckled Young's pants and found three bullet holes in the front of his hips, his pelvis shattered.

"Corpsman!"

Hn Armando Leal, one of the Navy Corpsmen attached to 2nd Platoon, was immediately on the scene and, after a quick examination, applied a battle dressing. Thankfully, there was little bleeding, but there was no way to repair the pelvis on the battlefield.

"There's nothing else I can do right now—"

With another cry for a corpsman, Doc Leal ran up the right side of the knoll.

Nunez squeezed his friend's hand.

"This is your trip out of here. You're going to make it, and you're going home to see Patty and your new son."

Cpl Nunez gave Young's hand one last squeeze and ran to catch up with 2nd Squad, which he now led. Once in position at the north side of the knoll, he spotted the twinkling flash of an NVA machine gun coming from the tree line in front of him. He called for an M72 LAW, a portable, one-shot anti-tank weapon similar to a bazooka. Nunez removed the pull-pin, extended the tube, and cocked the weapon. He then aimed the M72 LAW at the tree line, moved the safety to arm, and squeezed the trigger.

Nothing.

He pulled the trigger a second time, then a third and a fourth, but the M72 LAW failed to fire. He knew now that he would have to re-cock the weapon. Nunez engaged the trigger safety, laid on his back, and took a deep breath. When a M72 LAW failed to fire, there was always the chance that static electricity within the tube might cause the round within the cylinder to explode when it was re-armed. He exhaled sharply, and then re-cocked the weapon.

No explosion; he was still alive.

Nunez came to his feet, pointed the M72 LAW down range at the bursting flash of the enemy gunner, and fired. The rocket shot forward, exploded into the tree line, and silenced the NVA gun.

As he led his men forward, shrapnel slammed into Sgt Pete's face and neck, and a short time later, he took a bullet in the leg. As the mortars became a barrage and the enemy automatic rifle fire continued unabated, the Marine advance began to stall. With the exception of Sgt Peters, most of the leathernecks hit the deck for whatever nonexistent cover they could find.

"*I was really afraid to move,*" LCpl Elliot Rubenfeld said. "*I remember hearing crying, a lot of crying and yelling.*"

"*I saw Marines fall,*" Martinez said, "*and after about the third or fourth mortar round going off someone yelled—'Fall back!'*"

"*I remember mortars coming in, and we kept having to move back, move back, tightening it up, and tightening it up,*" Duca said. "*The perimeter was too wide spread. I can still hear in my head today—'You're too far apart; you're too far—'*"

Without an A-gunner to keep the belt of machine gun ammunition off the ground, Clark's M60 picked up dirt and jammed. The moment that his gun ceased firing was the opportunity that the NVA had been waiting for. In line to the left of Peters, Cpl Duca looked up at the woods and shook his head in disbelief.

"*Like an entire tree line, maybe one hundred feet from end to end, just got up and advanced forward, and I'm rubbing my eyes, and like, 'Am I seeing things?'*"

"Marines coming up on the right!"

"Them ain't no Marines! Shoot, shoot, goddamnit shoot!"

Like a nightmare appearing out of thin air, over one hundred North Vietnamese soldiers, supported by mortar, machine gun, and AK-47 fire, swarmed out of the forward cluster of trees toward the twenty exposed Marines. Wearing forest green utilities with foliage tied to their uniforms, legs, arms, and helmets, their camouflage was so effective that it appeared as if a whole stand of bushes had just picked up and moved.

"There they are!" Peters yelled. "There they are!"

Attacking from the front, the NVA swung hard and slammed into the Marines' right flank. Outnumbered five to one, the leathernecks now faced withering fire from two directions. The NVA were suddenly poised to roll up the thin American line, breach the company perimeter, and destroy the Marines piecemeal. The ambush had been nearly perfect.

"*The first mortar hit thirty feet away,*" Clark said, "*and then the next one hit like fifteen feet, and I was laying there in the fetal position waiting for the third one to hit as I watched a wave of them advance.*"

"Carlton, you're gone. This is it, man, I'll see you later—"

"*I was bidding myself farewell, and I don't know why, I just rolled over, and my eyes rolled up toward the sky, as if I had maybe died with my eyes opened, and I saw this image roll over the horizon. It was so huge that I couldn't get what it was, and it was frightening the way it just rolled up over in the sky. It was just a clear image of a man that was made out of the firmament, the clouds were going through it, and I couldn't believe what I was seeing. It was too frightening to look at, so I turned my head back toward the machine gun, thinking that I was going crazy. I turned my head to try to look at it again, and I started waving, you know, trying to clear my eyesight, thinking that it was smoke or that I was hallucinating. I then waited, thinking, 'Let me shake my head, clear my head, and take a good look.' When I did that, it actually got clearer, crystal-clear like a piece of china. I said, 'Oh, I'm having a trip or something. The clouds are shaping out of this—' and he looked like a god on a throne you know, you know, like the god of the universe. And when I was staring at it, it seemed like his eyes were staring back at me, so intense that it was unbearable.*"

"I'm gone—"

"*And I accepted the fact that we were going to get overrun, and then I was dead. Now, I'm up in heaven somewhere, and I said, "Oh, my God!*"

Clark then heard an answer that came on with a rasp.

"I'm all mans' God."

At first, it was like he was just mad at everybody. It was like a parent who was mad at his children for what they were doing out in the backyard. He came out there, and they were fighting, and he wasn't just our God—he wasn't just an American god—but he was God to the Vietnamese."

"Oh, God, Oh, God. Help me," Clark pleaded. "I'm getting ready to get killed—"

"Oh, ye of little faith—"

"OK, Lord, OK, Lord. I'm with you. You've got me from here. Even if I'm killed, I'm OK. OK, I'm here. I'm ready to go. Just let me hear you say, are you, God, are you?"

"The last words I heard were in an echoing sound—"

"I am—I am—"

"You are who? You are who?"

As he pleaded for an answer, Clark's machine gun opened up in the direction of the oncoming NVA. Cpl Jones, a veteran who Clark had a great deal of respect for, had shaken the dirt off the belt of ammo, reloaded the rounds, and begun firing on the enemy advancing on the Marine flank.

Clark, suddenly back on the battlefield, rolled to his right onto a dead Marine and caught sight of an enemy soldier but had no time to pull the .45 pistol strapped to his side. He grabbed the dead man's M16 and opened up on the NVA, who dodged behind a nearby bush. As he knelt and tried to zero in on his target, another leatherneck grabbed at his rifle.

"What are you doing?"

"You'll never get me," the Marine shouted, "you sons of bitches!"

Clark released his weapon, and the man charged toward the enemy, firing. Clark dropped to the ground again, crawled to another fallen Marine, and seized his weapon. This time, the dead man's rifle didn't fire as it, like countless others, had jammed. As he tried to clear the weapon, tear gas began to drift onto his position.

"We had dropped CS gas, and we had got the message to fix bayonets," Clark said, *"but my gas mask didn't work. I was trying to fend off this CS gas and cover my face and eyes, and I couldn't see the enemy, and it was smoke going on, and it seems like I could see souls, I could see the souls leaving people's bodies—"*

As he struggled to fend off the tear gas, Clark felt a tap on his shoulder. LCpl Albert Santos, a salt who had just thirty days left in-country and was due to head home the first week of October, held out his gas mask to Clark.

"I almost jumped out of my skin, but I turned around, and he give me his gas mask, and I put his gas mask on, and it felt like I was drowning in ten thousand feet of water, and somebody gave me their oxygen to breathe. I mean, I was dying with that CS gas hitting me. You cry, and you snot, and everything—

"And he give it to me, and it felt so good, and so I started feeling, like god, that was such an act of bravery. I was mad, so I pulled the mask off, gave it back to him, put myself in reverse, and made a retreat. I saw this crater, didn't know how deep it was, but I dove in it like Rambo, slid down on my forearms, rolled over still cradling this M16, and crawled back up to the top without exposing my head. When I dove into the crater, the stock of the M-16 broke completely off, and all that was left was a thin barrel."

As he came to the top of the crater, Clark's body broke out into uncontrollable tremors. *"I had to hit myself. I actually had to beat, you know, hit myself in the leg in order to stop shaking."*

"When we were online and got mortared," LCpl Tancke said, "we pushed ahead another couple of feet, were still getting mortared and getting machine gun rounds, and now we're getting attacked from our right flank from these guys in trees, bushes, and crap. Sgt Peters was giving directions, but then, it got so disorganized because we got hit so hard and so quickly that everybody's fighting for their life."

Tancke was able to fire off two magazines of M16 ammunition at the oncoming enemy before his rifle jammed.

"The only way to clear it was to pull back the bolt, take your cleaning rod, and knock out the cartridge because the extractor had ripped off the lip of the spent cartridge and fed another round in. You now got two rounds: one spent and you got a brand-new live behind it, so you had to pull it back, punch the thing out, and then manually reload one and fire."

Nearby, Pfc Martinez dove for cover into a hole and aimed his rifle.

"I couldn't see the enemy at all, and I couldn't see where the rounds were coming from. All I knew is that I could hear them all around us. I took a guess, got off one round, and my M-16 malfunctioned."

He fell back into the hole, struggled unsuccessfully to clear his weapon, and found another.

"By that time, everything was building, the battle was forming, the incoming was more intense, more fire, more automatic fire, more explosions, and as I peered over the edge of the hole, I saw Sgt Peters out in the open, to I would say about my 01:00 position, without a weapon and with blood on his hands."

"Get down, Sergeant! Get down—"

Cpl David Ryan, who was near Peters, tried to get the Marine to hit the deck out of the field of fire, but Peters resisted.

"Sgt Peters was standing out in the open," Martinez said, "and he was cussing at the enemy. I could hear him. I remember, I could hear him say, 'Come on, motherfuckers!' He was trying to direct the squad and fire, but he was also pissed off because he was hit."

A moment later, Martinez turned to his left and saw Father Capodanno and either Corpsman Leal or Phelps move out toward the wounded now beyond the retreating Marine line.

"Bullets are flying, mortar rounds are coming in, and we were in a mess," LCpl Rubenfeld said. "I was so scared somebody could kick me, pluck my eyebrows out, and I probably wouldn't have known much of a difference. We were pinned down, and nobody wanted to move. We didn't know what to do."

Everything was happening in a matter of seconds. Decisive action had to take place, and those choices had to be the right ones. Indecision or error meant death.

"One fuck up," Lobur said, "and you're dead forever."

As he lay there, hugging the ground for any cover he could find, Rubenfeld felt a swift kick in the ass.

"Move, move, you've got to get moving—"

Sgt Pete, blood on his face, neck, hands, and leg, oblivious to the fusillade of bullets and motor rounds, stood above him. Acting instinctively and by experience, the sergeant knew that they had to face and stop the enemy now or it would all be over. Leading by example and with tremendous control of his men, Peters began to pull the Marines back up the hill to face the devastating NVA threat to their right. Knowing how difficult it was to spot the camouflaged enemy squad fire teams as they zigzagged forward, Peters stayed on his feet so that he could spot the enemy and point them out for his men.

"When you're lying flat on the ground, it was very hard to see," Rubenfeld said. "These guys (the enemy) were so well-camouflaged, they were well-orchestrated, and they were well-trained. There was *no flank coverage, and the gooks were trying to cut us off, split us in half. Peters was trying to locate where they were at so that we could stop them. He was getting up into positions where he could point and direct fire, from whether it be a machine gun or whatever, into the enemy. He was getting us to fire and be effective, and the only way to be effective was to shoot at gooks rather than bushes.*

"But he also made it impossible not to get killed. There were so many bullets, so much going on out there that if you stuck your finger up, you were going to get it shot off. And he just totally exposed himself many times."

2nd Platoon Radio Operator Pfc Steve Lovejoy was coming down the knoll when the enemy burst from the tree line. Lovejoy hit the deck as small arms and mortar fire exploded at his front. Completely exposed, Lovejoy grabbed his radio, but it didn't work. He tried to fire his M16, but his weapon failed as well.

In a fighting hole nearby, 2nd Platoon Cmdr Lt Blecksmith was watching the NVA surge toward Sgt Peters's two squads when a crouched runner took cover next to him. Father Capodanno surveyed the scene, already littered with wounded men, and started to crawl back out of the hole. Blecksmith, surprised to see the Navy chaplain, grabbed Capodanno's pack and pulled him back.

"Stay here!"

"I've got to go out there—"

Blecksmith released his pack and watched as the priest scrambled back out onto the battlefield.

"I was pinned down," Lovejoy said. *"My radio didn't work, my rifle didn't work, and I knew if I stayed there that I was not going to survive. There was no shrubbery, foxholes, no bomb craters. Everybody down there was completely exposed, and the NVA killed everybody who stayed there. All of the sudden, just from out of nowhere, a pair of hands reached down and grabbed the back of my*

pack, hauled me up the hill, and threw me into a bomb crater. And until I was actually thrown into the crater, I didn't know that it was Father Capodanno. I remember the cool look about him as though he was saying, 'Do not worry; all will be OK.'"

Lovejoy grabbed his radio.

"We need help!" Lovejoy shouted. "We're being overrun!"

LCpl Albert Santos, now in the hole with Lovejoy, crawled to the edge of the crater, aimed his M16 in the enemy's direction, and fired.

Nothing. The rifle had jammed.

Lovejoy tried to radio the command group again.

"We need more help on the northwest quadrant of the knoll!"

No response. The radio was dead, and Lovejoy shook it in disbelief.

"How can the radio be dead after only ten minutes of battle?"

He tossed his rifle to Santos who was struggling to un-jam his weapon, changed the battery in his radio, and tried again.

"The enemy is closing in. We need help!"

Again no response, but he could now hear the broadcasts of other operators who, apparently, could not hear him. Santos cleared Lovejoy's M16 and fired until it malfunctioned again.

With two useless rifles and no radio, the two men were now defenseless and had no choice but to lie flat at the bottom of the hole as enemy rounds crisscrossed the air above them.

A moment later, after administering last rites to a dying Marine, Father Capodanno was back in the hole with Lovejoy and Santos as CS gas rolled over their position. The chaplain was now without a mask, as he had left his with Ericson on the backside of the knoll. Lovejoy reached for the gas mask in his pack and held it out to the priest. Capodanno waved off the offer.

"You will need it more than I will," he said as he crawled, once again, out of the crater.

Three other Marines had joined Pfc Martinez in his hole, but they only had two functioning weapons among them. He had gone through two M16s, both of which had jammed.

"We need men on our left flank!"

The call came from LCpl Andrew Giordano and Pfc Charles Martin, who were in a depression about ten feet to the left of his position.

One of the men in his hole looked at Martinez.

"You go."

"Why me? I don't have a weapon?"

Either Giordano or Martin heard him and answered, "We have one for you!"

Martinez counted to himself, "One, two, three," leapt from his hole, watched as Giordano provided covering fire, and grabbed the M16 that Martin held in his outstretched arm. Martinez dove to the ground as another Marine took a position next to him.

"I was exposed. There was no cover, it was out in the open, and there were no holes around that position."

As he hit the deck, Martinez spotted an NVA soldier about thirty yards to his front.

"I mean all this action is going on, and he's walking like it's a Sunday afternoon, just really calm and cool. I believe that he was trying to spot Marine positions. I had him in my sites, I pulled the trigger, and the rifle malfunctioned."

Martinez called to the Marine next to him. "There's a gook out there. Get him!"

The devil dog raised his head a little bit and said, "Where? I don't see him."

"He's right out in front of us; get him!"

"He said, 'I don't see him,' so I said, 'Give me your rifle; I'll get him,' and of course, he's not going to give up his rifle, and so I watched this North Vietnamese soldier just walk away and disappear."

In the depression nearby with Pfc Martin, LCpl Andrew Giordano spotted an enemy 60mm mortar less than sixty meters from his hole. Despite wounds sustained moments before, Giordano ran through the gauntlet of enemy fire to within fifteen meters of the enemy mortar team. He then threw four grenades in quick succession, killing three NVA and destroying the mortar tube. Seeing a fellow Marine fall, he ran to the wounded man and, while trying to help him to safety, was himself cut down by NVA machine gun fire.

Cpl Nunez, after firing his M72 LAW rocket launcher, found what was left of Sgt Pete's two squads in a defensive line along the crest of the knoll's right side.

"Over here!"

Nunez looked over to see LCpl Keith Rounseville waving him to a small depression barely a meter deep partway down the slope. Rounseville, at five-foot-four and one-hundred twenty-five pounds, was one of the smallest men in his platoon. Nunez made a low run and slid into the depression, while Rounseville and Pfc Dennis Fisher, the man who had bumped into Clark on the march in, provided covering fire.

"Get that gun!"

Sgt Red Manfra, the salt who had planned to go on R&R in Hawaii the next day, led a rocket team attached to Sgt Pete's two squads. Sixty inches long and weighing only twelve pounds when assembled, the M20 "super bazooka" rocket launcher fired a 3.5-inch rocket normally used against armor, bunkers, or dug-in troops. For this mission, Red armed the launcher with Willie Peter rounds that, when used against human targets, stuck to the skin and caused deep and devastating burns.

Manfra moved his team away from Peters' two squads in order to find an ideal position to direct the fire for his gunner with the launcher. As Lobur covered him with his M16, Manfra, standing on occasion, assessed the tree line, tried to see through the enemy camouflage, pointed, and ordered the leatherneck to fire. As the Marine launched a rocket, an NVA bullet cut the gunner down.

Manfra ran up to the position, grabbed the rocket launcher, and hearing a machine gun fire from a clump of bushes at the foot of the knoll, fired a second round. Lobur scrambled over to Manfra and reloaded the launcher, and Manfra fired again, taking out four enemy soldiers.

The rockets acted as a magnet for the enemy, and mortars began to fall onto Manfra and his team. Out of rockets, Lobur and Manfra grabbed their rifles and started to move back but not before a barrage of explosions knocked them to the ground and a bullet sliced through Red's right foot.

"By this time, we were really taking on a lot of fire," Manfra said. *"Mortars were coming in—people were screaming, bodies, and I screamed that I had gotten hit."*

"Sgt Manfra's hit!" Rounseville shouted, "Sgt Manfra's hit!"

Manfra turned back toward the enemy, struggled to his feet, and as he looked down the tree line, spotted two more enemy machine guns, one on the left and the other on the right with enough distance between them to ensnare most of Sgt Pete's men in a web of deadly fire. He aimed his M16, fired a few rounds, and then— nothing.

His rifle had jammed.

Manfra rolled to his side and opened the butt of the M16 in order to pull out the cleaning rod.

"Damn it!"

The rifle butt was empty. Thinking that he wouldn't need the rod while on R&R, he had given it to another Marine. At that moment, as he tried to clear his rifle, a 2nd NVA bullet slammed into the exposed leatherneck.

"It went in underneath my left arm, and it came out on the right side of my chest. It opened my chest, just ripped it open."

"He's hit again! Corpsman, up!"

"I'm hit. I'm hit," Manfra said, "My rifle's jammed—"

Without a helmet but with a white stole he wore around his shoulders when administering last rites, Father Capodanno and 2nd Platoon Corpsman David Phelps scrambled out to Manfra.

"I've never seen it so heavy," Lobur said, *"and I mean everywhere. Everybody is screaming and shouting, and there's Father Capodanno just walking around. Everybody is saying, 'Why is he here? He's not supposed to be here!' and I'm shouting at him, 'Get down! Get down!'"*

LCpl Rounseville, watching nearby from a depression, couldn't get to Manfra, who lay on the exposed slope under the crossfire of two NVA machine guns.

"There was really no place to go on that knoll," he said. *"We were exposed, and whatever little depressions or anything that we could get behind or into, we tried."*

"I was lying there," Manfra said, *"and I'm hurting, and I don't know how bad I am, but Father Capodanno appeared. He came up on me, and we were laying there, he grabbed my hand, asked me where I was hit, and asked me, 'Do you know the Lord's Prayer?'"*

"I don't know the whole thing."

"Well, I'll say it with you."

"So we laid there, and firing was going on all around us, and we laid there head to head, and we said the Lord's Prayer. He held my hand, and we said the Lord's Prayer."

Rounseville tried to provide cover for Father Capodanno, but—
"My rifle doesn't work."

The Navy chaplain grabbed Manfra's rifle, not knowing that it had malfunctioned, ran crouching to give it to Rounseville, and then returned to Manfra. "Be strong, young man. We'll get through this."

"Then somebody screamed, 'I'm hit,' and he said to me, 'I have to move on; I have to go.' So he crawled away from me, and a machine gun opened up, and I got hit again, and it flipped me right over on my back. That's how powerful it was."

Now, having been shot three times, Manfra watched as more enemy soldiers swarmed forward. Red knew that he was a dead man unless he reached some cover. Using his uninjured foot, he pushed himself against the hard ground to within a few meters of the depression where Rounseville and Nunez had taken cover until something caught on a snag. Thinking that it was his cartridge belt, he reached under his body and felt his own mangled left hand against a stump.

"Oh my god, that's my arm! My arm!"

The third enemy round had shattered his left arm, leaving it useless and numb at his side.

As he cried out, Manfra tried to push himself up.

"Stay down!"

"I kept yelling at Red," Rounseville said, "'Sgt Red, stay down! Stay down!' He was pretty well shot up, he kept trying to push himself up with his front two arms, and I see him take another bullet, and there was nothing that I could do for him."

A fourth shot rang out, striking Manfra below the right temple, blowing off the left side of his face. Red dropped to the ground, and even though they were only a meter away, the incoming fire was too intense for Rounseville or Nunez to pull him to safety.

Corpsman David Phelps, who had been near the back of 2nd Platoon when the ambush hit, had made his way forward to the sound of the fighting and the calls for a corpsman. Despite the hail of gunfire, and in order to keep Manfra from choking to death on his own blood, Phelps sat Manfra up with a bit of cover, applied battle dressings to his head and chest wounds, and then made his way toward the heavy gunfire.

Ten feet away in the shallow depression with Rounseville and Pfc Dennis Fisher, Cpl Nunez, who had found ammunition for his rifle, dropped a magazine, bent down to pick it up, and as he did, a bullet whizzed past where his head had been, striking and killing Fisher.

Cpl Joseph Fuller was in charge of a four-man machine gun team: one man on the M60, the other three armed with M16s. *"All three jammed. We didn't have any protection for ourselves except the machine gun. We saw about four of them moving to our direct front with heavy camouflage and automatic weapons. We opened up on them with the machine gun. We finally got a cleaning rod and cleared our M16s, but it seemed like every time we'd fire a couple of rounds, the M16s would jam."*

"They were thirty to forty feet, sometimes even closer," LCpl Fred Tancke said, *"and as most of the guys were pulling back, they were hit again by gunshot rounds."*

Tancke positioned himself like the hub of a wheel as the line pulled back up the hill. If the Marines didn't move fast enough, the NVA would outflank the two squads at his location and cut them off from the rest of the company.

"And so we start pulling back," Tancke said. *"I fire a couple of magazines, and I run into Leal, and he's by himself—"*

"Can you help me? I'm shot—"

Tancke saw a gaping wound inside the corpsman's right thigh.

"Put your fingers in there," Leal said. "Close off the artery—"

Tancke stuck his fingers into the warm blood and tried to stem the bleeding.

"The wound hadn't started pumping blood yet when he told me to help him clamp off the artery with my fingers," Tancke said. *"It then opened up, and the blood was pumping out quicker than I could close it off. My fingers kept slipping, and I was unable to clamp it and stop the bleeding. If I didn't clamp off that artery, he'd bleed right out, and it wouldn't take long: ten minutes, he's done."*

The corpsman couldn't stand, so Tancke grabbed him under his shoulder and began to scoot him back.

"I had hold of my rifle, and I got my left hand trying to squeeze off his artery. On my right side we're like scooting up, you know, on your butt, and I'm pulling him underneath his arms. I'm trying to drag him up the hill and trying to fight. I'm shooting gooks coming over the top of us, and my helmet fell off behind me, between my head and his head. I reached over to pick it up and 'boom,' it gets shot right out of my hand. The bullet shot the tip of my finger off, hit my helmet, and then a splinter must have gotten down into Leal. I picked my helmet up again, put it on my head, and said—"

"Oh Christ, let's get out of here."

"I can't make it—"

"You got to make it. You gotta help me because we're getting overrun. They're on top of us here—I gotta fire. I gotta try to keep them off of me. I gotta get you up—"

At that moment, fifty feet off the ground and about thirty feet northeast of Tancke and Leal, a Hu 1E chopper poured rockets and machine gun fire into the NVA advancing from the tree line to the north. His ammunition expended, the Huey gunner threw a red smoke grenade to the northwest about forty feet to mark the enemy position and left the battlefield. Four Marines then rushed forward to help Tancke with Leal, but the NVA were shooting at ground level.

"God, if you stood up, you were gone. Cornell was just standing up there, and I looked up, and before I could say anything, 'boom,' he got shot right in the chest. He was standing up there, coming down to help me."

"Get back up the hill!"

The men fell back with Cornell, and Tancke dragged Leal another meter while trying to fire at the same time. As he looked back down the hill, he watched an NVA soldier about thirty feet away boldly amble up to him with a machine gun in his arms.

"He came up on my left front, squatted down with the machine gun, and just sort of like laughed at me. I moved about four to six feet away from Leal to the left so I could focus in on the machine gunner and help conceal Leal from him. I was sure that I was going to take him out and aimed in on him."

Tancke aimed his M16 and pulled the trigger. Nothing happened, again.

"I looked down, and it had double fed. I tried to clear the weapon with the machine gun pointed right at me. I don't know why he didn't fire, but I just kept trying to clear the weapon, but it wouldn't fire; it wouldn't work."

The NVA soldier set down his machine gun onto its bipod legs, moved his finger near the trigger as if he was going to fire at Tancke, and laughed again. The soldier continued to laugh as Tancke, staring down the barrel of the enemy machine gun, struggled to clear his weapon. Failing that, the Marine reached for a grenade but couldn't open the brass clip on his pouch with his wounded hand.

"We gotta get out of here."

"No," Leal muttered. "Go."

"You gotta go; we gotta go."

"No, go."

Tancke turned back to the gunner, who now was no longer laughing. The soldier pressed the trigger of his machine gun, and with bullets tearing up the ground around him and whizzing by his head, Tancke clambered up the hill, dove into a large crater, and smashed his nose onto the inside of his helmet as he landed on a wounded Marine. As Tancke rolled over, blood pouring from his nose, the injured grunt he had landed on took another bullet.

"I'm bleeding all over the place. I jump and turn back around to see where the gunner is with Leal," Tancke said, *"and that's when Capodanno comes from my left side. The gunner must have spotted him from behind me, and as Capodanno comes running across in the open—"*

"Watch for the gunner!" Tancke yelled. "Watch for the gunner!"

"He just kept running across the hill between me and the gunner. It was like he was on a mission. He appeared to have been previously wounded, as I could see blood on his upper body. I couldn't fire my weapon, so I yelled again to get the gunner. The gunner opened up, and Capodanno fell in the area where Leal was. He went to his knees and fell facedown with several bullet wounds."

Tancke turned back to the Marines behind him.

"Corpsman, up! Damn—someone get that gunner!"

As he did, Tancke saw Corpsman Phelps to his left toward the top of the hill, leaning over LCpl Albert Santos, the salt who had offered Clark his gas mask and who had shared a fighting hole with Radioman Lovejoy.

"Santos had been shot in the head," Lobur said, *"and he lived a long time, maybe twenty minutes, half hour, and he was shouting the*

whole time for God to help him. I saw Doc Phelps lying alongside him just above the bomb crater where Lovejoy, Tancke, and others were. I remember glancing back and seeing Phelps look up, over our heads toward the advancing enemy. It seems he was putting a battle dressing on Santos 'cause they were both laying with their heads toward us."

As he tried to treat Santos, Phelps himself was shot in the head and killed.

2nd Squad Leader Nunez, positioned to the left of Tancke's crater and twenty-five to thirty feet from Capodanno (who was to the right), watched three or four NVA soldiers, one armed with a long knife similar to a machete, lunge toward the wounded chaplain.

"Capodanno threw his right hand up, and that's when the knife came down and hit his hand. He was trying to protect himself from the swing of that knife."

Nunez fired, hit some of the NVA, but ran out of ammunition.

"I was trying to find some ammo somewhere when they cut him, then they shot him and bayoneted him as they came over the top."

"Save your ammo!" Nunez shouted as he ran out of bullets. "Go to semiautomatic!"

As another Marine took out the NVA gunner with a grenade, Cpl Bert Watkins, a machine gun squad leader, came up and began firing where the gunner had been.

"We were now fighting off another attack from the direction of the village," Tancke said. *"Suddenly, there were other NVA soldiers just five or six feet in front of us popping up behind bushes between our crater and where the chaplain and Leal lay."*

In the nearby crater, 2nd Platoon Sgt Marbury called to out to Tancke: "Go see how close they are!"

Tancke stuck his head above the crater's rim, and a laughing NVA soldier popped his head up from behind a bush only two meters away.

Tancke ducked back down.

"They're right there!"

He then turned to the Marine next to him.

"Pull open my pouch."

The devil dog flipped his pouch open, and with his healthy hand, Tancke grabbed a grenade, pulled the pin, and lobbed it at the laughing enemy, taking him out.

A moment later, a second enemy soldier, this one carrying a chicom, a large grenade attached to the end of a stick, charged forward. Tancke tried to fire, but his weapon was still jammed. Lobur fired and dropped the soldier at the rim of the crater.

"He was just lying there looking at us with a grin, and he had the grenade in his hand, and he was dead. And then it was just a constant barrage of them charging up the hill, the left side, the right side—"

3rd Platoon

Back with the rear elements of the platoon in and around the village, Cpl Cummings and his squad were still reeling from the friendly fire of the Huey gunship as well as contending with the advancing NVA when they received the order to move up.

The leathernecks braved a gauntlet of bracketed NVA mortar explosions and small arms fire as they advanced in twos and threes through the draw toward Lt Cernick's position on the backside of the knoll. 3rd Platoon Radioman, Cpl Kevin Kelly, could hear the pleas for help from 2nd Platoon, but their radioman couldn't hear him. As he tried to raise Pfc Lovejoy, several Marines streamed past. As a bare-chested leatherneck, wounded with blood splattered on his forehead and side, stumbled past Cummings without a weapon, the squad leader grabbed him by the arm.

"What's the matter?"

"Oh god, they're carrying away the bodies—"

"Bodies? Who is carrying them?"

Cummings pulled the delirious casualty to the ground and called for a corpsman, who was quickly on the scene to hold the man down and patch him up.

"He was out of it," Cummings said of the casualty, *"very much out of it."*

"Spread your people out!"

Lt Murray appeared and directed 3rd Platoon to an area toward the lower part of the knoll along the east (right) side. Cummings directed his men to their new positions as 3rd Platoon linked up with the tail end of second to create a loose perimeter facing north/northeast toward the tree line.

"We did link up with 2nd Platoon to some degree," Goulet said, *"and it was a very loose perimeter. The enemy was in front, and we were in the rear protecting any assault that might come from that area."*

3rd Platoon began to take heavy small arms and mortar fire as the enemy tried to cut the men off from the rest of the company. Cummings' squad crossed a ditch, fanned out, and started to dig in. As Cummings and the two squads from 3rd Platoon moved, an NVA machine gun opened up on them from behind a tree, wounding Cpl Bill Moy with a bullet through his shoulder. As he maneuvered, LCpl Permenter spotted three Viet Cong running across his right front. He took them under fire and saw the middle soldier drop after one shot. Then his M16 jammed as the two standing VC dragged their wounded comrade to cover.

"This was the first time that I had ever seen an NVA soldier try to penetrate through our lines," Machine Gunner Cpl Joseph Fuller said. *"These NVA seemed to have no—seemed to have no regard for their*

self-safety. They just wanted to get into our perimeter, and they were doing it as best they could."

The devil dogs had to hold. While one grunt tried to dig a quick trench, which was nearly impossible in the rocky soil, another would provide covering fire, but that was often not enough, and the men had to pull back due to the intense enemy onslaught.

"The enemy was dropping mortars behind and walking them toward us," LCpl Permenter said. *"The noise was so intense and overwhelmingly loud it was impossible to hear anyone shouting. We each just kept an eye out, and when the Marine next to you moved, you did also, as it was imperative to stay together. Our squad was 'Tail End Charlie' (rear security), and we kept up with the rest of the platoon, all while shooting, throwing grenades, and unjamming our rifles."*

At his new position to the east (or rear) of the perimeter, Cpl Don Goulet, the fire team leader in 3rd Platoon who had cussed in front of Father Capodanno, began to lay down suppressing fire with his M16, only to have the rifle malfunction.

"So I picked up another rifle. Some Marine had been killed or wounded. I picked up that rifle and went to shoot it, and it was jammed so I threw it on the ground. I ran and I found another one and went back to my position, but that rifle had jammed. I picked up a third one, but that had jammed. So, between mine and those three, I went through four rifles that had jammed, and then the fifth one worked perfectly."

"Mortar rounds are coming in," Goulet said. *"It's hard digging in because the knoll was full of rocks and shovels aren't going in that good, a lot of lot of fire coming over that knoll, the green tracers, and you could hear it all over the place—"*

6

BIRD DOG

As the battle raged below, a Cessna O-1 Bird Dog, a single-engine, lightweight, two-seat observation aircraft circled at low altitude above, with veteran Marine Spotter Pilot CPT Tom Redmond at the controls and Co-pilot CPT Jan Nowak observing. As the tactical air controller airborne (TACA) responsible for the battle area, Redmond was, through FAC Goebel, Lt Murray's "eyes in the sky." His job was to sort out the situation on the ground, identify, and prioritize targets, then direct fixed-wing and helicopter gunship strikes against enemy positions. With no protection against enemy fire and no defensive weapons, Redmond had a vitally important and highly dangerous mission. Without knowing the location of Kilo 3/5 and the 1/5 Command Group, Redmond had to keep track of Bravo and Delta 1/5 near Đông Sơn and Mike 3/5 on the knoll as he put bullets, bombs, and napalm where those strikes were most urgently needed—and not on top of his fellow Marines.

3rd Platoon, Near the Backside of the Knoll

"I heard a transmission from the FAC," a radioman said. "It looks like a forest is moving our way!"

At that moment, an American F-4 Phantom jet came in low, between fifty and one hundred yards, slightly to the left of Cpl Cummings's position. As the F-4 approached, an NVA Quad 50, a 50 caliber antiaircraft weapon, opened up. As further evidence of the NVA's well-planned ambush, at least two Quad 50s, maybe more, were well placed in anticipation of American fixed-wing aircraft support.

"*The first jet came in very low, and we thought he was going to bomb them,*" Cummings said, "*but he didn't release. The second jet that came in released all his bombs, but we saw all these bullets and tracers go up in the air, and that meant there was a whole lot of NVA right in that area where he dropped the bomb. He took hits, started trailing smoke, and ended up ditching in the South China Sea.*"

As the Phantom vanished over the horizon, the North Vietnamese appeared.

"Here they come!"

A platoon of thirty-five well-camouflaged NVA had snuck undetected down a drainage trench alongside the knoll, and now, with a machine gun laying down a base of fire, charged toward 3rd Platoon in an attempt to pierce the Marine perimeter.

"*The enemy rushed from the east tree line where we had been,*" LCpl Permenter said. "*We took them under fire and shot them down as they rushed forward. With every round I fired from my M16, the next would jam in the chamber just when I most needed the ability to rapid fire.*"

"*When I seen them coming up the hill with the brush on their back and the weeds,*" Cpl Tylinski said, "*my only thought was 'I'll never see Michigan City again.'*"

Cpl Bill Moy, wounded in the shoulder by the machine gun just a few moments before, acted fast. Exposing himself to the heavy fire, he responded with his M16, pinpointing the enemy location for his fire team. The devil dogs exploded with small arms fire dropping at least fifteen enemy soldiers as one man managed to get within two meters of 3rd Platoon's line. The remainder of the enemy force retreated to the cover of the tree line, but they were far from finished.

The NVA knew that the Americans' rifles would often malfunction and that their supplies of ammunition had run low. Another attack on the weak back line of the Marine perimeter just might break their back. Within minutes, the NVA launched a second attack. Despite his wound, Moy continued to direct fire at the charging enemy, beating them back once more, but it seemed as if an endless supply of North Vietnamese soldiers lay in front of them beyond the tree line.

2nd Platoon

Due to the punishing attacks by a determined and tenacious enemy, the north side of the knoll was now in total chaos. Cpl Nunez watched as the NVA formed in the woods and moved forward once more in an attempt to overrun the thin line held by Sgt Pete and his two squads.

"Platoon-sized groups, thirty to fifty men each," Nunez said, *"were moving out of the tree line from our left front to our right front."*

Moments later, an F-4 Phantom II fighter bomber screamed over the battlefield and released a butterfly bomb, an antipersonnel incendiary fitted with folding wings that flutter and arm the fuse as it falls, onto the NVA advancing across the giant rice paddy. As its wings swung out, the bomb sailed past the Marines, landed in the middle of an enemy platoon, and detonated. That strike, along with the blazing napalm in the tree line, so close that the Marines could feel the searing heat, brought only a momentary respite from the unrelenting enemy assault.

Tancke, Lobur, and Sgt Marbury were in a crater below Nunez and Rounseville's depression. Martinez was off to the left, and Clark and his machine gun team were off to the forward right with an old bomb crater, about a meter deep and dotted with scraggly bushes, about nine meters further right and closer to the bottom of the knoll. It was in that old crater, with enemy fire now coming from the front, left, and right, that Sgt Pete made his last stand. Covered in dirt and undaunted by a gunshot wound to the leg and mortar fragments in the face and neck, he had fired his M79 grenade launcher until it was empty. He now stood in the crater with an M60 machine gun, the ammo belt draped over his left arm. Shooting from the hip, Peters fired burst after devastating burst as squads of camouflaged NVA advanced, forcing the enemy to disclose their positions with their return fire.

"He was not more than thirty feet from me," Nunez said, *"and every time the enemy would start their assault, he would stand up with his machine gun. You gotta recall most of his machine gun teams were down, were dead, or shot to pieces, and he would stand up and fire that M60 machine gun at the enemy.*

"You could see some dust from time to time come off of his battle jacket. It's what we called it. It was just nothing but a shirt, come off of his shirt, and it was bullets passing through it. I don't remember how many times he was hit; I just don't remember it—"

Peters dropped the machine gun and fell to his knees.

"I saw him shot down to his knees," Clark said. *"He had blood, and it seemed like it was coming out of his mouth, and he didn't have any ammunition, no weapon. As I was crawling toward him, I was saying—"*

"Get down, Sgt Pete! Get down!"

"Somebody get me a gun," Peters said. "Somebody get me a gun—"

"I was maybe about a body length from him," Clark said, intending to give Peters his .45 pistol, *"before rounds cracked out and cut him down from his knees, and he fell forward really hard, and it seems like it just took the wind out of him—"*

Clark froze.

"I thought the life immediately went out of him, but it didn't. Seconds went by, and then he started reciting the Lord's Prayer. It was an amazing thing. Here's the Lord's Prayer being said by this Marine who was fighting so ferociously and was shot down. He went from yelling 'Somebody get me a gun!' to 'Our Father, who art in heaven—'"

Clark listened quietly, and then Peters's voice weakened.

"I thought he was going to falter and not get all the way through the prayer."

But Peters started again and finished. With Sgt Pete's last amen, Clark looked up to the sky and watched as a Huey gunship came in like a spacecraft, hovered over the enemy, and unleashed a deadly barrage of fire onto the NVA.

1st Platoon

Pinned Down

On the front of the knoll near the large rice paddy Pfc Haney, pressed to the ground by his fifty-pound pack, lay facedown and unable to move, his limbs paralyzed from his massive chest wound. With his face to the side and looking to the sky, he could see the American fighter bombers dive and drop their loads.

"Where I was laying, I could see the flight pattern, and it appeared to me that when they were diving, I was the target. I would see them diving at us, and then, just before at the last second, they would turn to the right and drop napalm so close that I could feel the heat from it."

As the battle roared around him, a battle he could barely see and couldn't escape, every minute wounded Marines behind him screamed for corpsmen. When the air strikes came in so close that the concussive explosion bounced him off the ground and he could hear shrapnel scream just over his head, shredding plants, Haney thought, "Is this the time I'm going to die?"

"I was trying to keep myself alive and not knowing how to do it, as I was at the mercy of what was happening. It finally just got to a point to where I just had to shut down. I think my body just shut down, and it had to relax. I started drifting away a little bit, you know, 'This is it; I'm dying,' and all of the sudden the lights went on, and I'm like, 'I don't want to die,' and that gave me enough burst of energy to make it through the day."

"At that time, I wasn't a Christian. I became a Christian afterward, but on that particular day, I was definitely praying to God. I was looking for any help that I could get."

Sometimes he thought about his wife, and at times, he thought about his parents, but the main thought that popped repeatedly into his head was: "I want to live. I do not want to die. I do not want to die—"

At one point, he called to Swan, who remained pinned down in the large paddy.

"Listen to me, brother," Swan answered. "I've got a machine gun. I've got a sniper every time I stick my head up, and they've got me pinned. Can you patch yourself?"

"I can't move. My pack is on my back."

"Can you reach anything?"

"I've got my towel around my neck."

"Pull that towel off. Stick that towel, a piece of it, or the trunk of it, in that hole to stop that bleeding."

"That fear was there," Haney said, *"but you can work that fear if you can get a handle on it, which is very hard to do, but it can be done, and it can sustain you through things. You have to turn it around to where that's the only thing, you know. You just have to accept where you're at, the position that you're in. I mean, you can cry about it all day long, but it's not going to do you any good. I knew where I was at, I knew I couldn't move, I knew they would get to me, and I knew it was just when."*

An enemy mortar round exploded near Swan, and it sent pieces of hot shrapnel flying into his face, arms, and legs. Pinned down, cut off from his platoon, and out of ammunition, he had nothing else to do but slowly pick the hot metal from his skin.

"That day I felt like I was just so inept: out of ammo, sitting there, and not thinking cowardly but thinking, 'God, everybody is going to think I am a coward!' But, if I went back up that hill, I was dead meat. To try to run to a rifle would have been my demise, and I knew that."

In the pocket of his jungle utilities, Swan remembered a map, letters from home, and pictures of his parents and twin sister that he kept in a plastic bag. Remembering all the photos and letters found on the bodies of the dead Vietnamese that he had gone through, Swan dug a hole about a foot deep and buried the pictures of his loved ones.

"When I heard nothing but gooks behind me," he said, *"what I thought was behind me, this is before the sun went down, I went, 'Holy fuck, all of Mike Company is gone! They are going to come over the top here, and I am a dead motherfucker!' And I had the deepest fear run through my body at knowing I was out of ammunition and that I was a dead man. And as soon as that went through my body, I was flushed with the calmest feeling I have ever felt in my life."*

At about the same time, just a few feet to his left, the same sense of tranquility, knowing that he, too, was going to die, flooded through Howard Haney.

"I can't explain it," Haney said. *"It's not an acceptance of death; it's an acceptance of strength."*

"And it stayed that way," Swan added. *"I don't mean the rest of my life, but by God, that was me the rest of that day, and it was him the rest of that day. He accepted."*

Company Command

In the command crater, Lt Murray fielded constant reports from his platoons while simultaneously directing close air support through his FAC, Goebel, who was in contact with CPTs Redmond and Nowak in the Bird Dog flying over the battleground. The artillery officer along the company perimeter was coordinating artillery while Lt Hayden integrated the organic 60mm mortars near the village to the southeast while Cpl Fred Riddle coordinated the larger 81mm mortars located back at Hill 51.

In addition to the NVA attacking directly toward the knoll from the north, the enemy troops coming through the draw between the knoll and the village to the southeast needed countering. The command crater wasn't large enough to hold all of the Marines and sailors of the command group, and many had scattered nearby in fighting holes that protected the region east toward the draw. Combat engineers, scout snipers, helicopter support teams, and the division photographer had positioned themselves some ten to twenty meters east of the command crater to defend against infiltration by the enemy into the company's defensive positions.

Back up the hill, as wounded men staggered or crawled to the command crater, FAC Goebel was doing his best to coordinate air support when enemy mortars began to land near his position. As one walking wounded reached the edge of his hole, a mortar exploded into the man's back, killing him instantly.

"The senior corpsman was back to the CP and was trying to get everything squared away as far as the casualties were," Cpl Kelly said. *"We were starting to run out of battle dressings, and he was asking all the Marines that weren't injured to give them theirs."*

As the skipper pointed out positions he wanted the leathernecks to dig into, Kelly spotted movement thirty-five to forty meters to his right. Under cover of the deadly barrage, an NVA soldier, armed with a chicom grenade, had either emerged from a tunnel or slipped through the perimeter. He charged forward. Goebel pulled his .45 pistol, aimed, and pulled the trigger.

Click.

His gun was empty. In the urgency to get moving on Hill 63, Goebel had been too busy checking his radios to load his weapon. The soldier ran past the command crater and threw the grenade into a hole occupied by a Marine sniper team. One of the snipers, Sgt Forrest McKay, tossed the chicom back, killing the enemy as he retreated.

But for the air strikes and the presence of Marines on the north side of the knoll, the battalions of NVA streaming in from the river would have already swept over and overtaken Mike Company. There seemed to be an endless supply of expertly camouflaged NVA laying down a constant fire with deadly accuracy as they advanced. Outside of the reach of bombs and napalm, undaunted squads of the enemy were already climbing up the side of the hill and slipping into the perimeter, and the Marines didn't have enough manpower to stop them.

The American defense was weakest at the south (or backside) of the knoll and to the west. Reports came in that squads of NVA, resembling hedgerows bobbing up and down, had dug into within fifteen meters of the back of the knoll, and Murray was worried that they might move around to the left and hit them on the flank. With the NVA in danger of breaching the perimeter to the north and east, pushing through the draw to attack from the south, and the danger of being assaulted from the west, as well as reports of enemy already inside the perimeter—

"We may not get out of this."

It was the first time that thought had crossed Lt Murray's mind.

"Riddle, take some men and dig in on the left flank."

FO Riddle and a handful of Marines sprung from their holes into a storm of machine gun fire. As they struggled to dig shallow holes, they ran into more devastating mortar explosions, one round detonating between a man's legs and blasting him into the air.

Murray again radioed Col Hilgartner's command group.

"What's the status of the CS drop?"

The first attempt to drop CS gas on the company's position had been ineffective, as it wasn't able to reach all of the NVA, who were now close-in and about to breach the Marine perimeter. The only alternative was to make a drop of CS canisters directly on top of the Marines at low altitude, which would expose the aircraft, likely helicopters, to enemy fire.

"We're working on another method of CS delivery," came the response.

Murray tried to think of another tactic, another tool to keep the enemy from infiltrating the lines, but he had nothing. He had run out of options.

"Fall back!"

Murray watched as his order raced around the knoll, and the Marines began to pull back in a tighter perimeter. He then took a deep breath before issuing his next order.

"Fix bayonets!"

2nd Platoon

The remnants of Sgt Pete's two squads on the right side of the knoll were nearly out of ammunition when they were reinforced by 2nd Platoon's 3rd Squad after at least thirty minutes of fighting. Due to their faulty M16s, the grunts were having a hard time putting down a base of fire with what ammunition remained and were instead relying primarily on their M60 machine guns and grenades. The NVA, knowing that the Americans' rifles malfunctioned and that their ammunition was running low, were not charging up the hill but were instead maneuvering, avoiding Marine fire and using camouflage to get in close. The North Vietnamese were steadily taking over the knoll.

LCpls Lobur and Tancke, having long since fired all of their rockets and thrown their grenades, sat perched on the edge of a crater near the base of the hill, methodically shooting one round at a time with their M16s. The enemy, now that they were close, were easier to spot from the constant fire of their weapons.

"Our platoon was caught out there for an hour, maybe two, just fighting an onslaught," Tancke said. *"I mean, it was just a constant barrage."*

The NVA would emerge from the tree line, move forward to the bushes, pop their heads up, laugh at the Marines, and start shooting. As Tancke fired back, he remembered a shooting gallery at a county fair where targets pop up and players shoot them in a line: bing, bing, bing.

"While we were in this hole, the gooks were sticking their heads above the bushes about thirty feet from us," Tancke said, *"and as they would look over, I would fire and blow their heads away. At first, my rifle worked for about two or three magazines, and then it kept jamming up a little more, a little more, until I was firing one round at a time. I passed my rifle back to Lobur, and he cleared it and give it back to me. I'd fire it, just like in the old times with the muskets."*

"Berry broke his back! A water buffalo ran over him. Didn't you see it?"

Lobur spotted a wounded Marine lying five meters to his right but saw no sign of a water buffalo.

"Help me!" LCpl Jack Berry cried. "Help me!"

"I tried to get out of the hole," Lobur said, *"and so many bullets were hitting, it was almost like they blew me back, dirt flying and bullets smacking everywhere. I felt like hell, but I couldn't get him. You know, one fuck up and you're dead forever."*

"Hey, Lobur—"

Machine Gunner Watkins had set up a position higher on the knoll behind some bushes. With M16s jamming, the M60 machine gun was the only reliable weapon, other than hand grenades, to keep the enemy at bay.

"Go down there, and get me that gun ammo."

Berry, who had died just to Lobur's front, had two belts of M60 ammo on him.

"Can't do that. I just can't do that, man—"

"Go get the gun ammo off of Berry!"

"I can't do it. There's too much shooting!"

3rd Platoon

At the vulnerable backside of the knoll to the southeast, entrenched in the draw at the hill's bottom edge with his machine gun team, LCpl Baima had difficulty pinpointing each attacker for his gunner, while his assistant gunner fired with his M16. How the enemy's camouflage allowed them to advance from bush to bush with relative ease amazed Baima.

"I was directing fire for my gunner," Baima said, *"and I could see the enemy hopping from bush to bush. They were very well camouflaged, and they got right on top of us before they exposed themselves. I said to my gunner, 'Screw this. I want you to put a burst into each fucking bush right in front of you.'"*

Enemy soldiers fell dead and wounded all round as the M60 fired, only to have more surge forward to take their place.

"Goddamn it! My rifle's jammed. Anyone got a rod?"

"Who's got the cleaning rod?"

While the enemy advanced and as he ducked incoming rounds, Baima tore off his pack and began to rummage, finding the sections of his cleaning rod near the bottom.

"The ramrod came in two or three sections. You had to screw it together, and here I am in the middle of a goddamn fire fight trying to screw a ramrod together—"

"Damn it!"

He fumbled with the two pieces, screwed them together, and tossed the rod to his assistant gunner as more NVA appeared.

"He got his gun cleared, and then somebody else yelled for the ramrod, and he passed it down the line. While this was going on, we got the word to fall back and dig in."

"Fall back! Fall back!"

Lt Murray's order to tighten the perimeter raced down the American lines.

"Let's go—"

Baima, his team, and the remainder of the two other squads pulled back fifteen meters, broke out their entrenching tools, and hastily tried to dig trenches in the unforgiving rocky ground.

As Cpl Goulet stabbed with his shovel, the world seemed to explode, and everything went black. Moments later, he opened his eyes to find that the battle still roared around him. As he gasped for breath, blinding pain seared through him. A mortar blast had plunged shrapnel into his back within a quarter inch of his spine. Struggling for air from a punctured lung, he was quickly bundled up the knoll to a large bomb crater with other wounded when another order came down the lines.

"Fix bayonets!"

"Oh shit," Baima thought. "I've never heard that order before—"

Most of the Marines around him had bayonets, but a few didn't.

"Take them from the dead," Baima ordered. "They aren't going to use them now. Gather their grenades too, and stack them by the hole."

As they scrambled for grenades and bayonets, the men hastily prepared their new position farther up the knoll as enemy soldiers followed their retreat and continued to fire from behind the brush.

"We waited for the second assault, and then it came, and we could see the enemy hopping from bush to bush. We started firing again, and then the guns started jamming again, and I said, "Who's got the ramrod?"

No answer.

"Goddamn it! Who's got the rod?"

"I left it out there. I left it out there—"

"You gotta be shitting me. Where did you leave it?"

"Corporal, by that bush—"

"You're shitting me!"

"When we got the order to pull back, I just didn't remember it—"

"I'm going out to get it."

Baima knew that half of the twelve Marines around him needed that rod.

"Don't go out there—"

"If I don't get that ramrod, we're not going to make it. Cover me!"

As those Marines with working rifles laid down suppressing fire, Baima ran ahead outside the new perimeter, and as a mortar exploded to his left, he seized the rod and raced back to his men.

"I had about a squad, maybe twelve Marines around me, and at least half the squad was calling for that ramrod. And then we'd start firing again, and we'd fire three or four more rounds, and it would jam again, and you'd have to do the same thing over again. I saw three, maybe four dead Marines with ramrods down their M16s."

Although they were running out of ammunition, the Americans were able, for the moment, to hold back the NVA with each man firing just a few rounds before his rifle jammed and then clearing it with Baima's rod.

In a fighting hole nearby, Combat Engineer Ericson, armed with an M14 rifle, was thankful that Supply had not yet issued the M16 rifle to the engineers: thankful because the old, reliable M14 didn't jam. Supplied with about ten magazines holding twenty rounds each, he and the other two engineers, Braffett and Hilling, who were about twenty feet to his right on the ground without cover, laid down a steady base of fire when a corpsman came up to Ericson's hole with a wounded grunt.

"The guy had been shot through the right elbow," Ericson said, *"and every time his heart beat, the blood was squirting like three or*

four feet out of his body, so the corpsman knelt down by me and said—"

"I gotta get him in your hole. I gotta get him in your hole."

"Now, you have to realize what was going on. There was no way in hell I wanted to get out of that hole. But you do what you do. So I got out of the hole, as that grunt was going to bleed to death if that corpsman couldn't stop the bleeding."

As all three engineers continued to fire M14s from their stomachs or knees, an NVA soldier jumped to his feet about fifty feet to their front armed with a chicom grenade.

"He gets ready to throw a grenade, so I'm yelling at Hilling, 'Get 'em, Hilling! Get 'em!' as I'm trying to shoot the guy too. So Hilling shoots the guy. The guy falls down and gets blown up with his own grenade."

Just before the NVA grenadier appeared, but after he gave up his hole for the corpsman and the wounded leatherneck, Ericson saw what he thought to be a "strange thing" off to his right.

"There's a guy (Marine) kneeling down, and he's stripping film from his 35mm camera, stripping the rolls open and exposing the film."

Combat Photographer Warren Wilson was destroying the photographs he had taken, fully expecting the enemy to overrun the Marines.

"Well shit," Ericson thought. "This isn't good."

Now overflowing with wounded men, those still in the fight scoured the large bomb crater on the back of the knoll for weapons and ammunition. The wounded Goulet even had to give up his Ka-Bar fighting knife.

"Skipper says stay put," someone said. "The NVA are closing in."

"If a mortar doesn't blow us all to hell," Goulet thought, "I'll just have to give my best fight until they kill me."

Company Command

"Damn it, I have to find a way around this."

Lt Murray had almost run out of options. Bombs, bullets, and napalm from the air were killing hundreds of North Vietnamese, but with a good portion of his Marines armed with useless weapons, those who could fight running out of ammunition and the remainder dead or wounded, it wasn't enough. He had to find a way to break the enemy's never-ending assault, or he and his men had no chance.

"We'd had a huge amount of artillery, we finished off all our mortars, we had all kinds of fixed-wing come in, and I don't know how many series of bombings out in front, but they were still coming through," Murray said. "We tried everything we could, and it appeared that all of it was not going to work.

"If somebody is in a defensive position, you need seven-to-one odds to overwhelm them. They were attacking us; they know odds. So it became relatively obvious that they had overpowering forces. Once they take us on and they start intermingling with us, we are in deep trouble, and we need to find something to break that attack. When they started to break into the perimeter after an hour and a half, maybe two hours, of fighting, it looked like we would be completely overrun. They had us surrounded, and they were breaking through in various areas."

The commander of Mike Company had only one viable recourse. Scorching the eyes, skin, mouth, throat, and lungs of the enemy with CS gas would deter, at least temporarily, even the most tenacious foe. As long as his Marines had gas masks, they'd be safe, but for the wounded strewn across the battlefield without masks, or unable to access theirs, the drop might be a death sentence. Murray had no choice. With the enemy now poised for the final breach of his defenses, a gas drop directly onto his position was his only hope. He had to try again.

"Dream Hour, this is Connive Mike 6 Actual."

The call went to CPT Redmond, circling above in the Bird Dog.

"We have a shitload of bad guys in our position. Drop CS on top of us now, over."

"Connive Mike 6, this is Dream Hour. I have Deadlock 30 on station ready to drop."

The words were music to Murray's ears.

Deadlock 30 was an all-volunteer crew from Chu Lai who, after two hours of nonstop combat, arrived over the battlefield in two Huey helicopters. The first attempt at a CS drop by fixed-wing at high altitude had failed. If the gas was to have any chance of breaking up the enemy attack, Deadlock 30 would have to hover low when they made the drop with the chances high that enemy ground fire would send both choppers crashing down onto the Marines.

1st Platoon

Still pinned down in the rice paddy at the front of the knoll, Point Man Swan had been out of ammo for hours. Sweltering in the heat, he had long since consumed the water in both of his canteens and was now so thirsty from hours on the hot, dusty battlefield that he considered drinking his own urine. As the thought crossed his mind, he heard and then saw a Deadlock 30 chopper sweep overhead and felt a cloud of smoke roll over him.

"When the gas rolled down to me, I dug a hole in the corner of

this rice paddy dike, took my jacket and put it over my face, and stuck it down in that hole and covered dirt around it."

Command Crater

As the gas spread over the top of the knoll, FAC Goebel did his best to keep it from affecting the wounded in the command crater while trying, at the same time, to maintain contact with the aircraft.

"I recall the canisters resembling the 35MM individual roll film cans, about the size of a shot glass with a spew hole in the top," Goebel said. *"They landed all over the ground, and I had several brothers who did not have gas masks or were unable to use them. I remember trying to talk on the radio and rotate my mask around so the others could breathe and get the little canisters away from them and out of the hole."*

2nd Platoon

From his crater on the right side of the knoll, Lobur watched as a second Huey came into view. The Marine in the chopper held a lanyard attached to a two-legged contraption about the size of a backpack and covered with small holes. The helicopter came in dangerously low and held its position as enemy rounds began to pepper the skin of the vulnerable aircraft.

"He gives a yank on the lanyard and shoots about fifty gas grenades right at us—"

As small metal canisters shot through the holes and directly on top of the Marines, Deadlock 30, now taking heavy fire, whisked out of view as clouds of heavy white smoke swelled and billowed among the Americans.

"And its hotter than piss out there. It's always hot there, but it was really hot, and you're sweating, and this gas is just eating your skin up—"

With only a few masks available to the men in the crater, Lobur was able to take a few shallow breaths before his mask fogged up, preventing him from seeing in order to shoot.

Enemy fire increased once more, mortar rounds began to drop in, and—

"There they are!" Pfc Charles Martin yelled. "About twenty feet!"

"I tried to put a gas mask on," Lobur said, *"but it didn't work. It was too hot, it fogged up, and I took it off, and I was like Lamaze breathing with my face in the dirt, real shallow breathing. And I'm looking, and I'm crying, and snot's coming out, and it hurts so bad when your pores are open when—all of the sudden, I noticed, there's fuck—two hundred of them coming across that field, like it was a movie or something."*

Martin and Lovejoy began to toss grenades. Lobur knew that Lovejoy's radio didn't work, so he screamed toward the command crater:

"Do something! Get some air in here!"

"I saw them coming right at our front, then another rank and another, three or four ranks spread out like foot soldiers did. They had green uniforms, they had gas masks, and they had fully covered their mouth and nose, and they are coming across the field carrying their guns at port arms—"

"That's Kilo Company! They're coming to get us!"

Lobur knew that was bullshit.

"We're fucked!" Lobur said. "There's hundreds of gooks coming—"

"I'm shouting and shooting when they hand me a rifle, but that's like every thirty seconds, and that ain't going to do any good. The first

rank got to within maybe thirty yards, and I finally figured, 'This is it; should I shoot myself or what?'"

Nearby, 2nd Squad's leader, Cpl Larry Nunez, gathered an armful of grenades and crawled on his knees around the side of the knoll to a stand of brush about two feet tall. The Marines in his squad were now short of ammunition, and many of their rifles had jammed. The enemy was infiltrating their position and could easily take the high ground behind them. Supported by heavy and accurate grazing fire low to the ground, the enemy maneuvered in small units, twisting and turning toward the heaviest fire toward the Marines.

"You'd be looking at the side of a few enemy soldiers, and then you'd be looking at the face of a few from another angle," Nunez said. "They were just moving up there trying to find us."

Knowing that if he lofted the grenades into the air the enemy would see where they were coming from, he pulled the pins and instead tossed them low into the scrub brush, about five meters away. Nunez hoped the grenades would bounce up at odd angles and throw the enemy off as to where he was.

His strategy didn't work. As he pulled the pin on his last grenade, a chicom sailed in over the brush, hit the ground a few feet from him, and detonated. Pieces of shrapnel slammed into Nunez's head, but the grenade didn't kill him, as the chicom, for some reason, didn't explode with full force. Now unable to hear well, he caught movement to his right front, followed by a muzzle flash. By reflex, he moved his head as the NVA bullet passed his eye and sliced through his left ear. Out of grenades with his face and head bloodied, he scrambled back to his crater and gathered his squad.

The NVA had pushed Nunez's men back over the crest of the knoll. Nunez's squad had to push the perimeter forward, back up the rise of the hill thirty feet ahead. If the NVA gained that high ground, Nunez and the devil dogs with him would be sitting ducks for the enemy to fire down on them.

"Boys," Nunez said, "we're going to have to go take that back now, or they are going to be on top of us and shoot us—"

"We don't have any ammo—"

"We're gonna throw grenades. Everybody in the sound of my voice get a grenade, and we're going to throw them on the top of that ridge. Fix bayonets and throw grenades on my signal. We'll make the son of bitches wish they'd never been born."

Nunez noticed that the new guy, Martinez, didn't have a weapon. "Martinez, get a weapon. Get a weapon; they're all around you."

But there was no time to find an M16 that worked. Without a rifle, Martinez took a grenade, and when Nunez gave the order, he and the other men charged thirty feet back up the hill near the top of the crest, screaming at the top of their lungs and tossing grenades as they went.

"We blew them right off the top of that damn thing," Nunez said.

Now in a stronger defensive position, Nunez, either on his knees or standing, began to direct the fire of his squad when an NVA soldier broke cover and charged up the hill.

As the soldier brought up his rifle, Nunez brought up his, and both men fired. Rounds from Nunez's rifle smacked into the enemy, and as he ducked, the soldier's bullet smashed into Nunez's left shoulder. As the bullet hit, it knocked him back into the crater as a mortar sent pieces of hot shrapnel into Nunez's lower back, chest, and to the bone of his right forearm. Despite his multiple wounds and the fierce enemy attack, Nunez and his men held the high ground.

The Air Space Above the Knoll

"Connive Mike 6. You have three columns of Marines closing with your position on the north."

"We don't have Marines to our north," Lt Murray reported.

The location of Kilo and the 1/5 Command Group was, in fact, unknown but believed to be about six hundred meters south of Mike Company.

CPT Redmond took his Bird Dog into a steep dive to get a better view of the men he had spotted moving toward Mike Company. Two or three battalions, six to nine hundred soldiers in three parallel columns about two hundred meters apart, camouflaged with brush on their backs and branches on their helmets were moving fast, almost at a jog, from the south bank of the Ly Ly River across the wide-open dry rice fields toward the isolated Marines on the knoll.

The soldiers weren't Marines. Despite bombs, napalm, bullets, grenades, and CS gas, which had slowed the enemy, the NVA were closing in to finish off Mike Company with one final stroke.

"This is Dream Hour," Redmond radioed FAC Goebel. "There are hundreds more coming at you. Three files of them, one hundred fifty meters from your position—"

"Skipper," Goebel told Murray, "we got hundreds more NVA on the way."

"Thanks, Corporal. You obviously want to make my day."

Redmond rifled a Willie Peter marking round into the center of the advancing columns of NVA and called in bombers. As white smoke billowed up from the rice fields, the camouflaged soldiers continued moving south, undeterred, keeping to their single-file formations.

A flight of two Vought F-8 Crusaders, each carrying two one thousand-pound bombs, was orbiting on station. Attacking singly in a high angle dive out of the east, the Crusaders each lobbed both of their bombs simultaneously onto the enemy columns. The enormous explosions, followed by concentric shock waves, sent a storm of dust and debris airborne, momentarily obscuring the target from Redmond's view.

2nd Platoon

From his hole on the right side of the knoll, Machine Gunner Duca felt relief, even joy, as he watched the F8 Crusaders scream overhead. Braving enemy antiaircraft fire, the jet came in so low that he could see the facemask and helmet of the pilot. For Cpl Duca, it was as if he had been battling a guy bigger than he was, only to have a stronger buddy come to his aid.

Click. Click—

"I'm sitting in that hole," Lobur said, *"and here comes a Crusader hauling ass. Click, click. He drops two bombs. Click, click. He drops two more bombs, and he's down on the deck right across from me; that's how low he is—"*

As the jet banked away to the right, the leathernecks cheered as explosions rocked their crater. After the smoke and dust cleared, not a single enemy soldier was moving.

"Sweep the area for ammo—"

Men scrambled out of the crater to the dead and wounded lying outside the perimeter, scouring the bodies for M16 magazines, grenades, and more importantly, belts of machine gun ammunition.

"Suddenly Watkins runs past our hole," Lobur said, *"and he's out in the open, and he runs down there and gets those two belts of gun ammo from Berry, and he runs back."*

Now armed with two hundred rounds of machine gun ammo, the devil dogs could finally lay down an effective base of fire.

With the sun now beginning to dip toward the horizon, its dimming rays blurred and hazy in the dust and smoke, Cpl Nunez and his squad still held the crest of the knoll while Cpls Lobur, Tancke, and the others remained in the crater down the right side, the most forward position still manned. Many of the men, with useless weapons or out of ammunition, scanned the paddies and fields surrounding the knoll and prepared for another attack. But the enemy, it seemed, had fallen back.

With the fading light came the thunder of either a Phantom or an A-4 Skyhawk, and the dim silhouette of the jet came into view. Bright tracer rounds from two camouflaged enemy 50 caliber guns rose to greet the American as the aircraft swooped down and fired its 20mm cannons on the antiaircraft gun position. By coming in close to the battery to fire, the pilot dangerously exposed himself to the NVA guns, and a line of tracer bullets smacked into the jet's thin metal skin as it pulled up in a twisting right turn into the darkening sky.

The first aircraft had been the "bait," and now came the "switch." As the NVA gunner focused on the rising jet, a second American, this one with its lights off, followed in his comrade's wake, and as the men of 2nd Platoon cheered, wiped out the now exposed enemy gun with its load of bombs.

Standing left to right: LCpl Thomas Fisher, LCpl BJ Roraff,
Sgt Billy Jo Sims, LCpl Pete Schrader (KIA Essex).
Kneeling left to right: Pfc Richard Guerrero, unknown,
Sgt Sims's squad, 1st Platoon.
Photo courtesy of Ray Edwards.

Cpl Ron Mercereuio (left), 2nd Lt Ed Combs (right), 1st Platoon.
Photo courtesy of Ray Edwards.

LCpl Fred Tancke (left), Pfc Steve Lovejoy (right), 2nd Platoon.
Photo courtesy of Steve Lovejoy.

Cpl Bill Dubose,
squad leader, Delta 1/5
Photo courtesy of Bill Dubose.

Hn David Phelps at right,
corpsman, 2nd Platoon.
Photo courtesy of Jim Poindexter.

2nd Squad, 2nd Platoon. Front row kneeling from left to right:
LCpl Keith Rounseville, LCpl Richard Giebe (KIA Essex),
unknown, Cpl Larry Nunez.
Back row, standing: LCpl Carlton Clark, LCpl William Taliaferro,
Cpl Bert Watkins, LCpl Ron Pizana, Pfc Tony Martinez, Pfc John Noel.
Photo courtesy of Keith Rounseville.

LCpl Jack Swan, Point Man, 1st Squad, 1st Platoon.
Photo courtesy of Fred Permenter.

Sgt Larry Peters, 2nd Platoon.
Photo courtesy of Broome County
Historical Society.

From left to right:
Shirley, Larry, and Lynda Peters.
Photo courtesy of Broome County
Historical Society.

Sgt Larry Peters caring for Vietnamese children
in an orphanage, most likely in Da Nang.
Photo courtesy of Broome County Historical Society.

LCpl John Lobur (left), Pfc Steve Lovejoy (right), 2nd Platoon.
Photo courtesy of Steve Lovejoy.

Pfc Tony Martinez, 2nd Platoon,
in the field with M16, two belts
of M60 machine gun ammunition,
and grenades, similar to how
he appeared on September 4, 1967.
Photo courtesy of Tony Martinez.

Father Vincent Capodanno,
the Navy chaplain assigned to
H&S Company who accompanied
Mike 3/5 into the field on
September 4, 1967, despite
orders to remain on Hill 63.
Photo courtesy of JD Murray.

Left to right: Sgt Howard "Red" Manfra, Cpl Dennis Flood,
LCpl John Lobur, and LCpl Paul Gundlach, 2nd Platoon Rocket Squad.
Photo courtesy of Howard Manfra.

Combat Engineer Lief Ericson with a M14 rifle.
On September 4th, the combat engineers had yet to be issued
the new M16 rifle and instead fought with the outdated M14.
The M14s performed flawlessly, while the M16s repeatedly
malfunctioned. Photo courtesy of Lief Ericson.

Marines of Kilo 3/5 board CH-46 Sea Knight helicopters for transport
to the Quế Sơn Valley. Morning of September 4, 1967.
Photo courtesy of JD Murray.

Sgt Craig Sullivan (left), LCpl Larry Lukens (with his back to
the camera), Sgt Bill Lewis, 1st Platoon, awaiting transport
from Hill 63 to Quế Sơn Valley. Morning of September 4, 1967.
Photo courtesy of Bob Matteson.

Marine F4 Phantom fighter-bomber providing close air support
during the height of the Battle for the Knoll, September 4, 1967.
Photo courtesy of JD Murray.

Marines in the command crater wear gas masks in anticipation of
CS gas drop on Mike 3/5 during the height for the Battle for the Knoll.
Photo courtesy of Fred Riddle.

Command crater with captured NVA automatic weapons.
The RPG (second from left) was found 10—20 meters from the
command crater with a dead NVA soldier behind the sights.
September 5, 1967. Photo courtesy of Chuck Goebel.

1st Lt JD Murray, commander of Mike 3/5, eating C-Rations
on the morning after the Battle for the Knoll. September 5, 1967.
Photo courtesy of JD Murray.

1st Lt JD Murray, commander of Mike 3/5,
morning of September 5, 1967.
Photo courtesy of JD Murray.

Sniper with M40 rifle (right), Marine with M16 bayonet (left).
September 4 or 5, 1967. Photo courtesy of JD Murray.

Cpl Bert Watkins, 2nd Platoon machine gunner, showing bullet
damage to his helmet. September 5, 1967.
Photo courtesy of JD Murray.

Platoon Sgt Craig Sullivan, 1st Platoon.
Photo courtesy of Craig Sullivan.

3rd Platoon. Front row: Cpl Chuck Cummings.
Second row: LCpl Jack Garcia, Cpl Dennis Tylinski (with hat).
Very back row with hat: LCpl Vernon Randolph (KIA 2/7/68)
and LCpl George Iverson. Photo courtesy of Dennis Tylenski.

Marines identify comrades killed in action amid
captured NVA weapons on the knoll. September 5, 1967.
Photo courtesy of JD Murray.

7

Spooky and Company Command

Airspace and Command Crater

The NVA camouflage during the day had given the enemy a nearly insurmountable advantage over the Marines. Now, with twilight, came the even greater asset of darkness.

CPT Redmond, now low on fuel, briefed the new Bird Dog team of Fitzsimmons and Whitlow, then banked his Cessna north for the return flight to Da Nang. New to Vietnam, CPT Bob Fitzsimmons was flying one of his first missions while his spotter, Lt Rob Whitlow, had survived more than two hundred sorties in both Marine and Army Bird Dogs.

As they flew over the battlefield for their first close look, Blackcoat 3 set up a tight clockwise orbit nine hundred to a thousand feet above Lt Murray's command crater. Remnants of CS gas mixed with the dust and smoke from heavy bombs and napalm hung over the knoll and rice fields like a thin veil of dirty gauze, making visibility difficult.

"Dust and debris all over the place clouded the battle area," Whitlow said, *"but despite the monstrous blasts, the columns were still advancing to the south when the dust cleared."*

The NVA were still pouring from the tree line by the river across the large rice paddy and toward the knoll.

"There were only forty to fifty Marines still healthy enough to protect the perimeter," Fred Permenter said. *"We were precariously*

low on ammo, and the word came down to fix bayonets. If there were another assault, I knew we would be overrun and die on the little knoll before daylight. So, fatalistically, I thought 'Come and get us, you bastards.'"

Blackcoat 3 did its best to keep the air strikes coming in.

"Because of the limited visibility and because the NVA reinforcements were continuing their massive attacks from the north," Whitlow said, *"we continued to run flight after flight of bombers into the open paddies just north of M's location, working dangerously close to the Marines forward positions."*

At one point, Whitlow was coordinating six to eight flights of two attack bombers each, circling at two thousand foot intervals and flying without external lights. While he kept track of what aircraft and ordnance were available and how much time each jet had on station, CPT Fitzsimmons, as pilot of the flimsy aircraft, did his best to avoid getting shot down as an array of bombers, flying at five hundred feet, dropped their loads below the Bird Dog's orbit.

"The confusion was extreme and was heightened by the stress levels of anyone talking on a radio," Whitlow said. *"I made my best effort to stay calm and have a calming influence on the ground units, but I am sure my voice pitch elevated at least a few octaves. We had all the Marine ground companies, their battalion command teams, the regimental command team, and even the 1st Division CP on the radios."*

To make matters worse, Whitlow, at that time, had no notification by any command that another Marine company (Kilo 3/5) was even in the vicinity. Under the dim red glow of a small flashlight, which he hoped wasn't visible to the enemy, Whitlow tried to hold his map still in the vibrating aircraft as he surveyed the battlefield below. Now masked by smoke, dust, and darkness broken only by the flash of mortar rounds, he could no longer see the knoll, much less distinguish between American and North Vietnamese positions. Whitlow's greatest fear, even more than the NVA shooting him down, was to call in strikes mistakenly on the Marines below.

Whitlow radioed FAC Goebel in the command crater.

"What's your perimeter?"

"About a hundred meters across."

"Do you have a strobe light?"

"Hold on—"

Goebel rummaged through his supplies, and miraculously, pulled out a light.

"Got it!"

"I need a clear target. Can you mark the center of your perimeter?"

Not wanting NVA mortars to lock in on the command crater, Goebel climbed out, walked ten to twenty meters from its edge, turned on the blinking light, and held it as high over his head as he could. A thousand feet above, Whitlow watched as each pulse of light cut through the murky twilight.

"That takes guts," Whitlow thought.

"Where do you need the strike?" he asked Goebel.

"One hundred to one hundred fifty meters north of where I am standing now."

Whitlow called in the bombing run, and as the Crusader approached, Fitzsimmons flipped on the Cessna's landing light to avoid a collision. As he did, a stream of tracers from NVA antiaircraft fire rose up toward the Bird Dog. As the bullets just missed the wing of the small aircraft, Fitzsimmons cut the light and flew dark for the rest of the mission. The antiaircraft fire then zeroed in on the approaching F8.

To keep on top of any North Vietnamese who might be using the cover of darkness to advance on Murray and his men, Whitlow had to keep the Crusaders coming in with bombs. In order to protect the F8s, he had to deal with the remaining enemy antiaircraft guns expertly placed in a horseshoe around the ambush sight.

"Once it was dark, NVA antiaircraft guns opened up from around the valley, firing long streams of tracers into the night sky. The fireworks were made all the more spectacular by the fact that we were directly in the middle of the long arcs of tracers. The North Vietnamese gunners had planned their antiaircraft fire very well, probably knowing that the jets would make their run in from the open end of the valley to the east. They shot down one bomber and hit several others during the time I was overhead. The crew of the downed plane ejected over the South China Sea."

To deal with the antiaircraft guns, Whitlow made the decision to call in Spooky, the Douglas AC- 47 WWII era cargo plane fitted with three 7.62mm six-barrel rotary machine guns each with a rate of fire of two to six thousand rounds per minute. Affectionately known by ground troops as Puff the Magic Dragon, due to the glowing red tracers that lit up the sky and roar of the guns when fired, the propeller-driven Spooky was the first fixed-wing gunship designed by the Air Force for close air support of troops on the ground.

When Spooky arrived on station at just under ten thousand feet above the knoll, the Crusaders, flying below that altitude and with no lights, widened their orbits to avoid the fire of Spooky's devastating guns. In order to illuminate the targeted gun positions and to plan its line of attack, Spooky dropped a string of bright flares over the battlefield.

"Abort the flares! Abort the flares!"

Momentarily blinded by the sudden blazing lights, Fitzsimmons and Whitlow flew south into the darkness until their eyes recovered and the battlefield dimmed. In addition to disabling the all-important Bird Dog, the flares also illuminated, for the benefit of the NVA, the flight path of the slow flying AC-47, and the very guns that Spooky was to destroy quickly pummeled him.

The gunship responded with a stream of bullets and red tracers, only to have even more precise antiaircraft fire on them as the NVA guns locked onto Spooky's tracer stream. Spooky climbed toward its maximum firing altitude, likely about ten thousand feet, and let loose another torrent of red tracers and was again pounded by the enemy. Spooky fired once more, and for a third time, the NVA hammered him.

The pilot came over the radio.

"I can't operate in this environment."

With that, having failed in its mission and before the NVA shot him down, the old modified WWII warhorse departed the battle-field, at least for the time being.

In addition to the 50 caliber antiaircraft guns, eight to ten NVA heavy mortars had been battering the leathernecks on the knoll since early in the evening. One lucky enemy round could decimate the scores of American wounded who now crowded in one crater, while another could take out Murray and his command. If they could locate the mortar sites from the air, the devil dogs had to eliminate them as well.

A flight of Grumman A-6 Intruders, each armed with heavy bombs, sat stacked up with other aircraft over the valley waiting for the call to join the fray, but another strike from fixed-wing aircraft was fraught with danger. In order to hit the enemy, the jet pilots would have to make their drops perilously close to the Marine craters, a precise and difficult job even with unhampered visibility.

Not wanting to add to the confusion over the airwaves, Whitlow tried to remain calm as he spoke into the radio. He was working a bewildering range of FM and UHF frequencies, constantly switching channels to maintain radio contact with coordinating commands. At times, in a bid to disrupt communications, the enemy whistled and chattered into the radio traffic. On some frequencies, the North Vietnamese would speak in English with bogus commands in an attempt to confuse the Americans.

The Marine ground companies, the battalion command teams, and the regimental command, with occasional input from the 1st Division command post, all crowded the airwaves with problems and opinions but no real solutions. Bravo and Delta 1/5, the two companies that Mike and Kilo 3/5 had orders to rescue that morning, were still under attack west of the knoll and needed artillery strikes from howitzers located almost four kilometers away at Hill 51.

Those strikes, however, would interfere with the Intruder flight paths to the knoll battlefield should they need to call in the A-6s. The Marines had enough problems without having to worry about taking down their own jets by artillery fire.

The question, then, was crystal clear: who was under the greatest immediate threat, Bravo and Delta 1/5 or Mike 3/5?

From his vantage point in the air, Lt Whitlow had access to tactical information that no ground commander, despite his rank, had. Connive Mike was in a world of shit. If he didn't call in air strikes on the NVA battalions advancing from the river and into the draw, the enemy would wipe out Murray and his men. Whitlow radioed what he was seeing to regimental command and held his breath.

"Check fire," came the order.

To Whitlow's relief, the howitzers at Hill 51 received temporary orders to hold their fire. Seconds later, Blackcoat 3 spotted the flash of the mortar tubes and explosions battering the knoll. As Whitlow noted the position of the NVA heavy mortars fifteen hundred meters south of the battlefield, Fitzsimmons adjusted the orbit of the Cessna to avoid the trajectory of the incoming rounds.

Whitlow then radioed battalion and gave the coordinates.

"Request target clearance."

"Negative. Location of Kilo unconfirmed."

Whitlow's heart began to race, and he felt sick to his stomach. He had never received word that a fourth Marine company, 180 men, was near the battlefield.

"I didn't know that Kilo and the battalion command group were on the ground," Whitlow said. *"Nobody had briefed me, and they never made radio contact with me. The battalion command group, I think, had gone to radio silence, afraid they'd get overrun."*

No one knew for sure where Kilo Company was, and given the level of confusion and poor visibility, it was possible that the three assault columns that CPT Redmond had spotted advancing on the knoll, and subsequently bombed by the two F8 Crusaders, were not NVA but instead the Marines of Kilo coming to the aid of Murray and his men.

Whitlow tried to shake the possibility from his mind.

"Only the NVA wear foliage as camouflage," Whitlow thought. "We saw branches and leaves. Kilo would have radioed their approach. There was no call—unless their radios had failed—"

Due to the proximity of other friendly forces, Redmond, and now Whitlow, had sanctioned bombing runs only on precise and specific targets, at times using the burning pools of napalm to guide the flight paths of the Crusaders.

But stranger things have happened in the chaos of battle—
Whitlow's radio sounded. It was Battalion at Hill 51.

"If you see those mortar positions and you have positive identification, run the strike."

The two Grumman A-6 Intruders, twin-engine all-weather bombers seldom used for close air support of troops on the ground, were the next two aircraft in the rotation.

"I have the target in view," the flight leader said, "but I'm low on fuel. I'll have to drop everything on the first pass."

Coming in low from the east, the pilot of the lead Intruder, ignoring the streams of fifty caliber antiaircraft fire that rose up to greet him, rippled his entire bomb load down the long axis of the mortar position. An aerial onslaught of detonations plowed under the enemy guns, and concussive shock waves rocked the fragile Bird Dog, so much so that Whitlow feared that the Cessna's wings might snap.

"You hit us! The bombs hit our position!"

The despairing call came from the radio. It was Kilo Company.

"Abort! Abort!" Whitlow screamed.

As the second A-6 pulled out of its bomb run, a wave of nausea overwhelmed Whitlow, and for the first time that night, he lost his composure. Despite all of his care and attention to detail, his worst nightmare had come true. Because of his neglect, his error, scores of young Americans were dead. He grappled with the small window of the Cessna, stuck his head out, and tried to vomit. Nothing came up, and instead, the dry heaves overwhelmed him.

After several torturous moments, the radio lit up once more, the voice now calmer and more composed.

"No casualties," Kilo reported. "Repeat: no casualties, but the bombs were too close—"

Whitlow's retching eased, and now a draining weariness replaced the horror as Blackcoat 3 returned to its orbit over the knoll. With a maximum of four hours of fuel, the Cessna was nearly done in, as the Bird Dog's tanks were close to empty. Although it was a thirty-minute flight back to the air base at Marble Mountain, the two airborne Marines never discussed leaving Connive Mike without the protection from the air that the men on the ground so badly needed.

"We're going to go down in the middle of the fighting," he thought.

Whitlow loaded his M16 and .45 pistol, then tightened his helmet strap and shoulder harness as he and Fitzsimmons prepared for a crash landing.

"I'd better turn off that red flashlight before we hit the ground—"

If he somehow survived the crash, Whitlow didn't want to die by wearing a red light as a target.

• • •

Everything up to this point in the daylong battle indicated that the NVA would make another attack. With a seemingly endless supply of troops and a willingness to take heavy casualties, the enemy still enjoyed the cover of darkness, and despite every resource the Americans could throw at them, they remained poised to wipe the leathernecks off the face of that bare knoll. With every devil dog able to hold a weapon on the line, the seriously wounded consolidated in the command crater near the center, and the last of the ammunition distributed, Lt Murray readied his men by pulling back into an even tighter defensive perimeter.

Bleary-eyed, bone-weary, shell-shocked, and bloodied, every man stared out into the darkness and braced for the inevitable. Then something close to a miracle happened. The endless thump of mortars ceased. The flash of green tracers and the pop of AK-47s, the blast of chicom grenades, and the incessant ripping sound, like tearing canvas, of NVA machine guns, were coming to a sporadic end.

1st Platoon and Command Crater

"Holy shit. I hope they don't land too close—"

From his spot behind a rock near the front of the knoll, Lt Ed Combs watched as the massive air strike by the A-6 Intruder thundered across the valley. Still alive after sustaining a massive chest wound earlier in the day, Combs had survived two CS gas drops, incessant NVA mortars, small arms fire, and grenades but was still in a vulnerable position.

"At this time," Cpl Kelly of 3rd Platoon said, *"there were still people bringing back more wounded Marines, and they were really doing a great job. All this time that this was going on, the skipper was still directing artillery and other defensive fire and working with the Blackcoat in the aircraft."*

Cpl George Phillips, a weapons squad leader in 1st Platoon, had been walking near Vandergriff and the point squad when the ambush hit. Losing his rocket launcher to heavy machine gun fire, he had been manning 1st Platoon's thin line when a mortar hit him blowing him into the air and wounding his leg with hot shrapnel. Phillips was now one of the many walking wounded who were providing security for the command crater and helping to pull back the dead and wounded.

"I had picked up a rifle, and we began to assimilate a perimeter around this crater that was up on top of the knoll," Phillips said. *"We must have made twenty trips out and around the knoll bringing in*

wounded, bringing in weapons, bringing in anything we could find that was ours, and looking for anything that might have been theirs. It became clear we were not going to get resupplied. So we needed all the ammo we could get."

As he watched the company's west flank from a shallow hole dug to the left of the command crater, FO Riddle could see to the front and the open rice paddy.

"There was a lot of a fighting going on in the front, and I watched one Marine crawl down to where the wounded were in front of us, the 1st Platoon, and he drug back three or four guys to the bomb crater. I never knew who that was, but he definitely deserved a medal for what he did."

"We got to move back, Lt. We gotta start moving back—"

Phillips had been hesitant to try to move out to Combs, but with the unexpected lull in the incoming fire, the corporal knew that this might be his only chance to get the leader of 1st Platoon to the relative safety of the command crater. He and a fellow gunner scrambled down the front of the knoll and tried to pull the stricken lieutenant to his feet. Combs rolled over and struggled to his knees.

"Cpl Phillips, I think I can get myself back."

With his mind surprisingly clear, Combs came to his feet and, guided by Phillips, staggered back up the knoll, the sandy soil shifting under his feet, and slid over the top of FAC Goebel and into the crater.

Goebel looked down into the hole in Comb's chest that was the size of his hand, and as he tried to reposition the bandage that had somehow slipped off, a rock chipped off by a close mortar round knocked the man standing behind him unconscious.

"If there is anybody that can get out on the line," Murray said to his men, "we are going to need you out there."

With what little light available, Combs surveyed the crater filled with wounded Marines. "Shit, what if somebody throws a grenade?" he thought. "We're all dead."

As the lieutenant tried to sit up, everything around him started to blur. A corpsman looked at him and then turned and said something to Lt Murray.

"I'll be OK," Combs said, but he was losing consciousness, and his mouth was like sandpaper.

I can't say I have ever been thirsty like that before. It was just like your whole mouth was dry, and I think the dry was fear motivated, adrenaline motivated. And I didn't want to be a burden to anybody else. I didn't want to slow anybody else down from doing their job."

"Water, I need water—" he said.

Someone wet his lips.

"Water," he repeated.

"Lieutenant," Goebel said, "I can't give you any water."

The men were under specific orders not to let a man with a chest wound drink any liquids. The danger of aspirating and choking to death was too great.

Combs looked down again at his bleeding chest.

"I'm done," he thought. "Please, God, forgive me for my sins." He turned to a nearby Marine.

"I asked who I thought was Doc Phelps if he could baptize me because I didn't think I was going to make it. I was losing a little bit of my sense and kind of out of it at that time and asked him if he would baptize me."

"There's a guy over here who wants to be baptized," a Marine said to anyone in the crater. "Who is a Catholic?"

"I am."

Phillips had attended a Catholic seminary for a year before enlisting and knew that someone baptized in the faith could also perform an emergency baptism.

"He was a freaking mess," Phillips said, *"and we didn't think he was going to live through the night."*

"Are you sure you want to become a Catholic?" Phillips asked Combs.

"Yes."

Combs wasn't Catholic, but at the time, the distinctions of the various Christian faiths made little difference to him.

"Have you taken instruction in the Catholic faith?"

"I haven't."

Phillips knew that under normal circumstances an adult baptism required some instruction, and he knew that the critically wounded Marine might not intend to follow Catholicism should he survive.

"In the seminary," Phillips said, *"they taught us that you have to be sure that the person is serious. I didn't even think about it. I said, 'This guy's laying here with his chest blown open, and the only thing he can think about is being baptized. If that's not serious, I don't know what is. God can sort it out.'"*

Phillips retrieved his canteen.

"I baptize you in the name of the Father, and of the Son, and of the Holy Spirit."

He poured a bit of water onto Comb's forehead three times as he spoke.

"That thirty seconds it took to do it," Phillips said, *"and maybe the two or three minutes it took to discuss it, were the only peaceful moments in the night. I mean, everything was going on. Rockets are going off, bullets are flying, and all the shit is coming in, and people*

running in and out, but I remember for that two or three minutes it was, in my mind, it was absolute peace and quiet."

As he struggled to retain consciousness, Combs felt a breeze and thought he saw a leatherneck holding a small fan, but whether the vision was a dream or reality, he couldn't tell.

1st Platoon: Sergeant Sullivan's Crater

Although still under intermittent mortar and small arms fire, 1st Platoon Sgt Sullivan had been gathering his wounded, about thirteen men, and placing them into a crater at the right front corner of the knoll.

"My main goal was to organize the troops into a defensive position, and that never really happened because they were scattered out so much. So I was gathering up the troops and the ones that were still firing."

Before it got dark, Sullivan knew that he had to move the wounded to safety and that someone needed to find the command group and secure more ammunition.

"The plan was to leave there and go further back up the knoll to try to find the rest of our people," Cpl Ray Edwards said, *"and somebody suggested that one of us had to get out of the hole to help the wounded, so Guerrero got out and was laying pretty much flat on the ground—"*

Pfc Richard Guerrero and Edwards started to help Cpl Bob Matteson, who had taken an AK-47 round to his left leg, out of the crater.

"They pulled me out of the bomb crater," Matteson said, *"went to get a better hold on me to make sure my leg was over the other one so I could pull easy, and—"*

Boom.

"That's when Guerrero went down."

"He fell back in on me," Machine Gunner Fields said, *"and this is a big guy, he must have weighed 220. He fell right on top of me and went down into the bottom of the hole."*

An enemy round had struck Guerrero in the top of the left shoulder near his neck.

"I turned and looked, and he's down," Matteson said. *"I pulled his rifle out from under him, and I saw the guy who hit him, which was up the hill behind him between two little trees, and I put that guy down with Guerrero's rifle."*

A Corpsman or Marine pulled back Guerrero's utilities and stretched a sheet of plastic over the wound in his chest, but the stricken leatherneck wasn't getting enough air.

"He's turning blue!"

Sergeant Sullivan tried mouth-to-mouth resuscitation, but that didn't work. Thinking that something had obstructed his airway, Sullivan retrieved his Ka-Bar knife, and from his pocket, a Government Issue black ballpoint pen.

"I took a Ka-Bar, and I cut his throat, and I gave him a tracheo-tomy. I used a ballpoint pen, took all the guts out of it, and I put that down in his throat and then started puffing air down in there. And then he started getting color back, and then he started breathing on his own. Well, we thought he was going to be OK. Well, he was OK really, as far as that. I told them to keep an eye on him, so I got back up at the edge of the hole there and was trying to look out and see what was going on—"

Sullivan peered into the growing darkness.

"Sully, help!"

For a moment, the sergeant couldn't believe his ears. It had to be a wounded American, wounded and stranded out there, and the man was calling him by name.

"Sully, help!"

Sullivan lunged out of the hole, only to have a grunt grab him by the back of his belt and pull him back in.

"Sarge Sullivan, that's not one of our guys calling you!"

"What?"

"Yeah, that ain't one of ours! Listen!"

His ears still ringing from the mortar blast earlier in the day, Sully titled his head to the right in order to hear more clearly.

Soon the voice called out again.

"Sully!"

The accent was not American. The voice was that of a North Vietnamese soldier trying to draw Sgt Sullivan personally out of the hole.

"Shit—"

A moment later, the men heard rustling around them and the snapping of twigs. The NVA were preparing to rush the crater.

"Sergeant, they're up there. They're coming at us—"

With only a few rounds of rifle and machine gun ammunition left, the leathernecks couldn't respond to the enemy encroachment with firepower. All that they had were a few grenades, bayonets, knives, and clods of dirt.

"We'd kept hearing this rustling out there," Sullivan said, *"and everybody was scared shitless, so I crawled back up to almost the top of the hole to where I could listen, and I had them hand me one of those dirt clods—"*

Sullivan retrieved a grenade from his pack.

One of the men gave Sullivan a baseball-size clump of dirt. Sully waited and listened, and when he again heard rustling, he heaved the dirt clod at the sound.

One, two, three, four—

Sully pulled the pin on the grenade and lobbed it in the same direction. The explosive detonated, and an enemy soldier wailed in pain. In the darkness, thinking that the dirt clod was a grenade, Sullivan gambled that the enemy would get down, wait a few seconds, and then move again when he realized that the "grenade" was a dud. The second and real grenade had caught the man out in the open.

"*I heard all of this yelling, you know,*" Sullivan said, "*so I hit them sons of bitches.*"

Sgt Sullivan's deadly ruse had worked, while the enemy's, in trying to draw Sully out into the open, hadn't, but the NVA weren't finished. After Sully launched his grenade, the North Vietnamese opened up with a machine gun as enemy squads prepared to rush the hole, using the automatic weapon as suppressing fire. One of the men in the crater started to cry. Sullivan had to do something, right now.

"*I had this radio operator in there, one of the squad leader's radio operator, and he flipped his twig. He just started crying, and started screaming, and wanted to run out of the hole and run away, and wanted to fight everybody in the hole. They had to finally hold him down and sit on him. I mean, he was just hysterical.*"

Sullivan radioed FAC Goebel back with the command group. "Can I get an air strike? I need HE only."

"*I wanted to move the troops back, but I couldn't because of the intensity of the fire because they had us zeroed in with a machine gun, and they kept just grazing right across the top of that crater. So we couldn't get out of it. So I had called back to get an air strike.*"

"A plane is in the air," Goebel radioed. "Can you mark your position?"

Sully seized his pack, rummaged through it, and pulled out a silver tube. "I can do it with a white star cluster."

"Affirmative."

Sully turned to the other Marines. "Get down and start praying—"

He slapped the silver tube down on the palm of his hand, and the flare shot up, illuminating the area with little stars of white light.

"They're coming in for the run. Everybody, get down!"

Moments later, a plane approached from the back of the knoll, but instead of releasing the high explosives that Sully was expecting, a canister dropped from the weapons bay.

"Jesus Christ, it's friggin' napalm. We're gonna be cooked—"

As the leathernecks hugged the ground for dear life, the canister erupted in a hell-like fireball, sending a scorching wave across the rice paddy just outside the crater, momentarily sucking up all of the oxygen.

"When the napalm hit, it split over our hole. It hit, and went in a wave, and it went on both sides of us, and took our breath away. But nobody got hurt from that. And then they come in with the HE—"

Another bomber approached.

"Once that HE hits," Sully yelled, "We're gonna haul ass out of here!"

Several Marines lifted the wounded Guerrero and, with the other wounded, prepared to make a run, when another voice called out from beyond the crater.

"Sgt Sullivan—Sgt Sullivan—"

"Jesus Christ, who the hell is that?"

Sully peered over the hole and saw, crouching at the edge of the crater, a radio operator from the command group.

"They sent me here to get you guys out," Cpl Kevin Kelly said. "I'm going to lead you back to the CP."

Sully could have kissed the man.

As massive explosions erupted across the burning rice paddy, and as the NVA gunner, who had somehow managing to survive both napalm and HE, opened fire, the Americans clambered over the edge of the crater and scrambled up the knoll.

"They had Guerrero, and they had to lift him up, but he was really heavy. Hell, he was like six-three. As soon as we got to the top of the hole, damn if they didn't just open up a machine gun. They just tattered his body and just killed him. We carried him on back with us; we got him on back—"

Running and scrambling on their hands and knees, Sullivan and his men made it back to the top of the knoll and jumped into the crater that was being used as the company CP. Sullivan then took what was left of his troops fit to fight and reinforced the new perimeter at the top of the knoll.

• • •

Spared death by fire and bombs, Pfc Howard Haney still lay where he fell, in the now silent blackness, facedown in the rocky soil of the rice paddy. A burst of light and an enemy flare lit up the ground near Haney as the NVA scoured the area for movement. A few minutes passed, and a second flare followed.

Point Man Jack Swan crouched alone in an earthen trench and waited for a pause in the light. If he moved out to Haney as a flare went up, he was a dead man.

"Is there anybody from Mike Company down here?"

The low voice came from the top of the knoll.

"Over here!"

"I thought everybody else was dead," Swan thought.

"I've got two dead," Swan told the Marine when he reached him, "and one in bad shape. I need help to pull them back."

Keeping quiet but betrayed by the pounding of his heart, Haney heard plants rustle to his left.

"Jack was to my right," Haney said, *"and he had went down this little dried up dike, crossed over, and came back up on my left side. It took him probably thirty minutes to get to me, and about that time, he jumped over, landed right between my legs, grabbed me by the waist, and said, 'Haney!'*

"When he jumped over and grabbed me, I thought my heart flew out of my chest and then instant relief, but I think it scared him as bad as it did me because he didn't know what he was grabbing, and I didn't know who was grabbing me."

"Can you get up?" Swan whispered.

"No."

Swan retrieved his Ka-Bar, cut the straps of Haney's pack, and pulled the wounded man to his knees.

"He then stuck my left arm inside my jacket," Haney said, *"and I managed to crawl back into some cover, and there was another Marine there that was wounded. Jack then handed me a white phosphorous grenade."*

Crouching low and taking his chances that another flare would not expose him to the enemy, Swan moved out to check on another wounded man, scrambled up the knoll to the command crater, and with three other devil dogs, sneaked back to Haney through the thickets at the edge of the paddy. The men laid a poncho on the ground, eased Haney onto it facedown, and with a leatherneck at each end, lifted.

"When I first got hit," Haney said, *"it felt like somebody hit me with a sledgehammer, only I could feel the impact but not the actual*

pain itself. The real pain came when they put me in a poncho. My clavicle was broken, so when they would pick me up, it would twist my shoulder, and it would pop out, and that's when the pain came."

Haney bit his tongue as the men bundled him across the rough terrain, bore him over a dried up dike, and brought him down hard into a trench.

"They were running me, and we're going over these little one-foot dikes when they slammed my chest into the dike and slammed my shoulder, and I would yell, and I distinctly remember this guy telling me to 'Shut the fuck up!'"

The Americans made it to the command crater, eased Haney down next to Lt Combs, and then helped retrieve the bodies of LCpl Fisher and Pfc Mortensen. From the canteens of the dead, Swan was able, after hours in the blazing sun with his face in the dirt, to take a few gulps of precious water.

Despite the heat, both Combs and Haney could not drink water because they suffered from chest wounds. To give them at least a little comfort, Swan opened his pack, retrieved a small plastic fan sent to him by his mother, and turned it on both men. He would go through three batteries in the long night that lay ahead.

• • •

"It's now or never—"

Cpl Vandergriff, still in the hole where he had ducked down when the ambush hit, had noticed the letup in enemy fire. He took a deep breath, climbed out of his crater, and dashed up the slope toward the cover of some bushes, only to stare down the barrel of a rifle.

"Goddamn it, Bill," the Marine called out, "I nearly shot you—"

The leader of the point squad was soon back with what was left of his men.

2nd Platoon

"Clark," Sgt Marbury said, "I need you and another grunt on LP. Now."

Machine Gunner Clark, along with what was left of 2nd Platoon, had pulled back up near the crest of the knoll's hard-pressed north side and had begun to dig in. Now, with the pause in enemy fire, he received orders to man an LP, which meant he had to go back down the slope near the tree line. Should the bad guys initiate a night attack, it would be Clark's duty to warn the platoon.

"If you hear anything unusual, return to the perimeter and report."

Clark wanted to object but knew that he had to follow orders. Armed with a rifle and an M18 Claymore mine, he and LCpl Ron Pizana crawled slowly down the north side of the knoll past the Marine lines until they came to the body of Doc Leal.

"I think this is as far as we should go."

Using the dead corpsman as cover, Clark set the Claymore to the right front of the body, and in the path, he hoped, of any approaching NVA. Command detonated and directional, Clark could set off the mine by remote control, sending a wide pattern of metal balls into a deadly kill zone at any advancing troops.

The two men waited, and as the night wore on, fatigue brought on by the lethal day of fighting began to set in. Despite his best efforts, Clark's head began to nod, and his helmet finally fell off.

"I'm gonna report you," Pizana threatened.

"Promise?" Clark asked as he pushed his helmet back on. "If I get thrown in the brig, at least I'd be alive."

Clink—

The slight sound came from the now black darkness.

Clink. Clink.

"You hear that?"

"No."

"It's right off to the right."

Clark crawled back up the slope and reported what he had heard to Sgt Marbury.

"Return to your post and hold within the perimeter. If they attack, you'll know it."

Clark returned to the LP, and he and Pizana remained there for the remainder of the long night. He continued to hear soft clanking and shuffling coming from the direction of the enemy lines, and after a time, he realized what the sound was.

It was the sound of the North Vietnamese burying their dead.

• • •

"How do you feel?"

Pfc Steve Blackwood had taken shrapnel in the side of his chest and was struggling to breathe.

"I feel a little cold."

The thud of American shovels sounded across the north side of the knoll as 2nd Platoon continued to entrench. LCpl Lobur, kneeling next to Blackwood, a member of his rocket squad, had dug a strong hole for himself before crawling out to check on his comrade.

"OK. Hang in there. We'll get you out of here soon."

Lobur looked up to see a new guy, LCpl Clarence Boone, a man who had never seen combat before, lying silently in a trench with a bayonet-ready M16.

"I wonder what is going through that kid's mind?" he thought.

Lobur returned to his new position armed only with a rocket tube and one round. Although his side of the battlefield was now relatively quiet, there was always the danger of a night attack. He knew that an LP had gone out to warn them of approaching NVA, and he had orders to sit at the top of the hill and fire his last rocket at any enemy who came through the lines.

He sat and peered into the gloom as minutes, and then an hour, passed. Then he sat up, alert, as he thought he saw movement down the side of the knoll. His eyes scoured the darkness until, a moment later, he caught the silhouette of an NVA soldier with a bayonet fixed to his AK- 47 walking toward the wounded Blackwood and the new kid, Boone. The man didn't seem to be on patrol but was wandering around, almost as if he was lost. Was he looking to stab to death helpless Marines lying wounded outside the perimeter?

Lobur didn't have a rifle, and the rocket wasn't an efficient weapon for one-on-one combat, so he shouted down to the FNG in the trench. "Boone, there's a gook coming!"

Lobur watched in amazement as the new kid scrambled out of his hole to the enemy soldier, plunged his bayonet into the man's stomach, and pulled the trigger of his M16. The bullet cracked, the man crumpled, and the new kid ran back to his hole.

"It was as if he's been doing this his whole life."

Company Command

Low on ammunition and low on healthy Marines to man the new line, Lt Murray knew that a renewed enemy attack would finish off Mike Company. As enemy fire slackened after the drop of CS gas, Murray's first priority was protection.

"I was almost positive that they would counterattack during the night sometime. They were out there, our people could hear them talking, and at the same time, they were testing the lines to see what was vulnerable. The other priority was emergency resupply on ammo, medical supplies, and to get the serious medevacs out. We got no KIAs out that night."

Murray had established a tighter and stronger perimeter, but unreliable rifles, hastily dug and shallow trenches, claymore mines, flares, an occasional automatic weapon, and some grenades wouldn't be enough to bolster it. Establishing a LZ for medevac and resupply helicopters was, for the time being, out of the question. Even though pressure from the NVA had lessened as darkness fell, enemy squads still probed his lines with gunfire looking for weakness, and he had to assume that the enemy was regrouping for the final blow. His foe, however, had given him a respite, and Murray would make full use of it. He radioed Blackcoat 3, circling above and low on fuel.

"I want Puff all the way around, all night long. I couldn't give a squat how many Puffs you have to put up there, but we are not really sure what is going on down here on the ground, and I need protection."

"Roger that."

The heavy bombs from the fighter bombers had taken out the antiaircraft guns and heavy mortars, at least some of them, clearing the way for the Douglas AC-47 Spooky gunship to ring Murray's perimeter with crippling fire from its three 7.62mm Gatling guns.

Murray turned to Goebel, "I'm going to check our perimeter."

Goebel didn't like the sound of that. If the company lost its commander—

"If he gets killed," Goebel thought, "we'll never make it out of here alive."

"I'll go."

"No. That's my job."

Murray knew from experience that the devil dogs needed to see their commander. Nothing eroded the morale of a grunt more than the knowledge that while he was liable to catch a bullet and die at any moment on the front line his commander was back in the relative safety of a foxhole. While taking unnecessary risks was foolish, the men had to know that their leader was with them.

"I wanted to find out where we were, where we had holes in the line. So, I started with the second platoon, which was towards the Ly Ly River. I started walking around, and there were big differences in whole locations. In other words, some were close together and some were really far apart. And so I go from one hole to another and talk to them, and try and calm them down, make them feel good."

"The worst is over, hold onto your position, protect the folks on your left and right. Make sure you are in communications with them. We are going to pull through."

"Where is the next position?" he asked a group of Marines.

"We don't know."

"Okay, I am going over there to find out."

"I remember the skipper around that evening when it was dark," LCpl Permenter said, *"checking everybody, making sure everything was doing well, and the man's got guts, I'll tell you. It's a wonder we didn't shoot him."*

Murray stepped out into the pitch darkness in the likely direction, he thought, of the next leatherneck position. Finding no one, he soon realized that he had gone beyond the American line. The enemy or his own men, mistaking him for NVA, now could easily shoot him, so he turned back to where he thought the perimeter was and, after a few steps, called out in a loud whisper:

"This is Lt Murray. I am coming back in."

. . .

Stillness descended over the scarred battlefield. The enemy probes of the leatherneck line became fewer and then ceased altogether, the sound of small arms fire replaced by shuffling and the thud of shovels in the hard ground. The jets had stopped their bombing runs, and Spooky, when he came back on station, didn't take fire as he peppered the enemy with his Gatling guns.

"They had the gunship firing around our perimeter most of the night," Riddle said. *"It was pretty intense to look up and see the solid red stream of bullets coming down. It sounded like a heavy rain, and the dust was everywhere. You couldn't hardly see nothing because of the bullets kicking up the dust."*

To Goebel, it seemed as if the NVA were retreating and had left a rear guard to provide security for their burial teams.

"Mike 14, this is Loose Goose," Spooky's pilot radioed. "What else can I do for you?"

Goebel looked at Murray, who had returned safely to the command crater.

"Authorize resupply and medevacs," Murray said. "Have Puff remain available if we need him."

"Loose Goose, this is Mike 14," Goebel said after relaying the order. "God, I'd really like a cup of coffee."

As the NVA interred their dead, the Marines collected their fallen and staged the bodies on a patch of clear ground behind the knoll for removal after medevacking the wounded. Flares, which continuously lit the battlefield to catch enemy movement, ceased as the first relief helicopter came in. In order to avoid becoming a target for enemy fire, the first chopper arrived without lights, dropped crates of ammunition without landing or taking on any casualties, and left the area.

A second Huey, directed in by a Marine waving two red safety lights, was soon overhead. The pilot, sensing that antiaircraft fire was no longer a threat, flicked on his landing lights as he neared the ground. As he did, green tracers, seemingly from all directions, cut through the night toward the chopper and the exposed Marine.

Despite bullets that tore up the earth and sky all around them, the Marine never ceased giving landing signals, and the Huey pilot waited to douse his lights just before touching down. The chopper unloaded boxes of ammunition and other supplies and was soon back in the air. More helicopters arrived, braved the enemy fire, offloaded more supplies, and were able to medevac at least some of the critically wounded. Lt Combs, miraculously still breathing, and Pfc Haney were some of the first loaded onto the Huey.

"All that night Puff dropped illumination, and we received a few sniper rounds because choppers were coming in to pick up the medics and bring a resupply of ammo," LCpl David Jones of 1st Platoon said. *"Everything seemed to be all messed up the rest of the night because nobody knew really what was going on. We didn't know if any help was coming or how many of the enemy were still out there because all day we'd seen bushes moving and at night the wind was blowing. Everybody seemed to be real scared."*

After helping off-load ammo, LCpl Permenter helped ease the wounded Combs onto the chopper.

"After the chopper left I had this—all this liquid on me, and I couldn't figure out what it was. It was sticky, and it was slippery, and it was just—it was blood. I had blood all over me."

1st Platoon

Machine Gunner Fields, who had supported 1st Platoon from a crater at the front of the knoll, received orders to man the line near the crest, where he remained on alert with other leathernecks throughout the night. As dawn approached, and as the devil dogs resumed the grim task of recovering their fallen, Fields' new order was to provide cover for a detail of men who ventured down to the scene of 2nd Platoon's hellacious fight a few hours before.

The night was still pitch, as there was no moon, and Fields watched as two men emerged from the gloom with a poncho-covered body, which they laid down behind him. As the men returned to their duty, Fields became thoughtful as to the dead man's identity: if he was a friend or someone he only knew in passing.

"I pulled the poncho liner back to expose the face, and just as I did, a flare went off, and I saw a gold glint on the collar. I thought to myself, 'Well, this is an officer, so I reached down and looked at the emblem, and it was a cross, and I didn't know that we had a chaplain. I didn't know he was with us. His head was titled slightly to the right, just ever slightly, and there was a very calm look on his face, just a very calm look, and it was from the flare I know, but it was kind of a golden glow on his face."

Fields scrambled over the back of the knoll to the edge of a crater.

"Is somebody down there?"

"Yeah! This is the CP."

"We've got a chaplain up here that is dead."

"Damn! We didn't know he was with us!"

The news astonished Lt Murray. Father Capodanno must have arrived at the LZ on Hill 63 that morning unannounced and accompanied "his" Marines unofficially into the field. For Goebel, who was

Catholic, the revelation was especially disturbing. It was distressful enough for a Marine to have his chaplain, Catholic or otherwise, lying dead as a combat casualty, but seeing a Catholic priest KIA made Goebel doubt his own ability to survive.

"Please reconfirm that information."

The news shot through channels like a rocket when Murray made his casualty report to the 1st and then 3rd Battalion headquarters.

"When we found him," Pfc Julio Rodriquez wrote, "he had his right hand over his left breast pocket, as if he was holding his Bible. He had a smile on his face, and his eyelids were closed, as if asleep or in prayer."

· · ·

"I laid there, and it got dark," Red Manfra said. "Nobody came out. No corpsman came out, and I just laid there looking at the sky. I don't even remember them dropping gas, but they said that they dropped gas."

As he lay there watching mortars, artillery, flares, and Puff the Magic Dragon, he didn't dare move.

"You could almost reach out and touch them, that's how close they were. 'If I move, I'm dead,' and I thought I was dead anyway."

Breathing through the side of his face, his jaw shattered, Manfra was sure that the North Vietnamese would infiltrate his position and finish him off.

"When they overrun you, they just kill you if you're moving or if you're alive. They just kill you. I thought maybe everybody had gotten wiped out, and I was just waiting for, I was just waiting for whoever *was going to come get me, whether it would have been the Viet Cong or our guys."*

After the firing had stopped, a Marine detail found Manfra, eased him onto a poncho, took him back up the knoll, and placed him among the bodies of those who had died.

"I wasn't talking. I had lost a lot of blood, and I was in pretty bad shape, I guess."

8

FIRST LIGHT

Spent cartridges, rifles, and bloody clothes littered the red clay soil, while long ribbons of abandoned 35mm film, strewn along the bushes, waved in the occasional breeze. Blown bald by scathing small arms and machine gun fire, pockmarked from incessant mortar and grenade explosions, the knoll stood as mute testament to the Herculean struggle of the day and night before. Along its backside, and equally unspeaking as the ground they died defending, lay two rows of sixteen Marines.

At dawn, the men of India Company 3/5 arrived to provide security for the survivors and assistance for the wounded. After a brief and fitful sleep, Lt Murray ventured out of the command crater to where an enemy soldier's finger still rested on the trigger of his RPG.

"At first light, all I can remember is that NVA behind the RPG with his hand on the trigger and a round right through the middle of his forehead. And that RPG was aimed right at our hole, I would say somewhere between ten and twenty meters away."

Sixty meters away stood the bipod, base plate, and firing tube of an NVA 60mm mortar, so close that Lt Murray speculated that the soldiers removed fuses and fired rounds straight in the air to land on top of the Americans. The North Vietnamese had prepared well. During the chaos of the fight the day before, LCpl Permenter with

3rd Platoon remembered seeing a strange object toward the north of the knoll that was ten to fifteen feet up in the air.

"I couldn't figure out what it was until later on the next morning. It was a marking stick for the mortar team of the NVA. They had the whole place zeroed in."

The arrival of India Company and Major Black, the operations officer (S3) for Col Hilgartner's 1/5 Command Group, allowed Murray's embattled men to re-arm, reorganize, and conduct patrols around the knoll for any American casualties not found the night before, to count the Vietnamese dead, and to assess the remaining enemy threat.

"There was equipment and weapons all over the place," Murray said. *"We had started to bring in the KIAs, and the first thing I wanted to do was find out about any wounded and to get them as well as the KIAs medevacked out. It is tough on the morale to see the dead laying around and very tough on troops, especially if the people were close to them. My other big consideration was that we needed to get resupplied immediately, to continue with our protection, and to run the patrols ordered by 1/5."*

For the latter task, Lt Murray ordered Lt Cernick, commander of 3rd Platoon, to take a squad and a machine gun team to probe beyond the battle perimeter toward the tree line and the Ly Ly River, while another squad covered 360 degrees around the knoll.

"Major Black wanted us to run security patrols, specifically out to the Ly Ly River but also outside most of our area, just to see who was out there and if there was any North Vietnamese to take care of."

Spread out and silent with eyes peeled for any sign of movement, Cernick and his men encountered drag marks but initially no bodies on the outer edges of the knoll. As they ventured down the hill into the scrub, Cernick caught a glimpse of what looked like a backpack in a Vietnamese fighting hole. He crouched low and eyed his surroundings. The scrub could be teeming with camouflaged enemy eyeing the devil dogs at that very moment, ready to open fire, just as they were the day before.

Lt Cernick motioned to two of his men. The leathernecks retrieved grenades, pulled the pins, and tossed them into the hole. The explosives detonated, and Cernick approached, only to find the hole empty.

Cpl Cummings, who was part of Cernick's patrol, had no idea of the extent of the battle that he had been in the day before but would soon find out.

"What was in front of you—that was your world. I didn't know the extent of the 1st or 2nd Platoon's troubles that day. You pretty much are worried about what's in front of you and your people who are with you. That's all you know."

Hanging in the still air, the smell of burnt flesh, blood, and death grew stronger as the patrol approached the tree line and began to find bodies, intact and in pieces.

"There were several enemy troops that were napalmed," Motor Man John Bowers said, *"and that stench, that smell, it burst in your nostrils. They froze in the actual position that they were napalmed in. The guys (NVA) were down on the ground crawling, and they were, like, almost dead."*

Scalps, dismembered hands, arms, feet, and body parts littered the brush and the trees along with backpacks, canteens, gas masks, entrenching tools, and Russian and Chinese weapons. In all, fifty to ninety North Vietnamese corpses lay within one hundred meters of the American perimeter, with mounds of dirt marking those hastily buried in mass graves.

"*We found forty to sixty dead NVA out in front of us,*" Tancke said, "*and cleaned up all their gear. We found mortar tubes, tri-con rockets, AK-47s, one M16, gas masks, all kinds of grenades.*"

"*We would find two or three bodies tied together, being drug, and then they couldn't drag them anymore so they left them there,*" LCpl Keith Rounsvelle said. "*There was one little village we went into there was body parts in baskets, hands and legs. Of course, that could have been from the air strikes that we had throughout the night.*"

Lt Cernick and his men reached the river without encountering enemy forces, noted the presence of the NVA on the opposite bank, and returned to report to Lt Murray what they had found. Although instructed to cross the Ly Ly River, Cernick declined to obey that particular order.

"*I went up to the Ly Ly River,*" Cernick told Murray, "*but there were so many indications that the North Vietnamese were on the other side that I did not go across.*"

• • •

The triangular formation of three volcanic rocks, one of which might have been the rock that Machine Gunner Fields had slapped moments before the ambush hit, was over six feet tall.

"Hey, there are some gooks in the middle—"

Fields peered through a crack between two of the boulders and noticed that the center looked hollowed out from the top.

"Somebody said there're tunnels—that they were coming out of the ground."

Fields climbed up and looked down at an AK-47, a machine gun, and an RPG on top of the bodies of two NVA soldiers.

"Jesus Christ. Were they inside when I slapped the rock?"

. . .

"Bill."

Vandergriff turned from the large pile of resupply ammunition to see Sgt Sullivan. "I want you to take a patrol around the hill."

"I sent Vandegriff out with a few men. I think I had nineteen out of forty-nine," Sullivan said. *"I put together a mini-squad, if you will, and had Vandegriff go down to this one tree line and do a recon there to see what was going on down there."*

"The thing that struck me the most the following morning were the amount of people that weren't there," Vandergriff said. *"I looked around, and people started talking about who got hit, who got killed, and Jesus, what the hell happened?"*

After gathering some men from different fire teams, including Baima and his machine gun, Vandergriff began his sweep around the bottom of the knoll but didn't get far. There, from behind a bush, either grimacing in pain or simply grinning at the Marines, was an NVA soldier, fully alive, camouflage intact, his machine gun nearby.

"So, I gathered my guys up that were left," Vandergriff said, *"and we're walking down over the front of the knoll and coming back up the paddy, and there's a gook with his K50 machine gun just grinning his ass off at us. He'd been shot in the ass."*

The man was part of the machine gun team that had laid down a base of fire for the platoon of NVA that had attacked Cpl Cummings's 3rd Platoon Squad.

"We had a prisoner who had been wounded. He was shot all up," Sullivan said, *"a young kid, and he looked like he was about seventeen. As a matter of fact, I heard he had just gotten there that day and had come down the Ho Chi Min Trail and had just got with a unit."*

The grin was more than Vandergriff could take. "Shoot the motherfucker!"

The man made no move for his weapon. "No, you can't do that—"

The man just grinned, a big, shit-eating grin.

"I was really angry. I was really angry about the men we had lost and a lot of men that we had wounded, just the whole day. I guess part of that anger was focused at myself because I didn't do anything the day before. I don't feel that I did enough as a squad leader, as I was in no position to lead my men. I still feel that today; I still have that anger not at any particular one person other than myself."

Vandergriff backed away as other leathernecks moved forward.

"Wait! He could be booby trapped—"

After a battle, it was unusual for a soldier to remain behind, as the North Vietnamese recovered their wounded if they could. It was also not out of the realm of possibility that the NVA might rig one of their men with explosives in order to kill a few more Americans.

The Marines tied a rope around the man's ankle, dragged him from behind the bush, checked him for explosives and weapons, and brought him into the perimeter. A Kit Carson Scout, a former Viet Cong or PAVN soldier who had defected from the north, allied himself with the South Vietnamese, and then took part in a special Marine program that trained him as an intelligence scout and interpreter, approached the prisoner.

"The Kit Carson scout was trying to talk to him, and of course, the guy was close-mouthed," Fred Permenter said. *"And after a while, you could see the scout getting a little angrier, and he had a little swagger stick, like the British used to carry, about eighteen inches long. The scout rammed it through his wound, which I think he had got wounded between both legs, and the guy started talking."*

After questioning, a corpsman treated the prisoner's wounds and sent him out on the next chopper for further interrogation.

"I would say he was grinning because he was afraid," Vandergriff said. *"You know how sometimes everybody has a point when they're really afraid that for some idiot reason you'll grin? He was a good-looking young man. I was twenty-one at time, and I think he was probably around my age, and the thing is, he was just doing his job like I was doing mine."*

• • •

LCpl Lobur knew that his squad leader, Cpl Bill Young, had been shot in the pelvis early in the fighting and found him lying near the command crater at the top of the knoll, still awaiting evacuation.

"He was hit in the right groin about an inch or two below where you'd have an inguinal hernia. He was extremely pale, had no pants on, and actually moved the battle dressing aside to show me the wound. He was worried about his blood loss, but I told him that since he made it through the night he should be OK."

Lobur wandered over to the south rim of the knoll just past a large pile of useless, jammed M16s to two rows of dead bodies.

"I was looking for Gundlach, Blackwood, and Manfra, as they were in my rocket squad. I could see the faces at that time. They weren't covered yet, and they were laying on ponchos, as that's how we always carried the dead and wounded when no shooting was active."

As he walked among those who had died in the battle, he passed one body with so many battle dressings on his head that it was the size of a basketball.

"I could see his arms, very pale and heavily muscled, but I couldn't place the guy. As I passed by, I heard a loud whisper."

"Lobur!"

"I look around. I'm all by myself. It was one of the bodies, and I'm telling you this guy was so shot up that they thought he was dead. He had a battle dressing. Well, more than one—he had about five. He had a bunch of them wrapped around his head. It seems where his left eye was—it was just a big huge lump of battle dressing, and it's all bloody. He had a bunch of them around his chest, and someone told me he had a hole in his chest you could have stuck your fist in, and he had a bayonet taped to each humerus, each big bone in your arm, above the elbow. Somehow he'd broken both of his arms, and he had battle dressings on at least one leg, maybe both, in a big bloody mess."

Red Manfra, the Marine scheduled to go on R&R in Hawaii, shot multiple times, ministered to by Father Capodanno, and cared for by Corpsman Phelps, and who had lain motionless on the battlefield thinking, "If I move, I'm dead," had survived mortars, gas, Puff, grenades, and the NVA, and was now mistaken for one of the dead.

"I don't know how he saw me through all the bandages," Lobur said, *"but he did. I ran to the top of the hill where medevacs were in progress and dragged a corpsman to Red. He examined him, told me not to let him fall asleep, and ran off to get help. I talked to Red, and any time he didn't answer me, I'd gently nudge his wounded foot to get a response. When they loaded him on the chopper, I never thought I'd see him again. Somehow, Red made it, and Young did not."*

Later that morning, the devil dogs covered their dead comrades, lined them up, and prepared them for transport. Although Lobur thought he would survive his wounds, Cpl Young, married with a baby he would never see, would die twelve days later.

"As we went about our duties," LCpl Permenter said, *"everyone was quiet and in their own thoughts, wondering why we were alive*

and the others were not. Our fallen brothers were lined up in the center of our perimeter, each covered by a poncho. The memory of that long line of jungle boots protruding from ponchos is forever burned in my mind."

"I walked over to where the dead guys were," Ericson said. *"They had 'em wrapped in ponchos. I saw his boots sticking out underneath the poncho, and I could see the martini glasses drawn on his boots. That's how I knew Larry got killed."*

"Yeah, Doc got it," a grunt said, "and the chaplain got it too."

"It's just like somebody punches you in the guts. You're just drained. It just drains right out of you."

"It was then that I realized that Sgt Peters had died and other Marines that I knew," Martinez said. *"Martin, McKenzie, Mortenson, and Giordano. I thought of the picture that I'd given to Sgt Peters, not knowing that his family was going to see this picture or if he had a wife. I didn't know anything about his personal life, and I really hated the idea that that was going to be in his personal belongings, not so much because of the picture but because of the effect it might have on his family."*

"I saw him the next morning when I was looking at the dead," Fred Permenter said of his friend Steve Wright who, with the last mail call that morning, seemed relieved of some unknown burden before loading on the chopper. *"I was looking to see who was there, see if there were any of my buddies, and he was one of them. I think he just needed a letter from home. That's all. At least he got that letter. That's the main thing."*

"I saw Father Capodanno and Doc Leal," Sullivan said. *"Leal had a grazing wound to his head, and I'll never forget it because there was no blood, and it was just solid white."*

Also among the dead was Pfc Tony Gabaldon, the young-looking nineteen-year-old kid who had just arrived to 3rd Platoon that morning and cousin to Guy Gabaldon, the WWII Marine hero portrayed in the movie *Hell to Eternity,* the movie Dennis Tylinski had seen as a teenager.

• • •

As he policed outside the perimeter with other Marines, Jack Swan's emotions puzzled him. *"I remember saying to myself, 'Swanny, how come you don't feel any remorse?' And of course, this is my brain going one hundred miles with me. And, I said to me, 'It's fucking survival. It is mental survival.' But self-survival in Vietnam—if you fall apart, you are dead. If you mentally start whining about everything you've seen, you are dead meat, buddy. You aren't concentrating."*

Swan returned to the spot where the NVA had him pinned down in front of the knoll in order to retrieve the plastic bag containing the map and family pictures that he had buried when he was certain that he would not survive.

"The next morning, I went back out there. It was dug up. It was dug up and not there."

LCpl Hooley ventured back to his spot near the command crater and not far from the tunnel that the NVA had used to infiltrate the Marine perimeter. He was looking for the pack that he had discarded in the middle of the firefight.

"It was covered with ants, and there was three holes in the side of the pack."

The clear liquid that Hooley felt run down his back after he was hit by the NVA machine gun was syrup from the decimated cans of fruit that his parents had mailed to him from home.

"Where's Father Capodanno?"

Cpl Don Goulet, who had suffered a punctured lung from the mortar explosion, counted sixteen bodies as he waited for the medevac. He had heard stories that the chaplain had died in the field but didn't want to believe it. A Marine gestured toward one of the poncho-covered bodies, and Goulet moved toward it.

"Don't. He's cut up pretty bad."

Overcome by a wave of immense grief, Goulet stopped and climbed aboard an arriving chopper. As tears streamed down his cheeks and as he fought to catch his breath, he thanked God for Lt Murray, American close air support, and for giving him another day of life.

• • •

On September 4, 1967, Mike 3/5 was air lifted into the Quế Sơn Valley with approximately 165 Marines and Navy corpsmen. A day later, sixteen lie dead, another would later die of his wounds, and eighty-one would require medical evacuation. Many more walking casualties stayed in the field at their own request or by hiding their wounds in order to stay with the depleted company.

"There were people (in Mike 3/5) the following day who had gunshot wounds who didn't tell anybody about them because they didn't want to leave their buddies," Murray said. *"And these are gunshot wounds through and through. They didn't report them to the corpsman because they knew as soon as they did they'd be medevacked out. It wasn't so much the company as they didn't want to leave their squad or fire team where the people had to do their job or they were dead. So, this bond is just unbelievable. It is so strong that in many cases it is much stronger than a family tie—brother, sister, or parents.*

I don't know how to say it other than you want to be there with your buddies. You have experienced all these things together, and you don't want to leave them."

Two kilometers west of the knoll, amid the wreckage of two downed helicopters, twenty-eight more fallen Marines from Delta and Bravo 1/5, the men Mike and Kilo 3/5 intended to rescue, lay strewn among dead NVA who had breached their perimeter.

"When we connected with Delta Company the morning of the fourth," Navy Corpsman Casselman said, *"the one thing that I still remember is that there were at least half a dozen guys that weren't wounded but we had to medevac them because they were zombies. Whatever they went through that early morning, I mean, it just zoned them. They were just staring, some of them shaking, and looking pale and ashen. They were in shock and looked like they'd literally seen a ghost."*

One of the young Marines who required evacuation carried a burden that, if he is still alive, he carries to this day.

"One guy got killed by one of our own guys. He was crawling up on this big boulder during one of the firefights in the dark. One Marine saw this form crawling up this boulder, thinks it's the enemy, and shoots him. And I mean the blood, that boulder, was crimson red when I saw it. The guy that shot him was out of it. I can still picture his face, but I don't remember his name."

The dead included CPT Morgan.

"CPT Morgan was a fine man," Bill Dubose remembered. *"He was a fine Marine, and he was new to Vietnam. And me, being a corporal at the time, you know, he would talk to me. Usually the officers are sort of aloof; they don't talk much too much to underlings. He was a friendly guy, and of course, this is hindsight, but he didn't have the field experience that probably he needed, being that we didn't go to the high ground as soon as we crossed the river."*

• • •

On the afternoon of September 5, Lt Murray received new orders. Instead of returning to Hill 63 to reorganize and refit, Mike and India Company were told to saddle up again. Their new directive was to locate and destroy the enemy who had, just the day before, so cleverly and effectively ambushed Murray and his men. As they moved out, the Marines came across a fresh mass grave of NVA soldiers.

"We had to dig the damn thing up," Sullivan said. *"We counted the bodies then."*

Refusing evacuation despite shrapnel head wounds, Sullivan remained with his platoon for the duration of Operation Swift, which would last another eleven days. On September 6, two days after the fight on the knoll, Mike Company received fresh orders to come to the aid of both Kilo and India Companies, both partially overrun by a furious NVA ground attack.

"That evening, after we had set in, I think it was around 22:00, 10:00 at night, Col Webster called me and said, "JD, I need for you to move your company out and go over to help India and Kilo Company. They are surrounded, it looks very serious, and I need to commit you.""

"You couldn't turn on a light because they would see you, so we got three or four ponchos together, we sat down, and I briefed the platoon commanders and the platoon sergeants under these ponchos. We were going a thousand to fifteen hundred meters across terrain we had never seen before. The people settled in, they'd eaten, and they'd dug their foxholes. The lieutenants and sergeants had to go back, get their troops out of the holes, get them combat loaded and ready to roll."

Wearing gas masks because of a possible drop of CS on Kilo and India, Lt Murray's devil dogs advanced into the pitched darkness and crossed two streams over unknown terrain in their bid to once again rescue beleaguered comrades—surrounded, outnumbered, and outgunned by the NVA and receiving heavy small arms and mortar fire.

"I am back there now, man," Sullivan recalled. "I am walking in the damn water, and the moon is reflecting off that water, and then the closer we got, we could hear them screaming, and they were firing their weapons at ghosts because they didn't have any targets. They were just firing at ghosts. We finally got up there, and every time you would take a step, you would step on a dead Marine or a wounded Marine. I mean, it was just pure ghostly."

"The toughest part of it," Murray said, "in any type of movement at night, is insuring we don't get into a major fire fight with our own troops. I don't know how in the hell we did it, to be quite honest with you. It was one of the scariest moments of my life."

After reinforcing the two companies, the next morning Sgt Sullivan took his platoon past a hedgerow and a village to a large bomb crater that had partially filled with water.

"And there were Marine bodies everywhere. You could see bodies in that hole, and you could see where they had clawed the side of it with their fingers. You could see their fingernails were broke, and you could see the dirt where their claw marks were in the clay."

Sullivan's horror and anger grew when he realized that the enemy, most likely the Viet Cong, had mutilated many of the American dead, with bodies shot to pieces by automatic fire and arms twisted "like you take a damn rag and twist it."

"We had to take one of the Marine lieutenants and bury him," Goebel said, "because the NVA went up and down his body with a *machine gun and made him into hamburger. We buried him because of the troop morale. So we had a lot of bodies that we had to get out."*

To make matters worse, if that were possible, an eerie feeling came over Sullivan as he looked at one of the mutilated Americans.

"I saw a body lying next to that hole, and you know how you get an intuition, like you know somebody? Well, I had that feeling, like I knew this guy, and I told Mercereuio, my radio operator, I said, 'Mercereuio, I think I know this guy. Roll him over.' And he rolled him over, and sure enough, his mother used to wash and iron my daddy's shirts. He lived down the street from me, and he was younger than I was. He had been shot all to hell."

Sullivan didn't know that the young man from his hometown of Jacksonville, Florida, was in Vietnam, much less the Marine Corps.

"And about that time, I just started shaking. I flipped the hell out—I mean, I really did. When we had to gather all these people up, I had to go, I had to go sit down somewhere. And I went over, and sat down on a stump, and smoked a cigarette. I had to get myself put together because I was fixing to flip out. But I was very, very angry, and I could have killed anybody that day. Because there were so many Marines that had been killed and wounded, and then on top of that, they had to mutilate some of them. I could have killed anybody that day."

After encountering the horror of mutilated Americans, one of them a friend, and on the completion of Operation Swift on September 15, Sgt Sullivan and his radio operator earned a well-deserved R&R in Bangkok, Thailand. The two Marines weren't present when Mike Company went on Operation Essex, which lasted from November 6–17. When he returned, Sullivan's 1st sergeant asked him to come to his hooch.

"So we went over to his place, we got in there, and he shut the door, and he throwed me a Miller beer and told me to sit down. He had

something to tell me. He kind of walked around, you know, and he told me, 'Well, Sully,' he says, 'you don't have a platoon anymore.'"

With the exception of two Marines, all of Sgt Sullivan's comrades in 1st Platoon had been either killed or wounded on Operation Essex while Sully and his radio operator were on R&R.

"I didn't leave his hooch for about four days," Sully said. *"I got drunker than a damn dog. Cried in my beer. That just tore me up, you know?"*

Shortly afterwards, Sgt Sullivan, who now had two Purple Hearts for wounds sustained, received a promotion to assistant S3 Chief, a non-combat position in which he could help train new Marines.

• • •

On September 7, the morning after the terrifying night march, LCpl Fred Permenter once again found himself policing the battle-field looking for the dead and wounded. When he and his patrol came to several unmarked graves, his orders were to dig them up to determine if the dead were enemy or American.

"We buried them back 'cause they were definitely enemy. I, it was either me or one of the other guys, left an arm sticking up out of the ground, and one of the guys put a lit cigarette between the fingers as we marched on. That was a stress reliever. But, looking back at it, they were soldiers just like we were, trying to do the same thing, but they killed our buddies. We wanted to do as much damage to them as we could. That was our mentality."

Seeing a comrade of his, an engineer with a chest wound, being born on a stretcher, Permenter relieved one of the bearers to help carry his friend.

"I helped carry him down, and I guess the stress after three days of seeing nothing but carnage, I just broke down. I just went off to the side and just weeped a little bit, got it over with. That probably helped me out a lot though, you know, by doing that."

Later that day, after providing security for India and Kilo as they reorganized and called in supplies and medevacs, it surprised Lt Murray and the other officers when the commander of 3/5, Lt Col Webster, was unexpectedly relieved and replaced by Col William Rockey. When the new colonel called the company commanders together for a briefing, Lt Murray found himself on the receiving end of an unpleasant, and surreal, experience.

"Col Rockey royally chewed my ass out because I hadn't shaved that morning. It really pissed me off because we had now been in combat since the fourth. It had been very, very traumatic, and I am now getting chewed out because I didn't shave. Well, I really didn't have frigging time!"

On the night of September 15, 1967, as Operation Swift ended, Mike 3/5 was ordered by battalion to board trucks that would take the company from Than Binh to the 3/5 Battalion Firebase at Hill 63. From the 16th on the company was again in the regular routine of defending Hill 63 and providing troops for daily patrols around the base camp.

"The recovery was long and painful for everyone," Murray said. *"Grieving for fallen and wounded buddies—and the unjust incrimination by Division over lack of cleaning our weapons, affected the leadership of the company down to the fire team level."*

Rebuilding the company through new personnel, equipment, and training while still providing security for Hill 63 would dominate the devil dog's time and, to some small degree, help numb their losses.

9

THE NORTH VIETNAMESE

For Senior Col Le Huu Tru, commander of the 1st Viet Cong Regiment (VC) and the 31st and 21st regiments of the 2nd Division of the People's Army of Vietnam (PAVN), collectively known to the Americans as the NVA, CPT Robert Morgan's two isolated platoons (dug in near the village of Đông Sơn on the morning of September 4) presented a well-timed and favorable opportunity. After surviving several bitter and costly battles with the Marines during Operations Union I and II earlier in the year and having avoided a destructive confrontation with the Americans on Operation Cochise in early August, Tru waited to strike when the odds were in his favor. Should his troops succeed in inflicting heavy casualties on the Americans, as well as gain control of the Quế Sơn Valley, the North Vietnamese would be in a strong position to attack the vital city of Da Nang as part of the Tet Offensive planned for January 1968.

By August 30, two days after the end of Operation Cochise, Col Tru's men, having had the summer to regroup and refit after the fighting that spring, were once more ready for full-scale operations. Tru and his commanders predicted that the Americans would send a battalion of Marines into the region known as Doi Cam that September in a bid to take control of the Quế Sơn Valley.

CPT Morgan's two platoons, Tru calculated, were a reconnaissance in force for that planned attack. Tru ordered a battalion of the

1st Viet Cong Regiment, about four hundred strong, to attack Morgan's isolated men, outnumbering the Americans by at least five to one. He then dispatched a battalion from the 31st Regiment PAVN to deal with Bravo Company, the odds once again greatly in favor of the NVA.

With Bravo and Delta 1/5 heavily outnumbered and in danger of annihilation, Tru predicted correctly that the Marines would send in reinforcements for their beleaguered comrades. Anticipating that the Americans would advance west along Route 534 toward Đông Sơn and the Ly Ly River, Tru dispatched the 1st Viet Cong Regiment and the 31st Regiment PAVN to ambush the oncoming Americans, who had strengthened Tru's hand by landing Mike and Kilo 3/5 into separate landing zones, thus dividing their forces.

"We were caught out in the open," Murray said. *"We didn't have any position. We didn't have squat, and they were waiting for us to come in. They were smart enough to know that we had a tendency to guide on roads and where Bravo and Delta Companies were was right down toward the end of a large road (Route 534). They figured that was the route we were going to take, and they were right."*

"They anticipated the Marines would come that way," Whitlow said, *"because the landing zones had been used before, and there were only so many landing zones that could be used. They knew where they were."*

In 2009, a number of Operation Swift veterans, including JD Murray, Rob Whitlow, Chuck Goebel, and Craig Sullivan, met with their rivals of forty years earlier.

"When we asked the colonels, 'Why did you have the ambush there?' they said, 'We knew where you'd land. We always did.'"

The 1st Viet Cong, known as the Ba Gia Regiment, about fifteen hundred men, had orders to take up ambush positions in the rice paddy at the foot of the knoll that lay in the path of Lt Murray and his advancing Marines. Experts in unconventional tactics such as camouflage, mobile assaults, and surprise attacks, the regiment had earned its nickname after its victory, under the command of Col Tru, over South Vietnamese forces at the battle of Ba Gia in 1965.

"Bravo and Delta 1/5 we already trapped to the west at Đông Sơn," Whitlow said. *"These guys (Mike, Kilo, and the 1/5 Command Group) were trying to get to Đông Sơn before dark, so the North Vietnamese launched this major assault, thinking they had an entire Marine battalion trapped and caught, but they didn't. What they really had was the northern most unit, which was Mike Company: about 180 men."*

Tru's plan was to lure Mike 3/5, and possibly Kilo 3/5, into the open rice paddy, overrun the Americans with an overwhelming attack from the Ba Gia Regiment and a battalion of the 31st PAVN, a more traditional regiment in the NVA, and decimate the Americans in a quick and decisive battle before they could request reinforcements or close air support.

"They were very adaptive, and they obviously didn't have the same capabilities (air support) that we did," Murray said. *"They knew that if they can get to within fifty meters of us they're in fairly good condition, but if they're outside that, they're almost always dead because that is where we put our artillery and close air support. The idea was to sneak in as close as they could to us because the closer they were, the safer they were."*

NVA troops hidden in tunnels on the knoll were likely placed there to surprise the Americans from behind and prevent them from taking the high ground once they were caught in the open rice paddy.

"We think that the NVA probably left this platoon there to seal off the back side of the ambush site, which made a lot of sense," Whitlow said. *"If the Marines had moved through there and gotten in the paddies, these NVAs would have popped up out of their holes, and they could have kept the Marines from pulling back to that hill, but it happened that the battle broke out while they were still there."*

Thanks to Jack Swan and Vandergriff's point squad, the devil dogs were able to trigger the ambush prematurely and form a perimeter on the knoll before the trap had fully sprung.

Despite the handicap of a faulty weapon, the M16, Murray's men put up a ferocious defense, and with the arrival of close air support in the form of bombs, napalm, Spooky's Gatling guns, and CS gas were able to deny Col Tru his quick and decisive victory. By dawn on September 5, Tru's men, having suffered heavy casualties, had decided to withdraw.

Col Tran Nhu Tiep, who served under Senior Col Tru as the operations officer for the 2nd NVA Division, confirmed that at least four thousand Vietnamese troops surrounded the Marines, at least ten thousand held in reserve and another six thousand in the hills beyond.

"They (the NVA) had Bravo and Delta 1/5 surrounded," Murray said, *"and they were waiting for us to come in. My suspicion is that they probably had a battalion (about six hundred men) attacking us with another battalion providing suppressing fire and that there were as many as four thousand that were coming across or were available to come across. They had two regiments ready to tangle with anybody who wanted to come into the area. They really didn't care how big of a force we brought in because they had twelve thousand NVA ready to take us on and four thousand that were hitting our particular unit on that day."*

Doing rough math and assuming that Mike 3/5 had, at most, 180 men with the attacking NVA at about two thousand, the odds facing the Americans were at least eleven-to-one, if not greater.

"If you had that many men, why didn't you all just annihilate us?" Sullivan asked.

Tiep answered that the Marines were fighting so ferociously and bombarding so heavily that the NVA command made the decision to pull back and fight another day.

By September 15, after a series of bitter engagements that left his 2nd NVA Division severely weakened, Col Tru ceded control of the southern half of the Quế Sơn Valley to the Americans. Because of the casualties suffered by the North Vietnamese on Operation Swift, which included the death of Col Tru himself due to American helicopter gunship fire that December, the NVA were not able to mount a strong assault against Da Nang during the Tet Offensive in January of 1968.

At the cost of 127 Marines, 28 South Vietnamese, and 600 or more NVA, the United States achieved a tactical victory on Operation Swift. Although a victory for the Americans, the overall North Vietnamese strategy would ultimately prove to be decisive. The American casualties sustained in the bitter fights in the Quế Sơn Valley and throughout Vietnam in 1967, and the overall shock of the Tet Offensive launched by the North Vietnamese in 1968 would turn the home front in the United States against the war and would lead, ultimately, to final victory for the North Vietnamese in the spring of 1975.

10

VALOR, MISTAKES, AND THE LOST

"*I extended,*" JD Murray said, "*because I felt that I could save lives.*"

Murray's decision was not an empty sentiment. Because of existing Marine Corps and US Army policies, combat experience was a commodity vitally needed and often lacking among troops fighting in Vietnam. Individual replacements fresh from the states replenished veteran Marine and Army units with each man to serve a twelve- or thirteen-month tour of duty in- country. New company and field grade commissioned officers, the captains and lieutenants, spent half of the time in a combat role, the other half in a less dangerous posting. For a combat infantry company, this approach was, in hindsight, one of the worst policies of the war.

"*I had people on Swift,*" Murray said, "*who probably had been in-country less than a week and didn't know squat. By the time Swift occurred, I had spent almost fifteen months in combat, and there was nothing that I'd been involved in as fierce as Swift. I can't imagine what it was like for troops who had never seen combat, to be eighteen or nineteen years old and go through Swift without any real training. Our training over there was on the job, and you had to know what to do or you were dead.*"

Lack of experience and training were only part of the problem. For a small unit in battle, victory or defeat would often hinge on the degree of unit solidarity, combat experience, and competent leadership exhibited at the squad, platoon, and company levels. When the salts mixed with green additions fresh from the states, unit solidarity was severely undermined. Resented and avoided by the veterans, replacements such as Tony Martinez, Howard Haney, and Dennis Fisher often felt acute fear, alienation, and loneliness as they struggled to stay alive in a deadly world.

"It was the stupidest thing that the Marine Corp could have done, and you'll never see it happen again," Murray said. *"Only in Vietnam were we forced into a situation where a unit that was going into combat didn't train together. In all the other wars, every single one of them, unit training was extremely important because you find out the capabilities of each of your individuals, the good parts and the bad ones, so that you know what to do and expect from them in combat.*

"Hell, I didn't even know my three platoon commanders. They were brand-new. They had come in-country in June of '67, and I didn't take over the company until the end of July. I had them for one month, and they were split up all over the place. We weren't in one location, so I couldn't just round them up and talk to them. I had to travel to see each one of them, and I didn't know what their capabilities were until we were under the gun. Everything was exposed then."

While destabilizing for the combat infantryman, the individual replacement policy was particularly corrosive for his leadership, with new inexperienced officers rotating in every six months, only to leave once they had acquired some level of competence.

"Not only did the rotation policy foreclose the possibility of developing a sense of unit integrity and responsibility," argued Richard A. Gabriel and Lt Col Paul L. Savage in their work *Crisis in Command: Mismanagement in the Army,* "but it also ensured a continuing supply of low quality, inexperienced officers at the point of greatest stress in any army, namely in its combat units."

As a young lieutenant who had survived numerous battles unscathed, Murray repeatedly saw what happened when officers fresh from the states, who hadn't seen combat, got thrown into the fire.

"They made mistakes, and their mistakes cost lives."

On September 4, 1967, the men under his command were, in one sense, lucky. Murray's decision to extend his tour when he could have rotated back to a less dangerous job gave the leathernecks a competent, battle-tested leader when they most needed one, especially in light of the fact that Murray's three platoon commanders had no combat experience whatsoever. From the moment of the deadly ambush to the final withdrawal of the NVA that night, Murray's experienced leadership proved vital to the survival of the men under his command.

"If it wasn't for JD," Howard Haney said, *"we would not be here."*

"If it hadn't been for the skipper holding us together," Fred Permenter said, *"I think we would have been overrun; there's no question. As far as I'm concerned, he saved our asses along with Redmond and Whitlow up there in the Bird Dogs. I really thought that that was going to be it."*

When 1st Platoon came under devastating fire at the front of knoll, Murray quickly assessed the situation and sent two squads from 2nd, led by Sgt Pete, to their aid. When Combs went down, Murray, exposing himself to a deluge of fire, personally reorganized 1st Platoon by placing Sgt Sullivan in charge. While his outnumbered and outgunned leathernecks held the line, Murray skillfully called in artillery and mortar strikes as well as close air support in the form of bombs, napalm, CS gas, and the Gatling guns of Spooky, all of which had the combined effect of forcing the veteran and aggressive North Vietnamese to withdraw.

Murray's leadership would again prove crucial on the nights of September 6 and 10 when he skillfully led his bloodied Marines to the relief of other leatherneck companies surrounded and under attack by the NVA. For his bold initiative and aggressive fighting spirit, which undoubtedly saved the lives of countless Marines while accomplishing his mission, Murray received the Navy Cross, the Navy and Marine Corps' second highest decoration for extraordinary heroism in combat, second only to the Medal of Honor.

Fortunate to have Murray in command, the deck remained stacked against the devil dogs when they landed in the Quế Sơn Valley on the morning of September 4. The last-minute decision to drop Mike Company at a LZ separate from Kilo and the command group provided the NVA with an opportunity to attack Murray's men with a decided advantage in numbers. Poor intelligence also played a role when the Americans discovered a detailed map of the location of the North Vietnamese forces prior to the attack, but by the time the information went up the chain of command for evaluation, Mike Company had already walked into the deadly enemy trap.

"The information didn't get to us in a timely fashion," Murray said. *"If we had had people at a lower level, either battalion or regiment that could have read the maps and told us what they were, then we probably would have deployed differently. We would have known exactly where they were. Our intelligence failed us."*

No single factor, however, played a greater role in hampering the effectiveness of Murray's men in battle and in costing the lives of young Marines than did the repeated failure of the M16 rifle.

"The M16 was not a good weapon when we had it on Swift," Murray said. *"My guess is that from March to December 1967, close to one thousand Marines lost their lives due to the faulty weapons. In*

the early morning hours of September 5, it was obvious that close to half of the KIAs suffered by M Company had died while trying to extract spent cartridges from the chambers of their weapons. It was atrocious the number of people we lost."

The enemy was also well aware of the defects of the Marines' principle firearm.

"We got that rifle in March of '67, and that's when they had the hill fights up north, as well as Operations Union I and Union II. There were weapons left out in the middle of the battlefield because the North Vietnamese knew that they weren't good weapons. Very seldom did that happen."

It was not, as first alleged, the negligence of the individual leatherneck to keep his rifle clean that lead to the deadly malfunction but instead a simple matter of quality control up the chain of supply. The ammunition, not properly tested, delivered to the Marines, was found later to be incompatible with the rifle that the lives of the men depended on.

"Later we find out it was because the chamber wasn't chromed," Ken Fields said. *"The type of powder they were using was causing the chamber to carbon up, causing the round to jam in, and then the extractor would cut through (the casing) because it couldn't pull out the round. It was never a cleaning issue, but that is the stand that the military took, that we weren't cleaning."*

Mistakes by the Marine Corps at the tactical level occurred because of larger miscalculations in strategy as well. In previous conflicts, such as WWII, the Corps retained control of an area won in battle and rarely, if ever, relinquished conquered territory to the enemy.

"But we didn't do that in Vietnam." Murray said. *"Over and over again, Marines moved out of a combat base and took a hill after fierce*

fighting, and after they took that hill, they would move off it, and the enemy would return. Three weeks later, the same unit went out and tried to retake the same hill. So mentally, the men who repeatedly had to go out there are thinking 'What the hell is this? We keep on losing Marines trying to regain the same piece of territory that we leave, and they take over!'"

That strategy seemed to make little sense. Not only has the Corps in Vietnam come under criticism, but Murray's decision to call in CS gas on his own position has come under fire as well. For the commander of Mike Company, the tear gas drop by Deadlock 30 was a crucial element in driving back the enemy troops that had infiltrated the company's perimeter, and he remembers an immediate lull and a slacking of pressure after dropping the CS. Others, however, believe that seriously wounded Marines who didn't have gas masks or could not access the ones that they had, died because of exposure to the CS gas.

"I can understand that," Murray said, *"but it was my decision to call in the gas because I thought that a lot of people were going to die. So I accept that as a criticism, but somebody had to make a damn decision, and in my eyes, that was something that needed to be done."*

"The gas drop was a stroke of genius," Kevin Kelly said, *"It gave us ten minutes to reorganize before the gas lifted and the NVA came on us strong again."*

For Murray, full credit should go to all aspects of his fighting company for the successful defense mounted against repeated deadly and determined NVA attacks.

"Without the enormous support from air and artillery supporting arms, the troops fighting with inferior weapon systems but bravely fighting for each other, it could have been disastrous. A Marine is a Marine and willing to do almost anything for his buddy and his

unit. That is exactly what happened in Vietnam, even though we had so many things going against us."

For Craig Jackson, one of the beleaguered leathernecks with Delta and Bravo 1/5, the rescue mission of Mike and Kilo 3/5 was a godsend that prevented a catastrophe.

"If it had not have happened, they (the NVA) would have rolled over us, and there was nothing that would have prevented them from taking the Hill (the battalion fire base at Hill 51)."

From September 16 on, after Murray and his men returned to Hill 63 and out of the front line, one of the requirements of the officers and NCOs was to write award recommendations for those individuals who acted with great heroism during the operation. Unfortunately, with so many key personnel missing, and with witnesses killed or wounded and unable to testify, Murray is sure that many acts of valor did not get the recognition due to them. There were certain deeds, however, that no one overlooked.

In 1969, Father Vincent Capodanno was posthumously awarded, for conspicuous gallantry and intrepidity at the risk of his life above and beyond the call of duty, our nation's highest decoration for combat valor, the Medal of Honor.

"He was a wonderful man," John Costello remembered, *"but even more, you could tell he was something special, the way he cared, spoke to you, you could tell."*

When the Navy chaplain seized Steve Lovejoy by his radio pack, pulled him to his feet, and led him through machine gun fire to the safety of a crater near the top of the knoll, Lovejoy knew that the Navy chaplain had delivered him from certain death.

"It would be incorrect to only say that Father Capodanno had a profound impact on my life. Father Capodanno not only influenced my life; he saved it. Without his action, I would have perished on

September 4, 1967. My two wonderful children, Gina and Jeremy, would not be here. My three terrific grandsons, James, Joseph, and John, would also not be alive."

Throughout his life, Lovejoy had the honor of sharing the story of the heroic priest with his many relatives, friends, and acquaintances.

"I have been able to expose others to the power of God's love. Father Capodanno was truly one who radiated Christ. He was someone who was genuinely concerned with the well-being of others and one who put others before himself. Over the past forty-five plus years, I have hoped to be but a small equal to the giant of a man that walked that battlefield so long ago."

Don Goulet, the Marine who expressed embarrassment to have cursed in front of the priest, felt haunted by Father Capodanno's death long after he had returned to civilian life. He was working for the FBI when he decided to visit Capodanno's grave in West New Brighton, New York.

"It was extremely moving for me, of course. I had tears coming out of my eyes. I wanted my kids and my wife to know who this man had been."

George Phillips, the Marine who had baptized the critically wounded Ed Combs into the Catholic faith, felt inspired that day by the example set by the heroic priest.

"He would show up at the most amazing places. Father Capodanno was the only chaplain I ever saw outside the wire. He was a one in a million kind of guy."

"From the first day I met him," Byron Hill remembered, *"I knew he was a chaplain for the field Marine. Previous chaplains would disappear when we mounted out on an operation. However, it was clear that Father Capodanno knew where he was needed."*

As a young 1LT who served with the 11th Marine Artillery Regiment on Operation Swift, Hill sought guidance from the chaplain after seeing so many casualties among his fellow Marines.

"I spent countless hours talking with him: about faith, and just life in general, and I always found him a true inspiration. He regularly offered me communion and his blessings, and believe me, I welcomed the comfort he provided me. Father Capodanno was always there when we needed him, and I never knew of a Marine in 3/5 who didn't say how much they loved him, and that was long before he was killed."

One of Father Capodanno's final acts was praying with the wounded Red Manfra, who remembered the chaplain's devotion to his men.

"He was there all the time. If you needed to talk to somebody, he was always ready to listen to you. And if you wanted to pray, he would pray with you. He was an amazing man."

Dave "Doc" Magnenat still has the Bible that the chaplain handed him just before climbing on the helicopter at Hill 63 on September 4.

"I have used it a lot over the years. For the remainder of my military service, it was the last thing into my sea bag and the first thing out. Wherever I went, it had a place of honor."

Commissioned in 1973, the USS Capodanno, a Knox-class Navy frigate named for the fallen priest, received a papal blessing from Pope John Paul II in 1981. In 1976, the town leaders renamed the main thoroughfare in the chaplain's hometown of Staten Island, New York *Father Capodanno Boulevard.* In 2006, the Archdiocese for the Military Services declared Father Capodanno a Servant of God, formally initiating the cause for his beatification and sainthood. The Father Capodanno Guild, of which George Phillips was onetime chairperson, dedicates its service to the cause for his canonization.

In 2014, Father Capodanno's family donated his Medal of Honor to the Capodanno Chapel at The Basic School at Marine Corps Base in Quantico, Virginia. Through the medal, the intrepid Navy chaplain is with "his" Marines to this day.

"All I can say is to have known him was a great honor," John Costello said, *"and to meet someone of that quality in your life is a gift from God."*

"I'm going to come back with the Medal of Honor," Larry Peters told his mother when he left for Vietnam, "or I'm not coming back."

Like Father Capodanno, Sgt Pete had already served a thirteen-month tour of duty when, because of his love for and desire to help the Vietnamese people, he volunteered for a second tour. On his first tour, Peters had worked with a Marine Combined Action Program (CAP) unit and, in whatever free time he had, worked at a Catholic orphanage in Da Nang.

"Larry loved children," his girlfriend Gail Nelson said, *"and if he could, he would have adopted all of the orphans in Vietnam. He wrote to me discussing his heartache for their suffering. He not only gave his life for our country, but he gave it for the people and children of South Vietnam. He is a hero in so many ways."*

"Larry was all Marine," said Dave Harder, a childhood friend who grew up with Peters in Binghamton, New York, and who had served with him in the reserves, *"and he always strived to be the best he could. When he got into something, he put his heart and soul into it, and the Marine Corps did the same thing. He was very sharp, and I'm sure that when the fighting came down he was ready for it, and he was going to do whatever he had to do. That was the big thing about Larry: no matter what he was doing, he always took pride in it."*

When Lynda Peters drove Larry to the Marine Corps recruiting office while on semester break from college, she didn't expect to join up the same day as her younger brother. With two siblings in the Corps, Lynda stationed in San Diego and Larry in Vietnam, older sister Shirley joined the Navy and became a nurse, serving on the *USS Ticonderoga*. When the aircraft carrier pulled into port in San Diego that September in 1967, Lynda was standing at the gangway waiting to board to see Shirley, when someone called up to the quarterdeck with a message for her sister.

"Has Lt Peters gone ashore yet?"

"No, she hasn't signed out yet."

"I've got to find Lt Peters. Do you think you know where she is? Her brother has been killed."

Lynda overheard the conversation.

"My brother has been killed?"

"No, Lt Peters' brother has been killed—"

"I'm Lynda Peters. My brother has been killed—my brother has been killed!"

Allowed to board, a distraught Lynda broke the news to Shirley that their younger brother had died in combat, just twelve days shy of his twenty-first birthday.

In a letter to Harder, Peters had acknowledged that he might be die in battle.

"*It happens all the time,*" he wrote. "*Maybe it's fate. Who knows? Anyway, I'm a firm believer in when it's your time to go, you go. Regardless, I do believe that. The man upstairs calls the shots.*"

For his outstanding valor, indomitable fighting spirit and tenacious determination in the face of overwhelming odds at the risk of his life above and beyond the call of duty, Sgt Pete was posthumously awarded the Medal of Honor.

"*He believed that he was doing the right thing,*" Shirley said, "*that this was a war, we're to do good, and he was there to help people and help keep them safe.*"

When the Corps returned his belongings to his family, they found a picture of an unknown young woman among them. It is thought that the picture was the high school photograph of Tony Martinez's then girlfriend, future wife and mother of his oldest two children, the photograph that Sgt Pete was keeping safe for the new guy in his squad.

When Peters took a machine gun round to the leg as he rallied his two squads to the aid of 1st Platoon, it is possible that twenty-year-old Corpsman Armando Leal staunched the bleeding and applied the battle dressing.

Despite the constant enemy fire, Leal rendered first aid to wounded Marines caught between American and enemy lines until an NVA bullet severed his femoral artery early in the attack on 2nd Platoon. After undoubtedly saving lives, Leal would ultimately lose his to the same North Vietnamese machine gun that would kill Father Capodanno, and for his exceptional courage and unfaltering dedication to duty, Armando Leal received the Navy Cross.

"He was a very easily liked person," friend and fellow Corpsman Darryl Guidry remembered, *"who was admired by everyone who knew him. I can't remember him ever having a cross word to say about anyone."*

Fellow Texan Fred Riddle remembered Leal as a family-oriented, "really nice" guy with big ambitions.

"He was planning on being a doctor when he got out, go to med school, and become a doctor, and everything."

San Antonio's Southcross Junior High, where Leal graduated, honored Leal by renaming the school Leal Middle School, remembering him "as a good friend, always happy with a positive outlook and a good sense of humor. His determination, bravery, and commitment to his brothers in arms serve as an inspiration to all of us who are members of the Leal Middle School Community. We honor him and all that he stood for."

"Tom was an excellent Marine," Platoon Sgt Craig Sullivan wrote of LCpl Thomas Fisher. *"I could always depend on him, and he was well liked by all that knew him. Tom cared about what he was doing and always tried his best to do the right thing. He was always willing to help out wherever he could and always set high standards for himself and his fire team. He always put his men first; he was a team player and did his best to protect his men from harm."*

"I will always remember Tom," Fisher's friend Jim Christman said. *"We did a lot of cruising in his '50 ford. One guy that would not back down to anyone. Tom, you will always be a hero."*

When the ambush hit 1st Platoon, it was the twenty-year-old Fisher who immediately responded by directing his fire team to take out a camouflaged machine gun position. Undeterred and in full view of the enemy, Fisher silenced a 2nd NVA automatic weapon with his M16 before an enemy round shattered both his rifle and his arm. Despite his wounds and upon learning that the enemy had pinned Jack Swan down at the front of the knoll, Fisher braved a gauntlet of fire until struck down himself, and for his extraordinary courage, bold initiative, and selfless devotion to duty, Thomas Fisher posthumously received the Navy Cross.

Like Peters, Leal, and Fisher, childhood friends remember Andrew Giordano fondly.

"Andy was the younger brother I never had," Chris Argento said, *"a close friend who never returned, nor another friendship have I been able to make again. A handsome young man who had a great sense of humor, a bigger smile, and a heart of gold, he lives with me each and every day in my thoughts and prayers—faithfully a friend."*

Argento goes on to state that his sister Lynda, Andy's first true love, still mourns his sacrifices to this day and has never forgotten him.

"He was always the bright eyed and happy classmate in school and the smiling, easy going dude hanging out at the Pavilion on the Green in Valley Stream, New York," his friend Dan Reddan remembered. *"He remains, now and forever, the symbol of a regular guy doing the right thing at that time."*

When shells began to rain down on Sgt Pete's two squads from 2nd Platoon, Giordano braved a gauntlet of enemy fire to close within fifteen feet of on an enemy mortar team and, despite his wounds, threw four hand grenades onto the position, knocking out the weapon and killing three enemy soldiers. Moments later, while assisting a wounded comrade to safety, he died by enemy machine gun fire. For conspicuous gallantry and intrepidity in action, Andrew Giordano received the Silver Star, our nation's third highest military decoration for combat valor.

Jim Phelps, brother of 2nd Platoon Corpsman David Phelps, was fifteen years old when officers from the US Navy arrived at the front door of his family's home, and he didn't stick around to hear what they had to say. He already knew.

"Dave had talked to Dad via radio phone on his birthday in July. During that visit, Dave told Dad that he knew he would never make it back from Nam alive."

A high school basketball standout, Phelps was from the small, close-knit community of Williamstown, New York. He was the first to die in Vietnam, and the citizens placed a memorial in the center of town in his memory. At his high school, every year, the most improved basketball player at the end of the season receives The David C. Phelps Award.

For his valor in coming to the aid of multiple wounded Marines, undoubtedly saving the life of Howard Manfra and others, David Phelps was posthumously awarded the Bronze Star with Combat "V" on September 4, 2021, fifty-four years to the day after he was KIA.

The NVA struck down Phelps as he tried to provide medical aid to the mortally wounded LCpl Albert Santos. For Santos and many of the other young men killed on September 4, only snapshots of memories remain.

"The last time we spoke," Mike Hayes said about Santos, *"we were anxious about going home. We both had thirty days left on our tour, and we were going to be home the first week in October. Al was killed three weeks before he was to go home for good after two tours."*

"Memories are all that I have left of the time we got to spend growing up," Marion Kingery said of Pfc Gene Mortensen. *"I remember when you said you were joining up. Man, it was hard to think about not hanging out with you while you were doing what you thought best for you and your family. Who knew that summer would be the last I would ever get to see you again. As I grow old, brother, memories are all I have."*

Before he left his home in Yorba Linda, California, Jamie McKenzie gave away all of his possessions.

"You knew you weren't coming back," his nephew Gary recalled, *"which has always left a bit of a haunted feeling of loss to come. You gave me our slot car set, which on weekends you took me out to race, and you gave me your first and my first rifle. Your rifle is well cleaned and oiled and used to this very day."* Gary remembered fondly the egg fights Jamie and he had with friends in the orange groves of Yorba Linda and tubing down the Santa Ana River.

"Jamie was my best friend in Yorba Linda," John Walter remembered. *"He and his mom had this peach tree at their house. The highlight of our summer was to watch each peach come to age, pick them off one at a time, take it into his kitchen, and split it between the two of us. Many years later, every time I eat a peach, I remember him and me watching those peaches age to perfection, picking them, and eating them. He would have made a great father, and we would have continued our friendship."*

"Ray, you would always make us laugh with the 'Nyuk, nyuk, nyuk' and the full finger to the back (gently I might add)," a childhood friend remembered of Pfc Raymond Hengels, an FNG and ammo bumper for Carlton Clark. *"For a big guy, you were always very kind and gentle. You were so proud of your Marine uniform when you came to visit us on the football practice field that day."*

"Miss you every day, every hour, every minute," Norma Lakowski said of her brother Richard Guerrero. *"Thank you—always in my heart—never forgotten. Someday we will meet again."*

Pfc Dennis Fisher, the FNG who had bumped into Clark as 2nd Platoon approached the knoll and who the NVA shot dead when Larry Nunez bent down to pick up a magazine of ammunition, is well remembered by his high school friend Dick Moore.

"We were friends in auto shop at Chaffey High School. I was the kid on the outside, and Dennis invited me in. He was killed before I was even drafted."

"Jack was upbeat with a quick smile," Mike Bays remembered about his friend LCpl Jack Berry. *"A gifted woodworker. I still have the Remington Rifle with the stock he refinished for me."*

LCpl Steven Cornell, the Marine who, along with three others, scrambled out of the safety of a crater to help Tancke and Leal before machine gun fire struck him down; Cpl Bill Young, who sat by the old well with Larry Nunez before being mortally wounded as 2nd Platoon charged forward; and Pfcs. Charles Martin, Steven Wright, and Tony Gabaldon all will never be forgotten, their names and faces a silent testament to their sacrifice.

11

AFTERMATH AND HOME

Like the battles each man fought, each conflict was a microcosm of the greater war, a piece of a mosaic of violence, horror, and valor, often lonely, chaotic, confusing, and disconnected, yet inexorably intertwined with that endured by the man next to him, the story of the return home of each American who fought in Vietnam was isolated and dissimilar, yet in many ways, the same.

"When I read the list of those who had been killed, I was relieved that my friend Keith Rounseville wasn't on it," Red Manfra remembered. *"But when I saw Bill Young's name, I remember breaking down and crying. He was a Marine's Marine, and I thought he was invincible."*

Manfra, who was left for dead but found alive by John Lobur, was evacuated from the knoll and flown to a hospital in Japan where, due to the severity of wounds to his head, chest, arm, and foot, he underwent surgery and was once gain administered last rites. Later, the military flew him to Philadelphia where he would endure additional multiple surgeries, a severe infection, and the reconstruction of his badly misshapen face.

For his courage, aggressive fighting spirit, and unfaltering devotion to duty in deploying his squad, destroying an enemy mortar position, and in continuing to direct fire against the enemy despite his numerous wounds, Manfra received the Silver Star. Even though he never received his sea bag and belongings he left behind in Vietnam, the company clerk at Hill 63 honored Red's request and mailed nearly six hundred dollars, all of the money he had been saving up for R&R, to his mother in New Jersey.

Manfra would forever honor the memory of the heroic Navy chaplain who cared for him when he was near death, and Larry Nunez would forever cherish the chaplain's personal Saint Christopher medal, the silver pitted and tarnished, that Father Capodanno gave him that morning. For fearless leadership of his squad in the face of withering enemy attacks, despite numerous wounds that left him without the full use of his arms, Nunez also received the Silver Star. Like many of his brethren who fought in Vietnam, Nunez would go on to fight his own battle with cancer, a struggle he would lose in 2012.

"I had written my folks maybe the week before that time was getting close," Ken Fields said, *"and then I left ten days early. These were prop planes back in those days, and I flew into Wichita, Kansas, walked across the tarmac and through a set of double doors. And I am probably one of the first people out there, and I throw open those double doors, and there is my mother and father, standing right in front of me!"*

"What are you guys doing here?"

"Well, we sat down for dinner—"

Fields's parents had no idea when their son was about to return from Vietnam, but they lived under the flight pattern for the Wichita Airport and heard a plane fly over at five or six that evening.

"We looked at each other and said, 'Let's go to the airport!'"

"So they put their Sunday best on, and the very first plane they met from California was my plane. That was the first time they had been out to the airport. It was the first plane that they met, and there I was! Is it parent's intuition or what, I don't know. They had no idea. They knew I was coming home within the month, but they just happened to pick the right day!"

LCpl Fred Permenter and 1st Platoon Sergeant Craig Sullivan both experienced a different kind of homecoming. Permenter, wounded after Operation Swift, still walked with crutches when he returned to the US.

"I got accosted by a bunch of hippies in the airport when I went back to San Diego to see this one girl I met right before I left, and of course, I had my Marine Corps haircut and Marine Corps shoes on. One of these peace lovers actually threw a fist at me and knocked me on the ground, knocked me on the ground, and I'm on crutches.

"But I got him good; I got him good. As I was going down, that crutch went right up into his crotch. Brought him down. And luckily, there was business suits around, and they came running over and pulled me off him. This guy was not in very good shape after that."

"Well, that was a bad day," Sullivan said of his return to the US in April of 1968. *"We got a welcome home like we were bastards. That was, I think, one of the hardest things for me."*

Sullivan flew from Vietnam to Wake Island and then on to Anchorage, Alaska. After a long layover, he continued on to Travis Air Force Base in San Francisco. When his plane landed, instead of mortars, grenades, and machine gun fire, Sullivan had to brave a gauntlet of debris and insults hurled at him by a crowd of protestors, fellow Americans who seemed to loathe a Marine in uniform more than the North Vietnamese did.

"They had to have police cordoned off so they couldn't get out there to us. They started throwing damn eggs, tomatoes, and all this crap and called us baby killers, warmongers. 'Baby killers,' that was the biggest thing."

"I hated them. I could have killed them. If I had had a gun, I could have shot them and never batted an eye."

The following day, after experiencing several delays in his effort to get home to his wife and daughter in Jacksonville, Florida, Sully got on a bus to Los Angeles. The sergeant had with him a carefully wrapped doll as a gift for his daughter. The package had remained intact until security inspected it at the airport in LA.

"Here I've come clear around the damn world, and nobody messed it up. Well, I get there, and this woman ripped the package all apart and then just handed it to me all tore up. I was so mad I jumped at her, and they almost put me in jail."

After calming down, taking a shower in the airport, shaving, and changing into a clean uniform, he boarded a delayed flight to Chicago, where he would miss his connection to Atlanta. Sully would spend the next twelve hours waiting for a flight at midnight.

"Well, I go walking down the concourse, and I've got all my gear, my sea bag, and I got a clothing bag. And here I'm going, my little ass carrying all this shit, and I'm walking down this concourse, and all of the sudden appears about eight damn guys—hippies, and they made like a horseshoe, talking all this shit—"

Sully stopped, put down his gear, and took off his belt.

"I had my damn belt buckle—that you could shave with that son of a bitch, and I said, 'Well, we're fixin' to kick some ass here.' At about that time, I have this damn hand slap me on my shoulder and about drove me down in the damn concrete."

As he prepared to fight again, this time on his own soil and against his fellow Americans, Sully turned around and looked up into the face of six-foot-nine, three-hundred-pound professional wrestler Blackjack Mulligan.

"Sergeant, I'll take care of this." The wrestler pulled Sully to his side.

"You know," Blackjack said, "when I was a corporal in the Marine Corps, we always took care of our sergeants."

The hippies froze, and then began to back away.

"All right, boys. You want something, I got it for you—"

"They started to take off," Sully said, *"and he says 'Come here!' And they just froze."*

Blackjack ordered the hippies to pick up Sully's gear and said, "Let's go," and all of them started to walk down the concourse.

"These guys are all meek now, and they ain't saying shit."

Blackjack's entourage arrived at the airport bar to find four tables near the glass window that offered a view of the runway. Blackjack approached a couple sitting in the middle.

"Would y'all mind moving? I am fixing to have a party for this man who just got back from Vietnam."

"Well, he put all them tables together, and he said, 'All right boys, sit down.' He called the waitress over, and he said, 'Ma'am, this here is one of our Marines that just got back from Vietnam. Whatever the hell he wants you get it, and it's on these boys right here.'

"We got drunker than shit. We had steaks and the whole nine yards. They stayed with me until they walked me down to the plane to leave. We were singing and carrying on, and we had become good friends."

After braving a lightning storm during his flight to Atlanta, Sully finally made it to the front door of his home in Jacksonville early the next morning. As he fumbled for his keys in his sea bag, the porch light came on.

"This big damn Indian opens the door, standing there in his underwear, and he's got a big ponytail. He's about six-foot-four," and he says, *"Who the hell are you?"*

"Who the hell are you, and what are you doing in my fucking house?"

"Well, this is my house. I bought it six months ago. You must be that sergeant that was in Vietnam."

"Yeah."

"Come on in, son. Me and you need to talk—"

As the man's wife made a breakfast of eggs, grits, bacon and coffee, the man explained how he had bought the home from Sully's wife, who had not only moved with their daughter but had sold off all of Sully's possessions.

"I didn't even have a change of underwear."

The man was kind enough to drive Sully to his parent's home later that morning.

Craig Sullivan retired from the Marine Corps in 1981, having attained the rank of master sergeant. In 1991, the Marines called him back to active duty for four months for service during Desert Storm. Craig remarried and showed unrelenting courage and tenderness toward his wife of thirty-two years, Barri, who passed away in 2007 after a painful struggle with ovarian cancer. In 2016, he lost a son, Tony, to a heart attack.

For his courageous leadership, determined fighting spirit, and selfless devotion to duty in taking command of 1st Platoon after the NVA wounded Lt Combs, Platoon Sgt Craig Sullivan received the Bronze Star with Combat "V" device. He passed away from cancer in 2020, and his family remembers him as a Marine's Marine, loving husband, father, grandfather, great-grandfather, uncle, brother, and friend.

"He possessed a profound contrast of toughness, hardened by war and the rigors of life with an affectionate, gentle compassion rarely concentrated in a single person," his obituary read. "Yet, most of all, he was ever-present. He was always there for his loved ones."

For his aggressive fighting spirit and superb leadership of his fire team in beating back two charges of at least thirty-five NVA who sought to breach the backside of the perimeter, Bill Moy received the Silver Star.

For heroic achievement in a combat zone, Fred Tancke received the Bronze Star with Combat "V" device, the recognition coming for Tancke in 2011, forty-three years after his efforts to save Armando Leal on the knoll. Tancke's lifelong friend and comrade in arms, Steve Lovejoy, was present at the long overdue award ceremony.

In October of 2022, as this second edition of *Swift Sword* was in the late writing stages, Tancke provided to the author valuable clarification with regard to 2nd platoon's battle, especially as it pertained to the heroic actions of Corpsman David Phelps. Tancke died of cancer in January 2023, as the new edition of *Swift Sword* neared release.

Having achieved the rank of lieutenant colonel, JD Murray, commander of Mike 3/5 on September 4, retired from the Marine Corps in 1986 after twenty-four years of service. In 2021, he served as national commander of the Legion of Valor, our nation's oldest veteran service organization comprised of recipients of the Medal of Honor, the Navy Cross, the Army Distinguished Service Cross, or the Air Force Cross.

Chuck Goebel, Murray's FAC who braved enemy fire with a strobe light to direct bombers to their targets on the night of September 4, went to work for the Gardena, California Police Department when he came home from Vietnam. Known affection- ately as the People's Captain, he contracted leukemia, the cancer most likely the result of exposure to Agent Orange, a caustic defoliant used during the war.

"All of us walked through Agent Orange every day," Goebel said. *"They used it as a weed killer around our fire bases. So we may not have been exposed to it by being dropped on us or near the aircraft, but we were walking in and out of that dust every day."*

A proud father and grandfather, blessed with a fifty-one year marriage to the love of his life, Christy, Goebel passed away from cancer in 2020. For his bravery on September 4, he received the Navy Commendation Medal.

"When I left Vietnam," Point Man Jack Swan said, *"it was kind of like I welded the door shut and wrapped chains around it with a huge bolt. I have had people say, 'You came out with three Purple Hearts. You are a hero!' I say, 'No, the dead are the heroes. I am a survivor.'"*

In 2004, Swan, along with other survivors of Operation Swift, returned to Vietnam's Quế Sơn Valley and walked the site of the bloody battle so many years before.

"My heart is with every one of our fallen brothers," he said as he stood on the knoll, "but my heart is the warmest right now for those of you surviving, and what you have done for yourself since Vietnam, and how far you have come."

"And that is the truth. That is where my pride is, is them carrying on."

That bond was very evident at one of the first reunions of Mike Company held many years after the war.

"There were six new people from the 2nd Platoon who had never been to any gathering," JD Murray said, *"and you couldn't break those six people apart. It was the first time they'd seen each other in*

forty years. Nobody else was involved because it was so special to them because those people meant so much to them."

"I remember being in that bomb crater that night, just dying of thirst," Ed Combs said, *"and, of course, nobody would give me any water. And when I met with these guys, you know it had been thirty-four, thirty-five, thirty-six years at that time, I said, 'You know, for thirty-six years, I have had this ongoing dream every night about this thing. I remember this Marine cradling me in his arms and holding a fan over my face, one of these little fans.'*

"When I said that, Jack says, 'That was no dream, Lieutenant—that was me! My mom had just sent me one of those little plastic fans with the battery. And I was holding you. I couldn't give you any water. I was just trying to keep you cool."

At one reunion, Jack Swan had a surprise for his former lieutenant.

"I presented him a box with blue velvet inside, a blue fan identical that I held, that little hand held one that my mother had sent me with the brass up top that said, 'To Lt. Ed Combs, from 1st Platoon Mike Company, your greatest fan!'"

In 2007, Swan learned for the first time that Howard Haney, the FNG caught in the rice paddy with him when the ambush hit, had survived his critical wounds. Haney stayed in touch with Swan, who he called his brother, until Swan passed away from cancer in 2017. After the war, Haney went into construction and, in 1978, went into business for himself as a general contractor in Southern California building custom homes. He moved to Idaho in 1992, retired in 2002, and is now enjoying life with his wife, Bev. After Vietnam, Tony Martinez became a critical care nurse. Now retired, he lives in Wisconsin, stays active, and involved in his church and church choir.

On the night of September 4, the corpsmen medevacked 1st Platoon commander Lt Ed Combs to Da Nang, where he underwent immediate surgery for the massive wound in his chest. He had a second surgery on the hospital ship USS Repose and a third at the Navy's Bethesda Hospital in Maryland.

"I remember coming to, and there were four Navy chaplains standing there. And they were all Catholic. And I wasn't Catholic."

"Did you ask Cpl Phillips to baptize you?" one asked.

"Yes."

"Did you ask Cpl Phillips to baptize you in the Catholic faith?"

"Commander, at the time I didn't really care. I just asked to be baptized."

"Did you know that Cpl Phillips baptized you in the Catholic faith?"

"No, I did not."

"Does it bother you that you were?"

"No. Why would it?"

For heroic and meritorious achievement in a combat zone on September 4, Combs received the Bronze Star with Combat "V." After the war, Combs attended law school at the University of Louisville, started a small-town legal practice, and tried to bury his memories of Vietnam.

"In my town, my friends would look at me like I was an idiot when I told them I served in the Marine Corps in Vietnam. Neither my wife nor my children knew much about what went on there because there was no reason to talk about it, but there has never been one day in my life that I have not thought about what happen on September 4 and of the Marines I was with."

"I always wondered after that, whatever happened to Combs,"

George Phillips said. *"Did he stay a good Catholic, or was this just an insurance policy in case he went south that night?"*

In November of 2009, George Phillips received a call from a Marine Corps friend.

"Do you know Ed Combs?"

"I baptized a Lt Combs—"

"He says he's been looking for you for forty years!"

The grievously wounded young lieutenant and the corporal who had baptized him spoke for the first time over the phone, more than forty-two years after the epic battle.

"For me," Phillips said, *"it was pretty emotional, and I'm not a big emotional guy, but that got to me. I was just really—I was glad to hear that he was okay. And you know, we went back through the story and to hear him talk about how it was, you don't realize something like that can have a big impact on people's lives. That was, for me, that was pretty amazing."*

"Are you still a Catholic?" Phillips asked.

"Oh yeah, I got married in the Catholic Church, my whole family is Catholic, my children are Catholic, and my baptismal certificate lists the minister as Cpl George Phillips."

As a fire team leader in Combs's 1st Platoon, despite heavy enemy fire and a fragmentation wound to his leg, George Phillips was instrumental in not only enforcing the platoon's defense but in maneuvering his team forward on five separate occasions to bring the wounded into the safety of the company perimeter. For heroic achievement in a combat zone on September 4, Phillips received the Bronze Star with Combat "V" and would receive a second Bronze Star for valor on Operation Essex two months later. He retired after thirty years of service in the Corps and served for six years as chairperson of the Father Capodanno Guild, which seeks canonization for the heroic Navy chaplain.

3rd Platoon Cmdr Randy Cernick survived the war but died of cancer in 2006. Don Goulet, a corporal in 3rd Platoon who would later work for the FBI, passed away in 2014. For Chuck Cummings, a squad leader in Cernick's platoon, Swift was the third and worst of the 1967 Quế Sơn Valley battles.

"It showed the best of Marine infantry, airmen, air support, both enlisted and officer, and also the wonderful Navy Corpsmen: could not have been more proud to be with them."

"When I went to Vietnam," Ed Blecksmith said, *"I had one goal in mind: survive and come home, and I wasn't alone. Almost everybody I knew: that was their prime motivation."*

Despite mistakes made by the Corps, Blecksmith knew that the combat experience of Lt Murray and the training of the Marines are what made the difference between life and death on September 4.

"Everybody performed beautifully, the way they're trained to perform," he said. *"They were amazing men. I owe my life to them, and each of us owes their life to each other and the grace of God."*

Because of the randomness of death in battle, why some men die and others survive, Blecksmith has been motivated to live his life to the utmost for those who didn't come home from Vietnam.

"All you can do is dedicate yourself to live your life to its highest degree to honor those that didn't make it."

One of Blecksmith's greatest regrets was not contacting the families of those men whom he knew had been killed in Vietnam. He didn't fully appreciate their loss until his own son, 2nd Lt James Patrick Blecksmith, died by enemy fire in Fallujah, Iraq, in November 2004.

"I was never mad or angry with my enemy," Carlton Clark remembered. *"I loved the Vietnamese people. I had no problems with them whatsoever."*

Clark never wanted to be in a situation to kill others, but when forced to fight he had to defend himself and because of the vision he had on the battlefield, he has grown closer to God. *"There's been plenty of guys that's been to war and had terrible experiences, but I feel that one of the main things that I wanted to bring out was how God plays a part in our lives and how he's really there, whether we see him or not."*

"Many Marines went to war as innocent youth and returned home with both youth and innocence forever taken from them," Steve Lovejoy said. *"Upon my discharge, I was very disappointed with the way the Vietnam conflict ended. I felt that all of our casualties were wasted."*

Nick Duca and Donald Baima echoed Lovejoy's sentiment.

"The war always lives inside of you," Duca said, *"the hurt, and what you see, and what you experience. It's always there: the hurt, the pain. No matter how hard we try and no matter how productive we become in life and the things we accomplish, that era will never leave you because it's horrifying. It's horrifying. And to see what happened to your friends. God, it's horrible."*

"I spent years trying to forget it all, you know, doing my darnedest not to remember it," Ryan Hooley said. *"It never works, but I really try hard. I think every guy that went to Vietnam, a Marine, came home with post stress syndrome. I lay awake at night hearing machine guns, explosions, and mortars."*

Even though he did his best to put the war behind him, one night on duty as a Massachusetts state police officer would open old wounds for Donald Baima. After arresting a man for driving while intoxicated, the individual complained, "as he was a veteran who had served his country."

"I am also a veteran," Baima said, "and being a veteran doesn't give you the right to endanger others."

"What war did you fight in?" the man asked.

"Vietnam."

"Yeah, but I was in a war that we won."

Those cutting words would haunt Baima for many years to come.

"I'm still upset about walking away from that war," he said. *"Communism was a threat to the free world and threatened our way of life, our freedom, and I think that the four of us who joined the Marines together felt that way. We were definitely convinced that we were doing the right thing. We felt very patriotic about joining, and it is a shame that we just gave up and walked away."*

Donald Baima retired from the Massachusetts State Police and, at age seventy-five, still works for the US Marshals Service as a court security officer.

"I was very idealistic, and I felt that what we were doing was correct," JD Murray said, *"but I didn't have a view of everything. I wonder now, in hindsight, whether our government would ever have gotten involved as deeply as they did or how they did, if they, in fact, knew everything, as we found out later."*

In 2004, when Murray and other veterans of Swift returned to Vietnam and spoke with former members of the NVA, they were surprised to learn that many of the Vietnamese who they had fought against were not from the north but were actually from the south and more specifically from the region where the battles occurred.

"These South Vietnamese had gone north in the fifties and early sixties, believed in Communism, believed in uniting the country into one Vietnam, and viewed the rulers in South Vietnam as despots who

filled their own pockets with money at the expense of the people. These men would act as an advance guard for large NVA units who came south to their home areas in 1966 and 1967.

"*We called them North Vietnamese, but they were really South Vietnamese fighting for the north in their own territory. The Quế Sơns were a good example. If you are a Vietnamese villager in the Quế Sơn someplace and you have two options, to assist these white and black foreign people coming in or working with people that speak your language, look like you, some are you, and who are trying to help you out, which way would you go? Then, if you complicate that with some of the bombing that occurred, the killings. Wow! There is no doubt in my mind which way I would go.*

"*We never knew who was the good guy and who was the bad guy. In hindsight, it certainly makes things look a lot different than when we were over there fighting for our country, thinking we're doing everything correctly when, in reality, we were screwed from the very beginning.*"

Murray confirmed this sentiment when he and other veterans visited the knoll in 2004 and viewed gravestones scattered across the site.

"*I saw graves,*" Murray said, "*with September 1967 on them, which led me to believe that there were some locals who joined up with the Viet Cong. That entire area, almost every man, woman, and child in the entire Quế Sơns did not have a close affiliation with the South Vietnamese government.*"

"*I like to think I'm proud that I served, but I still have my reservations about our government,*" Dennis Tylinski said. "*Looking back at it years later, I remember being in boot camp and the drill instructor, as we're standing out there in the parade deck looking at Old Glory, and he'd say how we were to 'Stop them communists from coming into our country. We're to kill communists, stop them from making your mothers whores and your girlfriends whores, this and that, blah, blah, blah—'*

"*And boy, you get that lump in your throat, and the flag is flying up there, and now that I look at it years later, we fought there for ten years, fifty thousand people are dead, and we gave it back to the communists. So, I have a problem with that. I'm proud I served, but I'd never do it again. Under those circumstances, I would never do it again.*"

For Baima, it was John F. Kennedy who, in his inaugural dress as president in 1961, inspired him and countless other young idealistic Americans to enlist in the fight against communism. Kennedy's call, more than any other has, speaks to the true and noble legacy of the men who fought and died in the Vietnam War.

"Let every nation know, whether it wishes us well or ill, that we shall pay any price, bear any burden, meet any hardship, support any friend, oppose any foe to assure the survival and the success of liberty."

"*To put it all in perspective,*" Bill Vandergriff said, "*it seems now such a total waste, as all wars are. There was so much lost potential, so many young dying men. That granite wall in DC represents some of the finest young men that ever walked on the face of this earth. The war was something that our country asked us to do, but we did not fight for our country. We did not fight for mom's apple pie or any of that bullshit. We fought for each other. We took care of each other. That's who we fought for.*"

MAPS

Figure 1: Quế Sơn Valley Area Of Operations

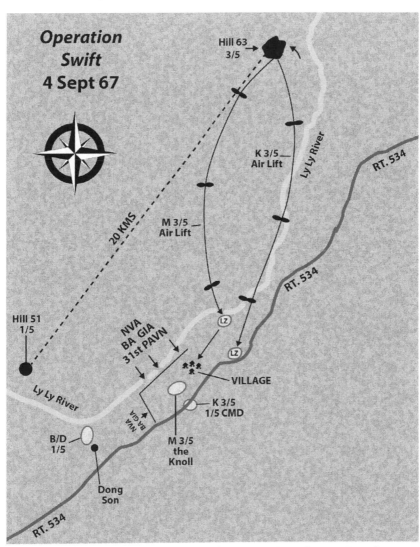

Que Son Valley area of operations for Marine Battalions 1/5 and 3/5 at the time of the ambush of M 3/5 on the knoll, 4 September 1967

Figure 2: Distance Map

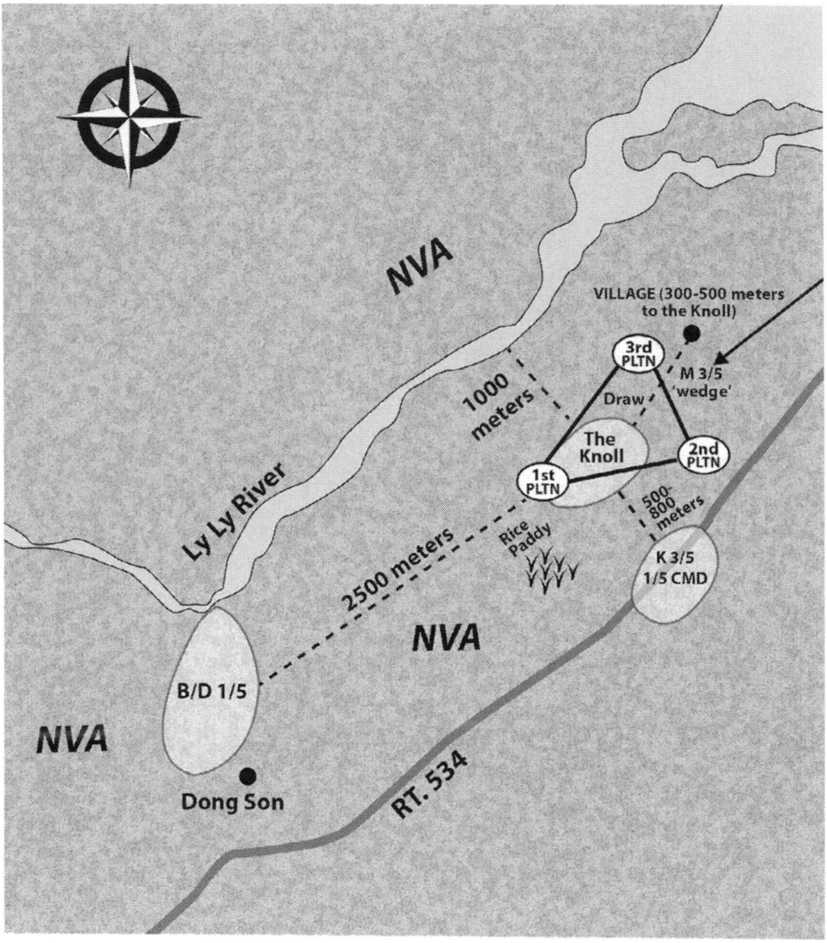

Approximate distances at the time of the
NVA ambush of M 3/5, 4 September 1967

Figure 3: Positions of Mike 3/5 at moment of ambush

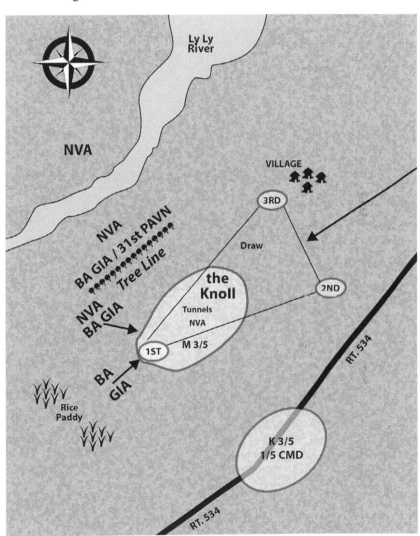

Positions of M 3/5 platoons, K 3/5 and 1/5 Command
at the moment of the NVA ambush, 4 September 1967

Figure 4: Sergeant Peters' Attack

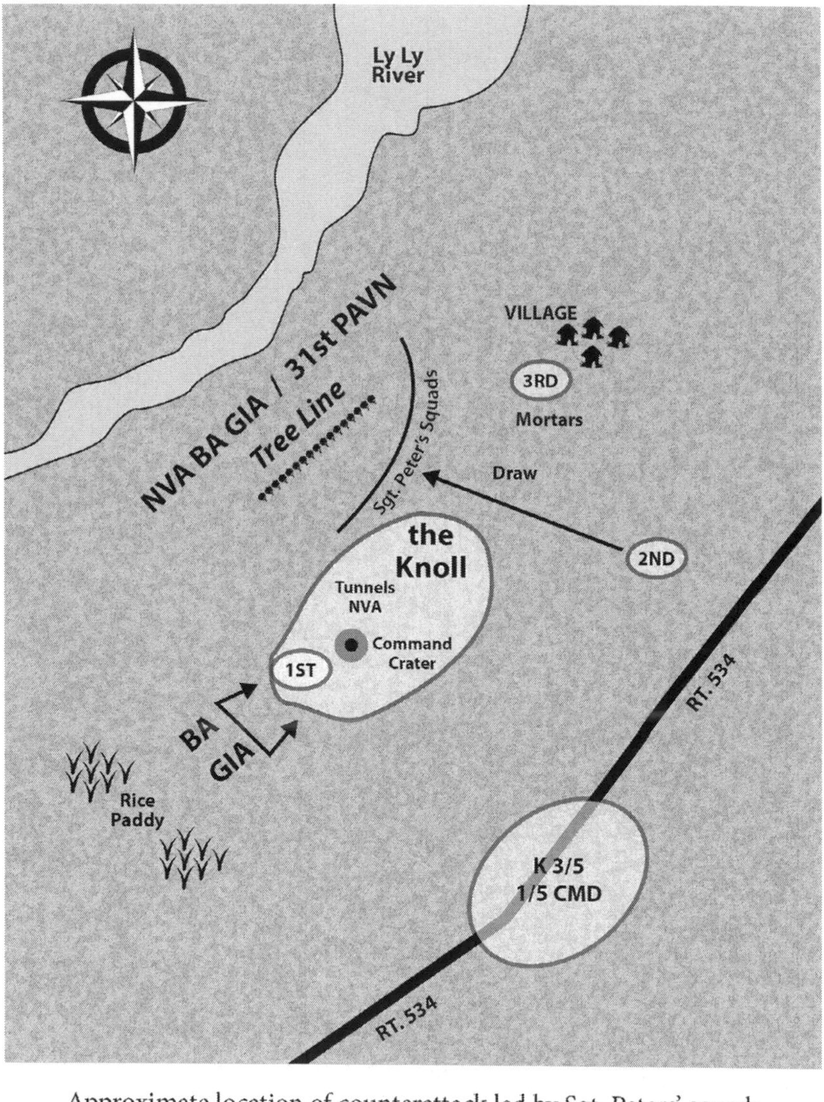

Approximate location of counterattack led by Sgt. Peters' squads
from 2nd platoon on NVA hidden in tree line shortly
after the ambush of 1st platoon, 4 September 1967

Figure 5: NVA counterattack on Sergeant Peters' squads

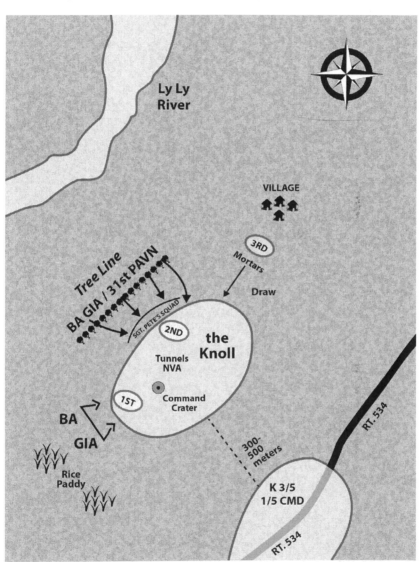

NVA units previously hidden in tree line attempt to envelop Sgt. Peters' outnumbered Marines and pierce the company perimeter before M 3/5 can consolidate on the knoll, 4 September 1967

Figure 6: Approximate Location of Mike 3/5 perimeter at dusk

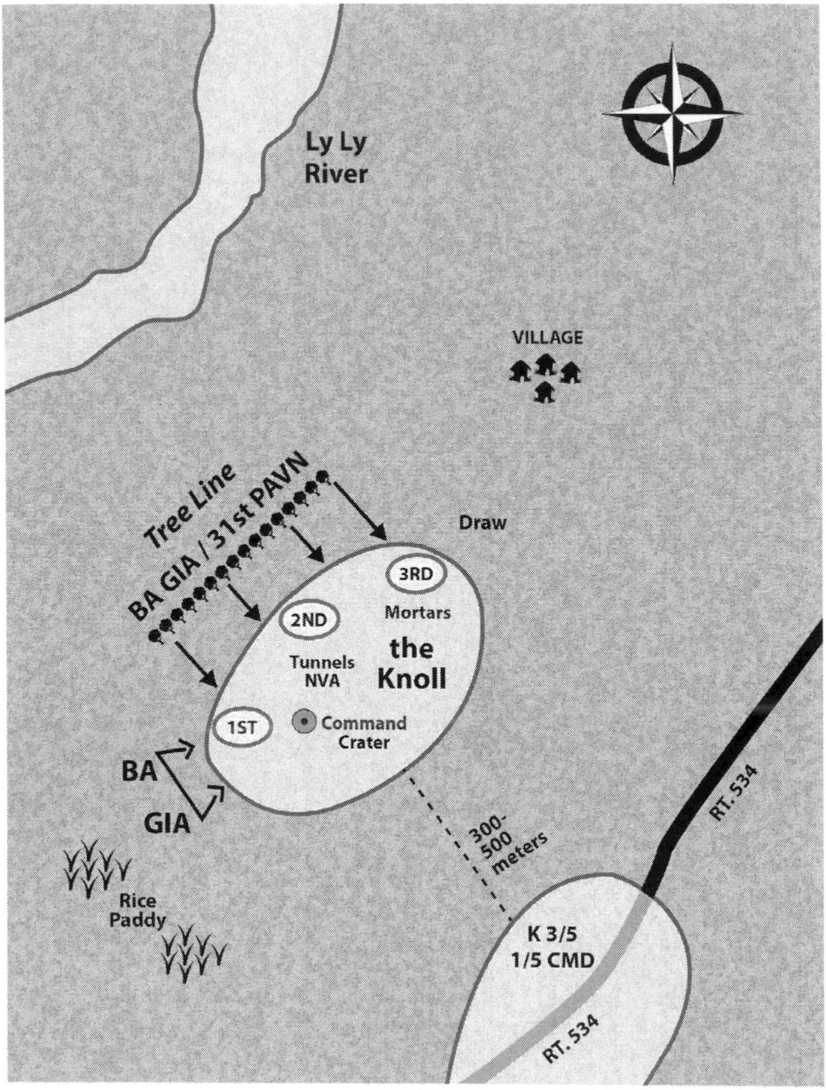

Approximate location of defense of M 3/5, with repeated attempts
of NVA to pierce the perimeter, near dusk on 4 September 1967

In Memoriam

Operation Swift began on 4 September 1967 and would last eleven days, claiming the lives of 127 US Marines and Navy Corpsmen as well as approximately 600 PAVN (North Vietnamese Army) troops. The purpose of this Memorial Page is to give a face to those Americans who lost their lives on the 4th and who are mentioned in the pages of this book.

Capt. Robert Morgan,
Delta 1/5

LCpl. Thomas W. Fisher,
Mike 3/5, First Platoon

LCpl. Richard Guerrero, Jr.,
Mike 3/5, First Platoon

Pfc. Gene Mortenson,
Mike 3/5, First Platoon

LCpl. Jack Berry,
Mike 3/5, Second Platoon

Lt. Vincent R. Capodanno,
Catholic Priest,
3/5 Battalion Chaplain

LCpl. Steve Cornell,
Mike 3/5, Second Platoon

Pfc. Dennis Fisher,
Mike 3/5, Second Platoon

LCpl. Andrew Giordano,
Mike 3/5, Second Platoon

Pfc. Raymond Hengels,
Mike 3/5, Second Platoon

Hn. Armando Leal,
Mike 3/5, Second Platoon

Pfc. Charles Martin,
Mike 3/5, Second Platoon

Pfc. James McKenzie,
Mike 3/5, Second Platoon

Sgt. Lawrence D. Peters,
Mike 3/5, Second Platoon

Hn. David C. Phelps,
Mike 3/5, Second Platoon

LCpl. Albert Santos,
Mike 3/5, Second Platoon

Pfc. Steven Wright,
Mike 3/5, Second Platoon

Cpl. Bill Young,
Mike 3/5, Second Platoon

Pfc. Tony Gabaldon,
Mike 3/5, Third Platoon

Editor's note: This is just a partial list of the 127 brave Marines and Corpsmen killed in action during Operation Swift. We honor their service and ultimate sacrifice.

ACKNOWLEDGMENTS

This account of the opening battle of Operation Swift could not have come together, much less be told, without the contributions of numerous individuals who helped shape it into book form for the general reader.

I would first like to thank my wonderful wife, Somer, my three incredible children Jake, Atty, and Myra Lee, and my mother, Myra. Without their love and constant support, I could not have written this new edition of *Swift Sword*. I am eternally grateful to my family for helping me make this book a reality.

I extend my deepest appreciation to my editor, Cynde Christie, whose wisdom and expertise helped mold a confusing and disjointed story into a cohesive and readable whole that is true to the historical record. To my book designer, Nick Zelinger, who not only supervised the layout but also helped create the maps of *Swift,* cover designer, Jun Ares, and copy editor, Jen Marshall, go my deepest thanks. I would also like to thank Jack Arnold, creator of my website and responsible for my social media presence and marketing gurus Rob Eagar and Kathy Lowenstern for their advice and support.

My greatest thanks, however, is reserved for JD Murray, commander of Mike 3/5 on Operation Swift, and to the fifty-one survivors of the operation who granted me the honor of interviewing them about the trauma of personal and deadly combat, an experience that haunts many to this day. Without their help and trust in me, I never could have told their story and the story of their comrades who lost their lives on Operation Swift. Without their words, *Swift Sword* would never exist.

GLOSSARY

3.5-inch Rocket Launcher: See Rocket Launcher, 3.5-inch.

782 Gear: See Individual Equipment.

Absent Without Leave (AWOL): The act of being AWOL, the subject of a punitive article (Article 86) of the Uniform Code of Military Justice, which proscribes unauthorized absence: "Any member of the Armed Forces who, without authority—

(1) fails to go to his appointed place of duty at the time prescribed;

(2) goes from that place; or

(3) absents himself or remains absent from his unit, organization, or place of duty at which he is required to be at the time prescribed shall be punished as a court-martial may direct."

Agent Orange: An air-delivered defoliant used on forested areas of South Vietnam in order to reduce the amount of overhead concealment of enemy ground forces.

Air Strike: Aerial delivery of ordnance on a selected target. See Close Air Support.

AK-47: The standard 7.62mm Kalashnikov assault rifle used by the military of the Warsaw Pact countries and their Communist Bloc allies, including China and North Vietnam.

Amphibious Ready Group: A small task force of three or four amphibious ships and their embarked battalion landing team (reinforced) of Marines.

Amphibious Reconnaissance School: There were two such schools at the time, one located at Landing Force Training Center, Pacific, Coronado, California, and the other at Little Creek, Virginia. Both schools screened and prepared Marines to conduct long-distance swims in open seas from small boats, submarines, or via helicopter insertion in order to conduct beach reconnaissance, off-beach reconnaissance, and hydrographic surveys to evaluate the suitability of beaches (and their gradients) as sites for potential amphibious landing by Marine or other forces.

Amphibious Warfare School: A six-month long Marine Corps formal school (then located at Quantico) intended for captains of all MOSs where the curriculum focuses on the planning, organizing, and conduct of amphibious and other infantry operations.

Amtrac: Acronym for amphibious tractor.

Armor Support: The use by infantry of tanks and amphibious tractors in support of any ground operation.

Army of the Republic of Vietnam (ARVN): The South Vietnamese Army.

Artillery: Large caliber weapons, such as cannons or howitzers, that are operated by crews and used to support infantry units/ organizations engaged in ground combat or to deny the use of an area to the enemy.

Assault, Frontal: The most basic of offensive tactics—attacking directly at the enemy usually because the terrain permits a rapid advance of the attacking force and is normally conducted in concert with a supporting artillery barrage or a base of high volume machine gun fire.

Aviator, Naval: See Naval Aviator.

Base of Fire: A force that gives support to the advance or attack of other units with its fire.

Basic School, The (TBS): The school at Quantico, Virginia, (Camp Barrett) where the five- to six-month course for newly commissioned second lieutenants is conducted—all Marine Corps officers who have just graduated from the Naval Academy, Officer Candidates School, Platoon Leaders Class, and NROTC attend this school to learn the basics of being a Marine Corps infantry platoon commander.

Battalion (Infantry): An organization normally composed of a headquarters and service (H&S) company and four "letter" companies, e.g. 1st Battalion: H&S, Alpha, Bravo, Charlie, and Delta companies (or batteries in an artillery battalion). 2nd Battalion: H&S, Echo, Foxtrot, Golf, and Hotel companies (or batteries in an artillery battalion), and 3rd Battalion: H&S, India, Kilo, Lima, and Mike companies (or batteries in an artillery battalion).

Battle Dressing: Large sterile bandages carried in individual first aid kits and by Navy corpsmen in their unit one(s).

Blocking Force: A stationary force against which a sweeping ground force pushes an enemy force in order to trap them between the two forces.

Boondockers: A combat boot with a shortened leather upper originally issued during WWII and worn with leggings—issued without leggings in the '50s and early '60s instead of a second pair of regular, high-topped combat boots.

Boot Camp: A euphemism for Marine Corps recruit training.

Bronze Star (with Combat "V"): The Bronze Star Medal is awarded to any person who, while serving in any capacity in the military of the United States, distinguishes himself by heroic or meritorious achievement or service, not involving participation in aerial flight, while engaged in an action against an enemy of the United States. The Combat "V" or Combat Distinguishing Device, when attached to the ribbon of the medal, denotes those individuals awarded the decoration because of direct combat with an enemy force.

Buddy Plan: An enlistment incentive that allowed friends to join the Marine Corps together and stay together through basic training.

Bug Juice: Government-issued insect repellent: it came in small, individual, plastic bottles.

C-4: A high quality, very high velocity military plastic explosive.

C-130: The Lockheed C-130 Hercules is a four-engine turboprop aircraft used as the primary tactical airlifter for military forces worldwide, capable of landing and taking off from short or unprepared runways. It was used as a troop transport, cargo carrier, aerial re-fueler, and gunship (Spooky) in Vietnam.

C-141: The primary strategic lift aircraft used by Military Airlift Command during the 1960s, 1970s, and 1980s. The C-141

Starlifter was a four-engine jet aircraft used for personnel and logistics transport.

C-Ration: Meal, Combat Individual (C-Ration) was the name of the field rations issued to Marines and Navy Hospital corpsmen in Vietnam. The ration consisted of a canned entrée (one of a dozen varieties), canned fruit, a B-2 unit containing cheese, crackers, and candy, and an accessory pack containing a can opener, a mix for a hot beverage, salt and sugar packets, a plastic spoon, chewing gum, a packet of four cigarettes, and several sheets of toilet paper.

Camp Geiger: Located near Camp Lejeune, North Carolina, it was the home of the Marine Corps' East Coast Infantry Training Regiment.

Camp Hansen: One of the Marine camps at Okinawa, Japan, it was used as a temporary stop for Marines en route to Vietnam and for those Marines who had completed their tour in Vietnam and were headed back to the United States.

Camp Lejeune: Located near Jacksonville, North Carolina, Camp Lejeune (named for Lieutenant General John Archer Lejeune, USMC, and the thirteenth commandant of the Marine Corps) is the historical home of the 2nd Marine Division.

Camp Pendleton: Located between Oceanside and San Clemente, California, Camp Pendleton (named for Major General Joseph H. Pendleton, USMC, who long advocated for a West Coast base for Marines) is the historical home (since WWII) of the 1st Marine Division.

Camp San Onofre: Located on the northwest corner of Camp Pendleton, it was the home of the Marine Corps' West Coast Infantry Training Regiment.

Candidate: An officer trainee who is undergoing the very rigorous and demanding training, evaluation, and screening process at the Marine Corps Officer Candidates School at Quantico, Virginia. The eleven-week process is designed to determine if the candidate has the requisite moral, intellectual, physical, and leadership potential to become a leader of Marines who is capable of handling the tremendous responsibilities of leading men in combat.

Caribbean Cruise (Also Known as Carib Cruise): A six-month deployment to the area of the Caribbean Sea by a Marine battalion landing team embarked aboard the vessels of a Navy amphibious ready group.

Chieu Hoi: A Viet Cong or NVA who accepted amnesty in exchange for his surrender. The phrase "Chieu Hoi" is a combination of two verbs "to welcome" and "to return." Those accepting the amnesty were frequently used as scouts (Kit Carson's) to lead US and ARVN forces to enemy supply bases and strongholds.

China Beach: A beach on the East China Sea just east of the city of Da Nang for in- country R&R provided to Marine Corps and other personnel.

Chinese Communist Grenades (Chicom): The general term used for enemy grenades fashioned in the manner of those manufactured by the People's Republic of China (communist China).

Chop Op Con: CHange OPerational CONtrol meaning an organization is removed from the operational control of their parent headquarters and placed under the operational control of another headquarters.

Claymore Mine (M18): A directional fragmentation mine, 8-1/2 inches long, 1-3/8 inches wide, 3-1/4 inches high, and weighing 3-1/2 pounds. The mine contained seven hundred steel spheres (10.5 grains) and 1-1/2 pound layer of composition C-4 explosive and was initiated by a No. 2 electric blasting cap. The M18 command-detonated mine was employed with obstacles or on the approaches, forward edges, flanks, and rear edges of protective minefields as close-in protection against a dismounted infantry attack. The mine propels a fan-shaped pattern of steel balls in a sixty-degree horizontal arc with a maximum height of 6.6 feet (two meters) and has a casualty radius of 328 feet (one hundred meters).

Close Air Support: Gun/cannon fire, rockets, bombs, and other ordnance delivered in very close proximity to friendly troops by friendly aircraft. Nobody is better at it than Marine aviators who train to be infantry platoon commanders before they attend flight school. Marine close air support was first demonstrated in Nicaragua during the Banana War era and was perfected during WWII and Korea. Close air support is also the reason each Marine division (1st, 2nd, 3rd and 4th*) is supported by a separate Marine aircraft wing (1st, 2nd, 3rd and 4th*) dedicated to providing fixed-wing and rotary wing (helicopter) aircraft support of ground combat forces. *The 4th Marine Division and 4th Marine Aircraft Wing are the Marine Corps' Reserve.

Close Order Drill: The procedure used to move a unit from one place to another in a standard, orderly manner while maintaining the best appearance possible and simultaneously teaching or reinforcing discipline by instilling habits of precision and automatic response to orders.

Code of Conduct: The six articles of the Code of Conduct define the serviceman's obligation while serving in combat and enumerate those things he may do or say, and conversely, may not do and may not say, if captured by the enemy.

Color Company (US Naval Academy): Of the thirty-six companies of Midshipman at the academy in any one year, the color company is the one that demonstrates through the accomplishments of its members that it has no peer in terms of its collective achievements in academics, professional skills, and athletics.

Combat Correspondent: Someone whose primary role is to observe combat operations and then record those observations in writing for public release, the historical record, and research purposes.

Combat Photographer: Someone whose primary role is to photograph (still photo or motion picture) combat operations for public release, the historical record, and research purposes.

Command Post (CP): A military headquarters, static or mobile, for a command group and its officers during an operation.

Command-Detonated Explosive: An explosive device, the detonation of which is initiated electronically or by other means by the person who implanted it or by someone acting as that person's agent.

Commissioned Officer: One who has been given a commission by the Congress of the United States to perform certain duties. Commissioned officers derive authority directly from the government and, as such, hold a commission charging them with the duties and responsibilities of a specific office or position. Commissioned officers are the only persons in the military authorized to exercise command (according to the most technical definition of the word) over a military unit.

Company: A unit comprised of a number of platoons, normally commanded by a captain, and the lowest level at which non-judicial punishment (Article 15 of the UCMJ) can be meted out.

Company Patrol Base: A piece of defensible terrain, normally fortified with earthen berms or sandbags, from which a company-size unit conducts day and night patrols of varying sizes in order to maintain observation or control over a much larger area.

Company Executive Officer (XO): Normally the second senior officer in the company; the second in command of that company.

Communism: The Marxist-Leninist version of communist doctrine that advocates the overthrow of capitalism by the revolution of the proletariat; a system of government in which the state plans and controls the economy and a single, often authoritarian, party holds power, claiming to make progress toward a higher social order in which all goods are equally shared by the people. A theoretical economic system characterized by the collective ownership of property and by the organization of labor for the common advantage of all members, communism is a form of socialism that abolishes private property and favors collectivism in a classless society.

Confidence Course: A series of high obstacles that must be negotiated by the individual Marine; successful completion builds an individual's self-confidence while teaching military skills.

Connecting File: The skirmish line of infantrymen that extends from the main body of a tactical formation to its flank security in order to maintain physical or visual contact.

Con Thien: A reinforced battalion-sized outpost located on a small cluster of hills (518- feet high) just south of the demilitarized zone. Con Thien was also the northwest corner of Leatherneck Square. (Dong Ha, Cam Lo, and Gio Linh represented the other three corners).

Cover Man: The infantryman, often a machine gunner, positioned immediately behind the point man in a tactical formation.

Daisy Chain: A series of explosive devices connected together by a common initiating device, e.g. detonation cord.

Da Nang: The major city in the I Corps area of South Vietnam. It had a large port, the largest airfield in I Corps, and was the home of III MAF, 1st Marine Division, 1st Marine Aircraft Wing, and Force Logistics Command headquarters.

Dear John Letter: A letter from a girlfriend back home telling her Marine she's found somebody else or is breaking off their relationship for some other reason.

Defense, Platoon: The tactical emplacement of a platoon's men and weaponry on a piece of terrain in order to defend against an enemy attack from the front, the flanks, or the rear.

Delayed Entry Program: A program which allowed young men to enlist in the Marine Corps but delay their departure for recruit training for some period after enlistment.

Demilitarized Zone (DMZ): An area, usually the frontier or boundary between two or more groups, where military activity is not permitted, usually by treaty or other agreement. Often the demilitarized zone lies upon a line of control and forms a de-facto international border.

Distinguished Flying Cross: A medal awarded to a member of the United States Armed Forces who distinguishes himself in combat in support of operations by "heroism or extraordinary achievement while participating in an aerial flight."

Division: Any one of the Marine Corps four infantry commands consisting of a headquarters battalion, three infantry regiments, an artillery regiment, and a tank battalion, amtrac battalion, engineer battalion, shore party battalion, reconnaissance battalion, motor transport battalion, and medical battalion (1967 T/O).

Dong Ha: Located at the junction of Highways 1 (north-south) and 9 (east-west). Dong Ha was part of four Marine combat bases that formed a quadrilateral extending about twelve miles south from the eastern DMZ area to the Cua Viet River at Dong Ha. The quadrilateral was known as Leatherneck Square and included Dong Ha, Cam Lo, Con Thien, and Gio Lin.

Drill Instructor (DI): The highly selected and highly trained non-commissioned officer or staff non-commissioned officer charged with the basic training of Marine recruits during the recruits' first three months in the Marine Corps.

Envelopment: A military tactic characterized by feinting an attack to the enemy's front while actually attacking from either of his flanks or both flanks (a double envelopment).

Esprit de Corps: A common spirit of comradeship, enthusiasm, and devotion to a cause among the members of the group. It implies devotion and loyalty to the Marine Corps, with deep regard for its history, traditions, and honor.

Executive Officer (XO): The officer second-in-command at company, battalion, or regimental level (same for Marine aviation squadrons and Marine air groups).

Field Gear: Also known as 782 Gear because of the form number of the receipt the Marine signs with the issuance of the gear. It includes items such as the helmet, helmet liner, camouflaged helmet cover, flak jacket, H-harness, equipment belt, canteens, canteen covers, first aid packet, ammo pouches, poncho, poncho liner, haversack, knapsack, entrenching tool, shelter half, bayonet (or KA-Bar fighting knife for those armed with a pistol instead of a rifle), etc.

Field Medical School (a.k.a. Field Med School): After completing hospital corps school, corpsmen who are to serve with Marines are required to successfully complete field med school, where they learn to perform their first aid and medical treatment functions in a field environment rather than a hospital.

Field Hospital: A large, mobile, expeditionary medical hospital unit, which resides in tents or tent-like structures, that treats and cares for casualties of war and offers many of the same services available in fixed hospitals.

Field of Fire: The area around a weapon (or group of weapons) that can be easily and effectively reached (in terms of range and declination) by gunfire from that (those) weapon(s).

Fighting Hole: A hole a soldier digs into the ground (foxhole) and is sometimes surrounded by a berm or sandbags, which provides some level of protection from direct fire weapons.

Fire Direction Center: Consisting of gunnery and communications personnel and equipment, the fire direction center receives target information and requests for fire and translates them into appropriate firing solutions in terms of range, azimuth (also called deflection), propellant charges, ammunition type, fuse settings, etc. that are passed to the firing batteries for execution.

Fire for Effect: The volume of fire (normally defined in terms of the number of artillery pieces or mortar tubes), duration of fire. or the number of rounds delivered on a specific point or area target in order to achieve the desired effect, e.g. Battery Six equals six rounds per each of the six artillery pieces in a battery or thirty-six rounds fired in rapid succession on the same target.

Firefight: The gunfire, normally small arms, exchanged by two opposing units in relatively close proximity to one another.

Fire Team: The smallest of infantry units (three fire teams to a squad) consisting of a fire team leader, an automatic rifleman, an assistant automatic rifleman, and a rifleman.

Fire Team Leader: The title of the leader of this smallest of Marine infantry units.

Flak Jacket: A sleeveless jacket holding protective plates of fiberglass bonded with resin that cover the chest, back, and abdomen. The jacket was designed to limit the damage done to the wearer's torso from the fragmentation produced by small explosives (hand grenades and small millimeter mortar rounds).

Flank: The right or left side of a military or naval formation.

Flank Security: That element of a tactical formation that extends out laterally to the left and the right from the main body to provide early warning of an enemy attack from that area.

Forward Air Controller (FAC): The FAC is normally the senior member of the TACP. An officer and designated naval aviator, he is the ground commander's advisor on the use of air assets. Utilizing the UHF communications capability of the TACP, he talks directly to the pilots of supporting aircraft to alert them to wind conditions and obstacles on the ground. He identifies ground targets and recommends run-in and roll-out headings for attacking aircraft.

Forward Observer (FO): An artilleryman or mortar man who accompanies an infantry unit to the field to request artillery or mortar fire support and then adjusts the artillery or mortar fire onto the target. He also plans defensive fire support in advance of actually needing it by plotting on-call fire missions.

Forward Observer, Artillery (a.k.a. Arty FO): That member of an artillery unit attached to an infantry unit for the purpose of requesting and adjusting offensive or defensive artillery fire and plotting pre-planned defensive artillery fire.

Forward Observer, Mortars: That mortar man attached to an infantry platoon or company for the purpose of requesting and adjusting offensive or defensive mortar fire and plotting pre-planned defensive mortar fire.

Foxhole: See Fighting Hole.

Free-Fire Zone: An area defined by map coordinates or prominent terrain features within which a unit/organization may fire without coordination with adjacent units/organizations and without permission from a higher headquarters.

Friendly Fire: A term used in reference to an attack on friendly forces by other friendly forces, which may be deliberate (e.g.

incorrectly identifying the target as the enemy) or accidental (e.g. missing the enemy and hitting "friendlies"). It is also known as blue on blue, which derives from mapping protocols where friendly forces are depicted on maps in "blue" and enemy forces are depicted in "red." The term "fratricide" can be applied if friendly forces are killed by friendly fire.

Galley: A kitchen aboard a naval ship or the food preparation area of a Marine mess hall.

Grenadier: The member of a Marine rifle squad armed with the M79 40mm grenade launcher.

Grenade, Concussion: A hand grenade packed with a significant amount of explosive and designed to kill through over-pressurization with the expanding gasses of the explosion within an enclosed or confined area, e.g. a tunnel or pill box.

Grenade, Fragmentation: A hand grenade whose serrated body or fragmentation coil is intend to fragment upon detonation and kill or injure with that fragmentation when those fragments impact the soft tissues of the human body.

Grenade Launcher, M79: A Marine rifle squad weapon resembling a short rifle with a very large bore barrel capable of launching a 40mm high explosive grenade out to a maximum of range of 300 meters.

Grunt: A euphemism for infantryman or anyone with an 03 MOS.

Guantanamo Bay: The oldest US Naval base located outside the continental United States, initially leased as a coal fueling station on the southeast coast of Cuba in 1903 with the acquisition subsequently formalized in a treaty ratified that same year.

Guard Duty: Performed at posts and stations around the world, a four-hour watch conducted for security purposes.

Guerilla: A member of an irregular force, usually an indigenous military or paramilitary unit operating in small bands in occupied territory, fighting a stronger force by sabotage and harassment.

Guidon Bearer, Platoon: The individual who carries the platoon's guidon during close order drill training, parades, and ceremonies, including recruit graduations.

Gun Target Line: An imaginary straight line from the gun to the target.

Gung Ho: An abbreviation for the Mandarin Chinese gongye hezhoushe, the phrase was clipped to the initial characters of the two words, "gung ho," which means, "work together." This clipping became the rallying cry for Marine Lieutenant Colonel Evans Carlson and his 2nd Marine Raider Battalion early in WWII and, by late 1942, was widely adopted throughout the Marine Corps as an expression of spirit, enthusiasm, and dedication" a can-do attitude.

Gunnery Sergeant (Gunny): A staff non-commissioned officer senior to a staff sergeant but junior to a first sergeant or master sergeant.

Hai Lang National Forest: A national forest located southwest of Quang Tri and northwest of Hue City in the I Corps area of South Vietnam.

Haiphong Harbor: The major seaport in North Vietnam used by communist bloc shipping throughout the war to deliver munitions to their allies in North Vietnam.

Hammer and Anvil: A tactic where a maneuvering ground force (the hammer) pushes the enemy back into a static ground force or terrain feature (the anvil) in order to surround and destroy the enemy with minimal numbers of enemy escaping the two forces.

Hanoi Hannah: An English-speaking female North Vietnamese radio personality who regularly broadcasted communist propaganda messages over the airwaves to US troops in South Vietnam, much the same as did Axis Sally (Germany) and Tokyo Rose (Japan) during WWII.

Helicopter Support Team (HST): Small groups of Shore Party personnel organized into teams that provide terminal guidance to helicopters landing in a HLZ. They also provide rigging for external lift by helicopters of equipment and supplies to forward areas.

Hippie: A term used to describe the rebellious youth of the 1960s and 1970s who opposed and rejected many of the conventional standards and customs of society. They eschewed Western middle class values and advocated extreme liberalism in sociopolitical attitudes and lifestyles, marked by resenting authority. They also advocated for legalized drug use and unlimited sexual expression.

Ho Chi Minh: The charismatic communist political leader of North Vietnam whose goal was the reunification of North and South Vietnam under communist rule.

Hoi An: A Vietnamese city located approximately twenty-five miles southeast of Da Nang.

Hollywood Marine: An ungenerous reference proffered by MCRD Parris Island-trained Marines about those Marines from the western half of the nation who received their basic training at MCRD San Diego.

Hooch (or Hootch): A makeshift dwelling fashioned from available materials, e.g. ponchos, shelter halves, et al. The term also refers to individual Vietnamese huts in a village.

Horseshoe, The: The name of a company patrol base north of Hoi An named for the geographical feature where it was located. It was on a piece of terrain similar in shape to that of a horseshoe surrounded and outlined by an inland waterway.

Hospital Corps School: The Navy formal school where new Navy corpsmen received hands-on clinical training in first aid and patient care.

Ia Drang Valley: The Ia Drang Valley is a valley located in the Central Highlands of South Vietnam and was the site on November 14, 1965, where 450 American soldiers of the Army's 1st Air Cavalry Division were airlifted by helicopter with the intention of locating and eliminating North Vietnamese Forces. The American soldiers were almost immediately surrounded by over three thousand soldiers of the People's Army of Vietnam (NVA), arriving in waves during this three-day engagement. Two hundred and forty-two American soldiers and over one thousand North Vietnamese soldiers were killed.

Illumination Round: An artillery or mortar round packed with a parachute flare that deploys and ignites at a predetermined altitude in order to provide spot or area illumination of the battlefield at night.

In-country: Meaning, in this case, located in South Vietnam, as opposed to supporting the war effort from bases outside of South Vietnam, e.g. Thailand, Guam, Okinawa, or The Philippines.

Indian Country: A reference to those geographical areas where the probability of coming in contact with armed Viet Cong or NVA was very high.

Indirect Fire: The use of artillery or mortars to fire at targets out of the crew's line of sight by firing in a high arc or angle out to long distances and/or over high terrain.

Individual Equipment: Also known as 782 Gear because of the government form number for the receipt each Marine signs to signify his acceptance of responsibility for those items listed and checked off on the form. The equipment consists of the field gear the Marine uses in field training and combat.

Infantry Training Regiment (ITR): Located at Camp San Onofre (for Marines graduating from recruit training at MCRD San Diego) and at Camp Geiger (for those Marines graduating from recruit training at MCRD Parris Island). Marines learned about crew-served weapons, map, and compass reading, use of grenades and other explosives, and numerous other basic infantry skills while participating in this four- to six-week training course.

Infantryman: One who serves in the infantry, as opposed to artillery, tanks, or other military occupational specialty fields.

Island, The: A platoon patrol base (located in GS 1757 of map sheet 7014-6640-1) just northeast of Hoi An and separated from the surrounding area by a river.

Judge Advocate General (JAG): The judicial arm of the United States Armed Forces, consisting of autonomous departments within the Marine Corps, Navy, Army, and Air Force. JAG's responsibility is the defense and prosecution of military law as provided in the Uniform Code of Military Justice. JAG officers also support military combat operations by advising commanders on the law of armed conflict.

Jungle Kit: Euphemism for the individual first aid kit.

Jungle Rot: A skin disorder induced by the tropical climate of South Vietnam. Also known as creeping crud. immersion foot as it applied to the feet. Small cuts and scratches quickly became infected.

Jungle Training: Training conducted in the jungle (Panama or The Philippines). The jungle is a very different environment than that where most Marines were trained and represented challenges in terms of terrain and land navigation, visibility, tactics, insects, reptiles, river crossings, etc.

Jungle Utilities: The Marine's combat or field uniform (called BDUs or fatigues in the Army).

KA-Bar: The standard Marine fighting knife issued to those for whom the .45 caliber pistol was the T/O weapon.

Khe Sanh: A reinforced regimental outpost located in northwest South Vietnam just below the DMZ. Khe Sanh was one of the most remote outposts in Vietnam.

Kin Village: The Okinawan village just outside the confines of Camp Hansen.

Landing Zone (LZ): An area of ground suitable for the landing of a helicopter or large numbers of helicopters.

Leave: A period of authorized absence. Each service member is entitled to thirty days of leave each year. Thirty days may appear to be a very generous amount of time away from duty, but service members, particularly those in combat, have little, if any time off. There are long deployments with frequent twenty-four-hour workdays and seven-day workweeks. There is no such thing as overtime pay in the military.

Legion of Merit: The Legion of Merit is awarded to members of the Armed Forces of the United States for exceptionally outstanding conduct in the performance of meritorious service to the United States.

Light Antitank Assault Weapon (LAAW): The LAAW, weighing only 5.2 lbs., was designed as a discardable one-man 66mm rocket launcher used primarily as an anti-tank weapon. In Vietnam, however, the LAAW was used almost exclusively as a bunker buster or for attacking entrenched enemies.

Listening Post (LP): Positions manned by one or more Marines at night and located outside friendly lines near likely avenues of approach in order to provide early warning of enemy movement/approach.

Lifer: Someone who elected to make the Marine Corps their career, not just a four-year enlistment.

LKA: Amphibious cargo ships designed to sail to the site of amphibious operations carrying equipment, cargo, and a limited number of assault troops. LKAs offloaded their equipment, cargo, and troops onto the ships' landing crafts. The crafts would then ferry the equipment, cargo, and troops ashore in support of an amphibious invasion.

Lock-on Training: A period of prescribed training (approximately four months in duration) that begins with fire team tactics and weapons employment and progresses through squad, platoon, company, and battalion tactics, weapons employment, supporting arms usage, and communications in day and night combat, both offensive and defensive, in order to train the unit/organization as a complete team.

LPA: Amphibious transport ships designed to sail to the site of amphibious operations carrying up to 1,500 assault troops and some of their support equipment. The LPA disembarked troops with the ships own landing craft. The ship would then stand off the beachhead ready to evacuate troops, casualties, and prisoners of war. In order to carry out its primary mission, LPAs had to provide all facilities for the embarked troops including, berthing, messing, medical, and dental care, as well as recreational facilities.

M14: A 7.62mm rifle that was standard issue prior to the adoption of the M16 rifle.

M16: The 5.56mm rifle that became standard issue in Vietnam in the latter part of 1967.

M60 Machine Gun: A lightweight, air-cooled, disintegrating metallic link-belt fed, portable or tripod/bipod mounted 7.62mm machine gun with an effective range of twelve hundred yards, a cyclic rate of 550 rounds per minute, and a maximum sustained rate of fire of one hundred rounds per minute.

Magazine (Ammunition): The ammunition accessory to a weapon (.45 cal pistol, M14, M16, etc.). A spring inside the magazine forces a round upward into the weapon's receiver. Once in the receiver, a round is pushed by the bolt into the chamber for firing. After firing, the same bolt extracts the round where it is ejected from the receiver. In Vietnam, the magazine for an M16 held twenty rounds.

Marine Corps: Short for United States Marine Corps.

Marine Corps Air Station El Toro: MCAS El Toro, California, was home to the 3rd Marine Corps Aircraft Wing and served as an aerial port of embarkation for many Marines en route to Vietnam via Okinawa.

Marine Reserves: The Reserve component of the United States Marine Corps consisting of a Marine Division and a Marine Air Wing Division. Members of the Reserve are initially trained on active duty for a period of six months (longer for technical personnel and officers) before they are released to their reserve units where they train one weekend per month and two weeks each summer for the remainder of their obligated service. They are subject to recall to active duty at the discretion of the National Command Authority.

MCRD Parris Island: The Marine Corps Recruit Depot located on the East Coast in South Carolina. All Marine recruits who live east of the Mississippi River attend MCRD Parris Island.

MCRD San Diego: The Marine Corps Recruit Depot located on the West Coast in Southern California. All Marine recruits who live west of the Mississippi river attend MCRD San Diego.

Medal of Honor: The Medal of Honor is the highest award for valor in action against an enemy force bestowed upon an individual serving in the Armed Services of the United States. Generally presented to its recipient by the president of the United States of America in the name of Congress, it is often called the Congressional Medal of Honor.

Medevac: The term used for medical evacuation from the field to a field hospital or hospital ship. In Vietnam, this was most often accomplished via a helicopter.

Mediterranean Cruise (Also Known as Med Cruise): The six-month deployment to the Mediterranean Sea by a Marine Battalion Landing Team (Reinforced) embarked aboard the vessels of a Navy Amphibious Ready Group.

Mess Duty: A temporary assignment of usually thirty days or less per year where a Marine of junior rank and any MOS serves in a galley, mess hall, or field environment to assist in the preparation and serving of meals to the rest of the unit/organization.

Midshipmen (Naval Academy): An undergraduate officer cadet. The word midshipman derives from the part of ship between the bow and the stern, "amidships," which was their traditional station at sea.

Military Occupational Specialty (MOS): A four digit number designating a specific military skill e.g. 0100 = administration; 0200 = intelligence; 0300 = basic infantryman; 0301 = basic infantry officer; 0302 = infantry officer; 0311 = rifleman; 0400 = logistics; 0800 = artillery; 1800 = tanks; 2500 = communications, etc.

Monsoon: A wind from the southwest or south that brings heavy rainfall to southern Asia in the summer.

Mortars: Crew-served weapons employed at the company level (60mm mortar) and battalion level (81mm mortar) used to fire high explosive, white phosphorous, and illumination rounds at a high angle trajectory out to a maximum of forty-six hundred yards. 4.2-inch mortars were also used by some artillery units in Vietnam.

Mud Flats, The: A company patrol base located west of Hoi An and characterized by clay soil that did not drain readily after rain, hence its name.

Mustang: Any Marine Corps officer with prior enlisted service but primarily an officer who rose through the ranks as an enlisted man and was selected to attend Officer Candidates School because of his demonstrated intellect and leadership ability.

NVA: North Vietnamese Army.

Naval Academy: Short for the United States Naval Academy at Annapolis, Maryland.

Naval Aviator: A Marine or Naval officer is designated a Naval aviator upon successful completion of flight training, which includes landing on aircraft carriers underway at sea.

Navy Corpsman: Trained Navy enlisted male and female medical personnel who provide first aid and medical treatment to sailors and Marines. Those serving with Marines in the field must be male and must complete field medical school to learn how to perform their medical treatment function in a field combat environment.

Navy Commendation Medal: Awarded to members of the Navy or Marine Corps who distinguish themselves by heroic action, outstanding achievement, or meritorious service, the Navy Commendation Medal falls between the Bronze Star Medal and the Navy and Marine Corps Achievement Medal in terms of precedence.

Navy Cross: The nation's second highest award for valor (along with the Army's Distinguished Service Cross and Air Force Cross) is awarded for extraordinary heroism while engaged in combat. The Navy Cross falls between the Medal of Honor and the Silver Star Medal in terms of precedence.

Non-Commissioned Officer (NCO): A corporal or sergeant in the Marine Corps charged with the exercise of leadership of other lower enlisted personnel.

Norton Air Force Base: Located in San Bernardino, California, Norton served as an aerial port of embarkation for most of the Marines en route to Vietnam via Okinawa as well as for service men from other branches of the Armed Forces.

Observation Post (OP): One or more positions normally manned during daylight hours by one or more Marines and located on terrain that afford(s) excellent fields of observation in order to provide early warning of enemy movement/approach.

Obstacle Course: A one-hundred-meter long series of obstacles that must be negotiated by the individual Marine in a prescribed amount of time in order to successfully complete the course.

Officer Candidates School (OCS): Located at Quantico, Virginia, OCS is where the Marine Corps screens and trains most of its future officers.

Okinawa: The largest of the Ryukyu Islands at the edge of the East China Sea and the Pacific Ocean, some 350 miles southwest of the Japanese Island of Kyushu and historical home of the 3rd Marine Division. Okinawa is where many Marines en route to Vietnam paused a few days to update vaccinations and store uniform items required while in Vietnam and as a temporary stop on the way back from Vietnam that allowed time for decompression and readjustment to life outside of a combat zone.

Operations Officer: The officer of a battalion, regimental, or division staff responsible for planning, organizing, and coordinating the training and the combat operations of that organization/command.

Ordnance: Military supplies, particularly weapons, ammunition, etc.

Patrol: Tactical movement through an area by a squad, platoon, or company in an effort to gain information and/or to locate or make contact with the enemy.

Physical Conditioning Platoon (Special Training Branch): A platoon within the Special Training Branch, a part of the Recruit Training Regiment, where recruits who are not performing at an acceptable level physically are temporarily assigned (a few weeks to several months) to build strength and endurance so that they can return to a regular recruit platoon to successfully complete the remainder of their training.

Physical Training (PT): Any physical activity involving calisthenics, aerobic exercise, long distance running, and negotiating the obstacle course or confidence course.

Platoon: A small unit, usually infantry, led by a lieutenant and consisting of three squads, a small command, and a communications structure.

Perimeter: The distance around a given two-dimensional object tactically speaking, the trace of a defensive line.

Perimeter Defense: A defense without an exposed flank, consisting of forces deployed along or around the perimeter of the defended area.

Platoon Commander: The officer who leads a platoon (a.k.a. platoon leader).

Platoon Guide: The NCO, junior to the platoon sergeant but senior to the squad leaders, who draws and distributes the logistic support needed by the platoon when in the field or garrison.

Platoon Honor Man: The recruit who graduates with the highest academic, physical fitness, marksmanship, and leadership grades in his platoon.

Platoon Patrol Base (PPB): A small piece of defensible terrain, normally fortified with earthen berms or sandbags, from which a platoon-size unit conducts day and night patrols of varying sizes in order to maintain observation or control over a much larger area.

Platoon Sergeant: The senior enlisted man (normally a SNCO) in a platoon; the senior enlisted assistant to the platoon commander.

Point: The point man or point element of men providing security and/or early warning at the head of a tactical formation.

Point Man: The individual providing security and/or early warning at the head of a tactical formation.

Popular Forces: South Vietnamese National Guard-type local military units.

Post-Traumatic Stress Disorder (PTSD): A psychiatric disorder that can occur following the experience of life-threatening events such as military combat. People who suffer from PTSD often relive the experience through nightmares and flashbacks, have difficulty sleeping, and feel detached or estranged. These symptoms can be severe enough and last long enough to impair significantly the person's daily life. PTSD also manifests by clear biological changes as well as psychological symptoms and frequently occurs in conjunction with related disorders such as depression, substance abuse, problems of memory and cognition, and other problems of physical and mental health. The disorder is also associated with impairment of the person's ability to function in social or family life, including occupational instability, marital problems and divorces, family discord, and difficulties in parenting.

Puff (Douglas AC-47 Gunship): An Air Force aircraft mounted with three Gatling guns on the port side, each of the guns (a.k.a. "mini-guns") capable of firing one hundred rounds per second (six thousand rounds per minute PER GUN). Puff was the forerunner of the larger Lockheed AC-130 Spectre gunships. Known in Vietnam as Spooky.

Purple Heart: The medal awarded in the name of the president of the United States to any member of the Armed Forces of the United States who, while serving in combat, was killed or wounded by enemy action.

PX: Abbreviation for Post Exchange. A retail outlet aboard a military base where uniform and sundry items can be purchased.

Quang Tin Province: Located twenty-three miles northwest of Chu Lai in the Phuoc Ha and Quế Sơn Valleys.

Quang Tri Province: The northernmost of South Vietnam's provinces.

Quantico: The educational home of the Marine Corps. Located in northern Virginia, it is the home of the Marine Corps' Officer

Candidates School, The Basic School, Amphibious Warfare School, Marine Corps Command, and Staff College, et al. Also the home of the FBI Academy.

Quinceañera: The traditional celebration of a girl's fifteenth birthday in Mexican, Puerto Rican, Cuban, and South American cultures.

Quonset Hut: A lightweight prefabricated structure of corrugated steel having a semicircular cross section. Its components could be shipped anywhere in the world and assembled without skilled labor.

R&R: Rest and recuperation, rest and recreation, rest and relaxation. Terms used by the US military for the one-week vacations given to members of the Armed Forces serving in combat areas.

R&R (In-country): A brief respite from combat (two to three days) taken in areas within theater not prone to enemy attack, e.g. a beach in a rear area.

Radio Watch: A period of duty (normally two to four hours) where a Marine listens to the unit's radio receiver/transmitter for incoming radio traffic, records those messages, and sends responses to those messages or other sitreps/spotreps as directed by the duty officer or commanding officer.

Radioman (Company, Platoon, Squad): A Marine whose primary function is to carry and operate the unit's receiving and transmitting radio, monitor the unit's tactical radio net, record radio transmissions in his message book, and send messages as directed by his officer-in-charge.

Rear Guard: The element of troops that protects the rear of a tactical military formation.

Recon: The act of conducting a physical reconnaissance of a geographical area or a reference to a reconnaissance team, company, or battalion.

Reconnaissance: The act of inspecting or exploring a geographical area, especially one made to gather military information/intelligence in preparation for an offensive operation.

Reconnaissance Battalion: Composed of four "lettered" reconnaissance companies and a headquarters and service company, the reconnaissance battalion's primary mission was to conduct clandestine surveillance and intelligence gathering along with occasional limited scale raids in support of the division.

Regional Force (RF): South Vietnamese militia units organized within each district in South Vietnam to engage in offensive operations against local Viet Cong forces. RF units were better paid and equipped than PF units and could be assigned duties anywhere within their home district.

Reverse Slope Defense: A reverse slope defense is characterized by the location of defensive forces on a slope of a hill, ridge, or mountain that descends away from the enemy thereby providing cover from the enemy's direct fire weapons while it exposes (in silhouette) the attacker's lead elements to the defender's defensive fires as the attackers crest the hill in the attack toward the defender's reverse slope position.

Rifle Company: Comprised of three rifle platoons and a weapons platoon (a total of six officers and 210 enlisted men). There were four of these "lettered" rifle companies per battalion.

Recoilless Rifle, 106mm: A long barreled, jeep, mechanical mule, or Ontos mounted-weapon that fired a high explosive anti-tank projectile. There was no recoil because the propellant gases were exhausted to the rear from the breach simultaneously with the firing of the weapon; one could be killed simply by standing behind the weapon when it was fired.

Recruit: An individual undergoing Marine Corps basic training; a recruit is not called a Marine until he has successfully completed the training and earned the title and the cherished eagle, globe, and anchor: the official emblem of the United States Marine Corps.

Regiment: A training, infantry, or artillery organization normally composed of three battalions and a headquarters company.

Reserves, Marine: See Marine Reserves.

Rifleman: Every Marine is trained as a rifleman before being assigned an MOS, and in combat, every Marine can be called upon to act as a rifleman when needed. Also the billet title for one of the four members of a fire team.

Rocket Launcher, 3.5-inch: There were six of these anti-tank, bunker-busting rocket launchers in the weapons platoon of each rifle company. An earlier generation of this weapon (the 2.75-inch "bazooka") was used by infantry units during WWII and Korea.

Rocket Propelled Grenade (RPG): A hand-held, shoulder-launched anti-tank weapon capable of firing an unguided rocket containing an explosive warhead. Due to advances in armor design, requiring more precise aiming to hit weak spots, most modern tanks were largely immune to unguided anti-tank weapons. RPGs were very effective against light-skinned vehicles or unarmored wheeled vehicles, as well as against buildings and bunkers. The term is most often applied to the Soviet model RPG-7.

Rocket Squad: Composed of two three-man assault rocket teams and a squad leader, there were three such squads in each weapons platoon. One squad normally attached to each of the three rifle platoons.

Rockets: A reference to the 3.5-inch M20A1B1 Rocket Launcher. Also a short reference to the team, squad, or section employing such weapons.

Rules of Engagement: Directives issued by competent military authority that delineate the circumstances and limitations under which United States forces will initiate and/or continue combat engagement with other forces encountered; such rules, both general and specific, that dictate when, where, and how force shall be used.

Salt: Short for "old salt" or someone who's been around for a while. A soldier with a longer period of active service than others in the unit.

Sampan: A flat bottom Asian skiff usually propelled by sail or one or more oars.

San Diego: See MCRD San Diego.

Sand Dunes, The: A company patrol base located north of Hoi An and named for the terrain where it was located.

Sapper: An enemy soldier or para-military man who lays mines or booby traps.

Scout/Sniper: See Sniper. One who employs camouflage, reconnaissance, stalking techniques, and long-range marksmanship skills in order to acquire and kill enemy personnel at great distances (thereby demoralizing/disheartening any enemy personnel who observe or learn about the incident).

School Yellow: The school solution (the correct or best answer) to a tactical problem at The Basic School or Amphibious Warfare School was always printed on yellow paper and provided to students after they had attempted to apply their own solutions.

Scorpion: A euphemism for a fire team or squad-size ambush set up outside of friendly lines at night to thwart or deter enemy movement through one's area of responsibility.

Sea Bag: A cylinder-shaped, tall canvas bag used to transport one's uniforms and personal items from duty station to duty station.

Seabees: The members of one of the Naval construction battalions that build Naval aviation bases and shore facilities in an amphibious objective area once the area has been secured by Marines.

Search and Destroy: A military strategy that came into use during the Vietnam War because it seemed to be ideally suited for guerilla/jungle warfare. The insertion of ground forces into hostile territory to locate and destroy enemy forces and then withdrawn immediately afterward.

Section Leader: The NCO in charge of a crew-served weapons section, e.g. machine guns, mortars, assault, etc.

Semper Fidelis: The Marine Corps motto. Latin for "always faithful."

Sergeant Instructor: Performs the same function at Officer Candidates School as drill instructors do at the two Marine Corps recruit depots.

Shrapnel: Fragments from an exploding artillery or mortar shell, grenade, bomb, or mine.

Silver Star: The nation's third highest award for valor (gallantry and intrepidity in action) against an armed enemy in combat. The Silver Star falls between the Navy Cross and the Bronze Star in terms of precedence.

Situation Report: Periodic reports (normally hourly) submitted to higher headquarters via radio that address what has transpired in the past hour that did not require immediate action.

Six-by: The short title for the M35A2 6 x 6, 2.5-ton cargo truck.

Small Arms Fire: That gunfire produced by small arms, e.g. rifles and machine guns.

Sniper: A highly trained and skilled expert military shooter whose job is to spot and shoot enemy soldiers at a great distance while remaining concealed in a well-camouflaged shooting position.

Sniper Platoon: A small platoon of expert marksmen located at the regimental level. Members were routinely attached to the regiment's subordinate battalions during combat operations.

Speed Reaction Course: The course consisted of a series of twenty problem-solving exercises, each contained in a walled-off area the size of a racquetball court. The speed reaction course evaluated an individual's ability to guide a small group in the solution of a difficult problem in an uncertain environment;

solving the problem was secondary to how the leader demonstrated an understanding of sound leadership principles while executing the task. One particularly difficult exercise, for example, required student teams to transport a fifty-five-gallon drum across a twelve-foot river using only three wooden planks, none of which were long enough to reach the other side. Key learning points were the importance of quick thinking and decisiveness in time sensitive situations, as well as flexibility and risk-taking when operating in an uncertain environment.

Spooky (Lockheed AC-130 Spectre Gunship): Spooky had the same mission as Puff but was a newer, larger, faster Air Force aircraft mounted with four General Electric MXU-470 7.62mm miniguns and four 20mm GE M-61 Gatling guns.

Spot Report (SpotRep): A report submitted to higher headquarters that addresses something of significance that is time sensitive and can't wait for the hourly situation report.

Staff Non-Commissioned Officer (SNCO): An enlisted member of the Marine Corps, (staff sergeant through sergeant major). A position of leadership over NCOs and other enlisted personnel.

Staging Area: An area where forces are brought together immediately prior to being tactically deployed.

Strategy: The science and art of using all the forces of a nation to execute approved plans as effectively as possible during peace or war. Also the science and art of military command as applied to the overall planning and conduct of large-scale combat operations.

Stokes Litter: A stretcher manufactured with steel netting and steel frame that is designed to hold an injured or wounded individual to be lifted by wire from the ground to a hovering helicopter when no safe landing zone is immediately available.

Supporting Arms: Assets used to deliver high explosive and/or high volume firepower, e.g. aircraft, artillery, naval gunfire.

Squad: A small infantry unit composed of a squad leader, a grenadier, and three four-man fire teams. Includes a small unit tasked with the tactical employment of two teams of crew-served weapons, e.g. machine guns, rocket launchers.

Squad Leader: The individual responsible for the tactical employment of three infantry fire teams or two crew-served weapons teams. An infantry small unit leader.

Sweep: An infantry tactic of moving through an area across a broad front in order to locate and clear it of opposing forces.

Table of Equipment (T/E): A listing of the equipment and weaponry required by a unit, organization, or command in order to perform their function.

Table of Organization (T/O): A graphic depiction of the various components which make up a unit (platoon or company), organization (battalion or regiment), or command (division) delineating the numbers of personnel necessary to fill all the billets in that unit, organization, or command and the individual and crew-served weapons with which they are armed.

Tactical Air Control Party: Consisting of a Naval aviator (an officer pilot/forward air controller) and his supporting radio operators for the tactical air request high frequency (HF) net radio, the tactical very high frequency (VHF) radio net of the supported unit/organization, and the tactical air control ultra-high frequency

(UHF) radio net which permits him to talk with fixed-wing or rotary-wing aircraft overhead or en route to provide the requested air support.

Tactical Area of Responsibility (TAOR): A geographical area delineated on a map by grid coordinates or easily recognized physical terrain features, e.g. rivers, hill tops, ridge lines, tree lines, or a combination of these within which one's unit or organization was responsible. In size, it was appropriate to the size of one's organization/unit and the resources an organization/unit had to cover it. No friendly forces entered or fired into your TAOR without your unit's or organization's approval.

Tactics: The military science that deals with securing objectives set by strategy, especially the technique of deploying and directing troops, ships, and aircraft in effective maneuvers against an enemy.

Tour of Duty (Vietnam): Time spent away from the United States while in Vietnam (thirteen months for Marines, twelve months or less for the other services). It ended with the arrival of one's rotation tour date (RTD) when one had completed thirteen months and was ready to return to the United States.

Tracer: A small arms projectile, e.g. a bullet, which was manufactured with a colored phosphorous coating so that its trajectory, once fired, can be observed by the gunner to more effectively adjust his rounds on target.

UH-34: The medium lift Sikorsky helicopter used by most Marine medium helicopter squadrons during this period for troop lift, logistics re-supply, and medevacs.

Uniform Code of Military Justice (UCMJ): A Federal law enacted by Congress under which military justice is administered to members of the Armed Forces, e.g. non-judicial punishment, summary courts-martial, special courts-martial, general courts-martial, etc.

Unit One: The designation of the Navy corpsman's medical kit containing first aid supplies and some surgical instruments.

United States Marine Corps (USMC): "America's 9-1-1 Force." One of the two co-equal branches of the military within the Department of the Navy. "On November 10, 1775, the Continental Congress authorized the raising of two battalions of American Marines, 'particular care be taken that no person be appointed to office or enlisted into said Battalions, but such as are good seamen, or so acquainted with maritime affairs as to be able to serve to advantage by sea,' thereby creating the legendary institution today known as the United States Marine Corps. From the Nation's birth to the present day, the Marines represent a proud culture of service and contribution in defense of the values and freedoms at the heart of the American experience."

USO: Abbreviation for the United Service's Organization, a volunteer organization chartered by Congress as a non-profit charitable corporation to provide morale, welfare, and recreation-type services to uniformed military personnel.

Utilities: The Marine field or combat uniform.

Vietnam (a.k.a. South Vietnam): A country in Southeast Asia bordered by Cambodia, Laos, North Vietnam, and the South China Sea.

SOURCES

From 2007 to 2011, I interviewed fifty-two American survivors of Operation Swift, two sisters, a friend of one Marine KIA, and a former operations officer for the 2nd NVA (PAVN) Division. Those interviews, as well as twelve after-action reports given by Marines within weeks of the conclusion of the operation, comprise the vast majority of information in MD this book. I am eternally gratefully to these veterans of the Vietnam War and to their friends and family for trusting me with their story.

For those men who lost their lives on September 4, 1967, or who would die due to wounds sustained on that day, I have relied on remembrances posted on Debbe Reynold's wonderful page (combatwife.net) and on the Wall of Faces (xxx.com).

Additional sources reviewed and websites consulted are listed below.

Marines and Navy Corpsmen Interviewed
Mike 3/5

1st Platoon	2nd Platoon
Ed Combs	Ed Blecksmith
Ray Edwards	Carlton Clark
Ken Fields	Nick Duca
Howard Haney	Paul Gundlach
Ryan Hooley	John Lobur
Bob Matteson	Steve Lovejoy
Bill Nicholson	Howard Manfra
George Phillips	Tony Martinez
Craig Sullivan	Larry Nunez
Jack Swan	Keith Rounseville
Bill Vandergriff	Elliot Rubenfeld
	Fred Tancke

3rd Platoon
Donald Baima
Chuck Cummings
Don Goulet
Kevin Kelly
Fred Permenter
Dennis Tylinski

Command Group and Attachments
John Bowers
Lief Ericson
Chuck Goebel
Forrest McKay
JD Murray
Fred Riddle
Rob Whitlow
Warren Wilson
Lynda Peters,
    sister of Larry Peters
Shirley Peters,
    sister of Larry Peters
Dave Harder,
    friend of Larry Peters

Delta 1/5
Larry Casselman
Bill Dubose
Craig Jackson
Maloey Jones
Allen Morris
Brian Spradling
Bob Warren
Steve Wilson

Colonel Tran Nhu Tiep,
2nd NVA Division (PAVN)

After action reports conducted by Marine Staff Sergeant Joseph H. Lutchens, September 19, 1967, of Mike 3/5 Marines
Joseph Fuller, 3rd Platoon
Thomas Haga, 2nd Platoon
David Jones, 1st Platoon
    (KIA 11/8/67, Essex)
Kevin Kelly, 3rd Platoon
Lenard Kelly, 3rd Platoon
Steve Lovejoy, 2nd Platoon
David Pizana, 2nd Platoon
Craig Sullivan, 1st Platoon
Fred Tancke, 2nd Platoon
Bill Vandergriff, 1st Platoon
Bert Watkins, 2nd Platoon
John Wiggins, 2nd Platoon

REFERENCES

Memorial Page for the Marines and Navy Corpsmen of Mike 3/5, Vietnam, 1966-1971 *(www.combatwife.net)*

The Wall of Faces, Vietnam Veterans Memorial Fund *(www.vvmf.org/Wall-of- Faces/)*

Communist Party of Vietnam Online Newspaper *(https://en.dangcongsan.vn)*

"Battle of Ba Gia," Wikipedia, (Communist Party of Vietnam Online Newspaper *(https://en.dangcongsan.vn)*

Provincial Communist Party Committee of Quang Ngai, "Reunion of the ex-soldiers of the Ba Gia Regiment in the old years, May 29, 2009 *(http://www.baoquangngai.vn/channel/2023/ 2009/05/1709652/*

Telfer, Gary (1984). *US Marines in Vietnam: Fighting the North Vietnamese 1967.* History and Museums Division, Headquarters, US Marine Corps. ISBN 978-494285449

Operation Swift, Wikipedia, *(https://en.wikipedia.org/wiki/ Operation_Swift)*

"Sorting through the chaos of Operation Swift in Vietnam," *(https://www.dailypress.com/military/dp- nws-evg-vietnam-marine-20150906-story.html)*

"Lost Battles of the Vietnam War"
(http://www.g2mil.com/lost_vietnam.htm)

Military Wiki (https://military- history.fandom.com/wiki/
Operation_Swift)

Hoang Van Thai, Hoc Tap (Studies), Hanoi,
No 9, September 1965, pp. 38-47

Survey on Ba Gia and its significance in the Vietnam War,
Lucas Le, July 26, 2009

"Otto Lehrack on Operation Swift," VFW
Magazine, September 2017
(http://digitaledition.qwinc.com/publication/
?i=425867&article_id=2843462&view=artic
leBrowser&ver=html5)

"Vietnam War Commemoration" (vietnamwar50th.com)
(https://www.vietnamwar50th.com/1966- 1967_taking_the_
offensive/Operation-SWIFT-Begins/)

Delta Company, First Battalion, First Marine Regiment Vietnam
1965–1971 (https://www.delta-1-1.net)

Mike Company, Third Battalion, Fifth Marines, RVN, 1966–1971
(http://www.securenet.net/3rdbn5th/mike35/ citation.htm)

"The dramatic story of the priest who died on a Vietnam
battlefield," The Catholic World Report, May 24, 2020,
(https://www.catholicworldreport.com/2020/ 05/24/the-dramatic-

story-of-the-priest-who-died-on-a-south-vietnam-battlefield/ #sdfootnote2sym)

"49 Years Ago, This Priest Earned 3 Purple Hearts and a Medal of Honor," by Johan Bennett, September 7, 2016, "The Stream," *(https://stream.org/49-years-ago-priest- earned-3-purple-hearts-medal-honor/)*

"Medal of Honor Monday: Navy Lt. Vincent Capodanno", April 1, 2019, US Department of Defense News, *(https://www.defense.gov/News/Feature- Stories/story/Article/ 1798399/medal-of- honor-monday-navy-lt-vincent-capodanno/)*

Obituary of Lynda L. Peters *(https://www.hccommunityjournal.com/obit uaries/article_148bdc44-6d2c-11e5-8252-3b8186d7153a.html)*

All Marine / Sgt. Lawrence D. Peters / Local Vietnam War Stories, WSKG Public Media, *(https://www.youtube.com/watch?v=BT2tvt uOAgQ)*

https://www.fordham.edu/about/leadership-and-administration/ administrative-offices/office-of-the-president/hall-of-honor/ vincent-r-capodanno/

Leal Middle School website, *(https://www.harlandale.net/ domain/1470)*

"Vietnam War: The Individual Rotation Policy," by Mark Deep, 11/13/2006, Historynet, *https://www.historynet.com/vietnam-war-the-individual-rotation-policy/*

Crisis in Command: Mismanagement in the Army by Richard A. Gabriel and Lt. Col. Paul L. Savage

Obituary of Clyde Craig Sullivan *(https://www.adignifiedalternative.net/obitu ary/clyde-sullivan)*

Obituary of Chuck Goebel *(https://www.mccormickandson.com/obituaries/ print?o_id= 8049863)*

"Que Son Valley and Nui Loc Son" by Eric Hammel, reprinted from 'Vietnam Magazine' *(www.wvam.com/vets/queson.html)*

Obituary of Don Goulet *(https://www.dignitymemorial.com/ obituarie s/auburn-me/donald-goulet-6112285)*

Misfire: The Tragic Failure of the M16 in Vietnam, Bob Orkand and Lyman Duryea, Globe Pequot/Stackpole Books *(https://rowman.com/ISBN/9780811737968/ Misfire-The-Tragic-Failure-of-the-M16-in-Vietnam)*

"Marksmanship, McNamara and the M16 Rifle: Organizations, Analysis and Weapons Acquisitions" by Thomas L. McNaugher (Rand Corp., 1979)

"The M16 Controversies: Military Organization and Weapons Acquisition" by Thomas L. McNaugher (Praeger Scientific, 1984)

"Tales of the Gun: M-16" DVD (History Channel, 1998, available at *History.com*)

The Hill Fights: The first Battle of Khe Sahn by Ed Murphy (Presidio Press, 2003)

"The Vietnam War from the Other Side: The Vietnamese Communists' Perspective" by Ang Cheng Guan, 2002, Routledge Curzon, London

Medal of Honor Citations
   Vincent Capodanno
   Lawrence Peters

Navy Cross Citations
   Thomas Fisher
   Armando Leal
   J.D. Murray

Silver Star Citations
   Andrew Giodarno
   Howard Manfra
   Bill Moy
   Larry Nunez

Bronze Star Citations
   Ed Combs David Phelps
   George Phillips
   Craig Sullivan
   Fred Tancke

About the Author

Doyle Glass is an author, historian, and sculptor dedicated to honoring those who fought for freedom. He is a master at recounting true stories of brave men and women who, outnumbered and out-gunned, continued to battle toe-to-toe with ferocious opponents in wartime.

His first book, *Lions of Medina,* gives a firsthand account of the sacrifices made by the Marines of Charlie Company during the Vietnam War.

His second book, *Swift Sword,* chronicles the gut-wrenching story of valiant Marines in Vietnam who endured a horrific firefight isolated on a lone knoll in the Quế Sơn Valley.

Coming in 2023, *Benoist's War* will reveal the harrowing story of Robert Benoist, a famous French Grand Prix World champion in the 1920s and Le Mans race winner in the 1930s, who risked everything as a British secret agent to help rid France of the Nazi occupation during WWII.

Doyle Glass was born in Midland, Texas, among the fifth generation of a pioneer ranching family. The Glass family prided themselves for an appreciation for hard work, adventure, and honor. After earning degrees in history and law from Southern Methodist University, he completed law school and worked as an assistant district attorney in Texas. Later, he served as assistant attorney general in Kentucky, prosecuting some of the worst violent crimes in the state.

In 2000, Glass turned to the arts as a way to tell stories of his childhood heroes. He conceived and sculpted a bronze statue of

John Squires, who braved enemy fire to save others during WWII and received the Medal of Honor. The statue stands in *The Kentucky Medal of Honor Memorial* in downtown Louisville, Kentucky, as a reminder of the sacrifices made by local citizens who fought and died for freedom.

In 2008, Glass designed and sculpted the *Texas Medal of Honor Memorial,* dedicated to George O'Brien, who earned the Medal of Honor during the Korean War. The memorial stands at the International Artillery Museum in Saint Jo, Texas, as a symbol recognizing those who earned America's highest award for combat valor.

Besides writing and sculpting, Glass's greatest pride is being a loving husband and father to his wife and three children where they reside in Dallas, Texas.

Left to right: John Lobur, Ed Henry, former NVA colonel Tran Nhu Tiep,
JD Murray and Steve Lovejoy on their return to the knoll in 2009.
Photo courtesy Steve Lovejoy

Made in the USA
Columbia, SC
17 March 2023

13881746R00163